BLACK RESISTANCE/WHITE LAW

UNDER   THE   EDITORIAL   SUPERVISION   OF   ARTHUR   S.   LINK

MARY FRANCES BERRY

BLACK RESIST -ANCE WHITE LAW

A HISTORY OF CONSTITUTIONAL RACISM IN AMERICA

ACC

NEW YORK

APPLETON-CENTURY-CROFTS

EDUCATIONAL DIVISION

MEREDITH CORPORATION

741-1

Library of Congress Card Number: 78–151970

PRINTED IN THE UNITED STATES OF AMERICA

390–08840–4

For
my mother,
who paid her dues,
and for Minerva

Contents

Preface

This book is an attempt to describe and analyze constitutionally sanctioned violence against blacks and violent suppression of black resistance—the outgrowth of a government policy based on essentially racist, not legal, concerns—throughout the American experience.

Black people have been a disquieting presence in America since the arrival of the first twenty slaves at Jamestown in 1619. To most blacks, their status, usually as slaves until 1865 and as second-class citizens thereafter, has been unacceptable; to some, it has been intolerable. Before 1865, in addition to aiding in the suppression of slave revolts, the national government ignored or approved—on constitutional grounds—white mob violence directed at blacks and their few white supporters even when local officials participated in the violence. Those blacks who did not become involved in conspiracy and rebellion before the Civil War were not necessarily "docile"; they lived in the grip of a system of violent control institutionalized under the Constitution. The years since Reconstruction, when blacks became nominally free, are littered with incidences of white riots against blacks, burnings of black homes and churches, and lynchings, while federal and local law enforcement agencies stood idly by. And while federal law enforcement disregarded white violence, pleading lack of jurisdiction under the Constitution, it endorsed and contributed to rigorous campaigns of surveillance and control of rebellious blacks, using "constitutional" military force against them with impunity.

Whether its policy was action or inaction, the national government has used the Constitution in such a way as to make law the instrument for maintaining a racist status quo. Some legal theorists might describe the American political system as one in which law represents the will of the majority while providing room for the protection of minority rights, but this is not an accurate description of the system in operation. Though the Bill of Rights, the Civil Rights Act of 1866, and the Fourteenth Amendment purport to protect individuals in their lives, liberties, and property, these ringing phrases have in fact afforded little protection to black people as a group. Law and the Constitution in the United States have been a reflection of the will of the white majority that white people have, and shall keep superior economic, political, social, and military power, while black people shall be the permanent mudsills of American society.

I am especially indebted to Elsie M. Lewis of the History Department at Howard University for continued suggestions, encouragement, and moral support. William R. Leslie, who was my doctoral adviser at the University of Michigan, provided the benefit of his wisdom derived from years of constitutional analysis. John W. Blassingame of Yale University asked the right questions as he always has since our student days together at Howard. James M. McPherson and Arthur S. Link of Princeton University, James P. Shenton of Columbia University, and William Strickland and Vincent Harding of the Institute of the Black World read the manuscript and provided helpful commentary.

Librarians and archivists at a number of institutions gave me willing assistance. I received the complete cooperation of Alfred Blair, Donald Mosholder, and Sara Jackson at the National Archives; of William Ewing, curator of the manuscript collection at the Clements Library at the University of Michigan, which permitted the use of the papers of Lord Lyttleton and General Anthony Wayne; and of John Fenker, documents librarian at Eastern Michigan University.

Gerald C. Poindexter, my classmate at the University of Michigan Law School, and Carol Muehling, a graduate student at American University, provided valuable research assistance. I would also like to thank Joyce Simanek, Sandra Shields, and Demaris Booker for typing the manuscript.

Despite the contributions made by these persons indicated, any defects in this study are mine alone.

M. F. B.

BLACK RESISTANCE/WHITE LAW

"Law and order must prevail" has become the cliché of the 1960's and the biggest lie, because the American black man has never known law and order except as an instrument of oppression; and it has prevailed upside his head at every available opportunity. It exists for that purpose. The law has been written by white men, for the protection of white men and their property, to be enforced by white men against blacks in particular and poor folks in general.

Julius Lester

(from *Look Out, Whitey! Black Power's Gon' Get Your Mama!*)

1 Foundations of Repression

The federal pattern of constitutional interpretation, which has been successfully utilized to maintain the continued social, economic, and political subordination of black people, evolved from policies and theories developed during the British colonial period. The British theory of federalism, the division of power and responsibility between the central and local governments, which arrived in America with the first colonists, has become a handy philosophical tool for maintaining white superiority. Federalism as a policy has been advanced to explain national noninterference when state agencies refused to protect nonconforming blacks from white violence intended to keep them in their place; and then, it has been cited to explain the compulsory use of national force when state agencies found themselves unable to successfully ward off black attacks on white persons or their property.

Black suppression in America began with the introduction of the system of slavery in 1619. Slavery was permitted and even encouraged by the British government, even though slavery made blacks a potential enemy in the midst of the colonists. Very early, the rapid increase of the slave population and the rebellions that followed brought the need for an adequate instrument of defense. The British federalist policy placed the responsibility for the use of force on local colonial officials because the British government was unwilling to use military force unless all civilian and local police measures were exhausted.[1]

The colonists' principal instrument of slave control was the local militia. By the time the American colonies were established, the militia in England was largely a debilitated institution; however, the establishment of the colonies demanded it be revived as the primary military organization in America. Although the king technically had full authority over the militia, these groups were largely supported and controlled by the individual colonies, with the governor of each colony acting as commander. In times of crisis, such as slave revolts, British regulars supplemented colonial militia forces.[2]

As the number of blacks increased alarmingly in the colonies, some southern colonists made efforts to control the slave trade. However, slavery had become such an economic boon to British merchants that every attempt to interfere was vetoed by the British government. A body of custom, judicial sanction, and statutory law evolved to institutionalize the system. Slavery was officially recognized as an institution in colonial laws by the 1660s. In 1697, Parliament expressed the view that blacks were property of great value to the kingdom, and ten members of the Court of King's Bench agreed that slaves were merchandise that could be regulated under the Navigation Acts.[3]

When the Treaty of Utrecht ended the war of Spanish Succession in 1713, the British government expanded its interest in slavery by obtaining a British monopoly on the colonial slave trade. Having no control over the increasing number of slaves arriving in the colonies, the colonists began to strengthen the militia. The most critical areas for slave control were those in which the slave population was large, the white population small, and the distance between the settlements great. Bands of hostile Indians greatly aggravated conditions in several colonies. In 1710, the population of the colony of Virginia was at least twelve thousand blacks as compared to eighteen thousand whites. At this time, the governor confided to the legislature that the militia was in such a disreputable state that he expressed fear should the word reach the slaves and Indians. In an effort to obtain revenue to arm the militia more adequately, the Virginia legislature enacted a duty in 1723 on the importation of liquor and slaves, to be paid by the importer.[4]

The colony of Carolina, with its extremely small white population, the presence of hostile Indians, and the large number of slaves, was particularly concerned with slave control. There were 10,500 blacks and 6,250 whites in Carolina in 1715; in 1724, there were three times as many blacks as whites; after the split of the colony into North and South Carolina in 1729, the situation was not significantly changed. By 1765, there were an estimated 90,000 blacks and 40,000 whites in South Carolina. Selected slaves were used to augment the militia against the Yamassee Indians in 1715, but a slave uprising in 1739 shattered confidence in the employment of blacks for defense and led to renewed efforts to strengthen the militia. Numerous programs for increasing the white population were debated in the colonial assembly, but no resolution was adopted. After 1743, the British government responded to requests for aid by stationing three regular infantry companies under the control of the governor of South Carolina to protect that colony and Georgia from possible slave revolt.[5]

Despite the presence of regular British troops, the fear of insurrection persisted in South Carolina. In 1757, at a meeting of the governors of North Carolina, Pennsylvania, Virginia, and Maryland convened to plan colonial defense for the duration of the French and Indian War (the Seven Years War, 1754–1763), South Carolina's predicament elicited great concern. In a letter to Lord Lyttleton, governor of South Carolina, the governors stated that British regulars would remain stationed at Charleston so that the local militia could be moved to defend the frontier. The British soldiers were intended to keep the blacks "in awe." [6]

Numerous other instances of actual or feared slave rebellions occurred during the colonial period, and the statute books were peppered with legislation designed to control the slave population. Blacks could not gather in groups, carry weapons, or travel without the permission of their masters; white males periodically searched black quarters for weapons and kept the blacks under surveillance. Militia laws were primarily designed for slave control. Internal control of blacks by militia and adjunct patrols, assisted in times of stress by British troops, was a well-established system by the time of the American Revolution.[7]

During the American Revolution, colonists in the South continued to express fear of black revolt. The defection of large numbers of slaves to the British compounded these fears. Southern delegates to the Continental Congress expressed unwillingness to use their militias outside their own borders. In 1779, a committee of the Continental Congress reported that South Carolina could provide very little manpower for the war effort because the militia was needed as a home guard to suppress rebellious movements among the blacks.[8]

As a result of the American Revolution, state governments were free to make whatever regulations they desired on slavery and the control of blacks. Article II of the Articles of Confederation recognized the retention of state control over domestic institutions—which included slavery. The national government under the Articles had neither the authority nor the force to suppress domestic disturbances. It followed, therefore, that in cases of black revolt, states would be forced to rely on their own resources. The end of the British government in the colonies marked the end of British protection.[9] Since the northern states soon either abolished slavery or put it on the way to ultimate extinction, constitutional and legislative provisions for slave control were of minor importance above the Potomac. The southern state governments recognized the continued existence of slavery as an institution by reenacting and expanding the body of colonial laws on the subject. The militia and citizen patrols remained primarily responsible for control of the black population.

As the confederation moved toward constitutional government, issues of internal security were found to require careful consideration. The maintenance of the system of slavery through the use of force was a primary problem of colonial defense. The fear of black insurrection, the absence of regular troops to augment local militia, and the obvious inability of the central government to suppress internal disorder hastened the development of an adequate military system patterned on the federalist model. Black oppression through the system of slavery had survived the Declaration of Independence and American Revolution and would now become an integral part of American constitutional law.

NOTES

1. For information concerning the establishment of slavery and other aspects of black history, see any number of general surveys. E.g., John Hope Franklin, *From Slavery to Freedom* (New York, 1969); Andrew C. McLaughlin, "The Background of Federalism," *American Political Science Review* 12 (May 1918), pp. 215–40.

2. John R. Western, *The Militia in the Eighteenth Century: The Story of a Political Issue,* 1660–1802 (London, 1965), pp. xii–xv; Louis Morton, "The Origins of American Military Policy," *Military Affairs* 22 (1958), pp. 75–82; John W. Shy, *Toward Lexington: The Role of the British Army in the Coming of the Revolution* (Princeton, 1965), chap. 1, *passim;* Herbert Osgood, *The American Colonies in the Eighteenth Century,* 4 vols. (New York, 1958), 1:99, 151; 2:349.

3. John Russell, *The Free Negro in Virginia 1619–1865* (Baltimore, 1913), chap. 2, *passim;* Leslie Fishel and Benjamin Quarles, eds., *The Negro American: A Documentary History* (Glenview, Ill., 1967), pp. 18–20; Kempes Schnell, "Court Cases Involving Slavery: The Application of Anti-slavery Thought to Judicial Controversy, 1830–1860" (unpublished doctoral dissertation, University of Michigan, 1955), pp. 2, 3.

4. Osgood, *American Colonies,* 2:218; Franklin, *From Slavery to Freedom,* p. 73; Herbert Aptheker, *American Negro Slave Revolts* (New York, 1943), pp. 14, 176–7.

5. Shy, *Toward Lexington,* pp. 12, 33; Franklin, *From Slavery to Freedom,* pp. 79, 82. *See* Thomas W. Clarke, "Negro Plot, 1741," *New York History* (April, 1944) and Joshua Coffin, *An Account of Some of the*

Principal Slave Insurrections (New York, 1860) for information concerning conspiracies in the north.

6. Lord John Campbell Loudon to Lord William H. Lyttleton, 24 April 1757, MS, Clements Library, University of Michigan, Ann Arbor, Michigan.

7. Aptheker, *Slave Revolts,* pp. 74–8; Robert Taylor, "Slave Conspiracies in North Carolina," *North Carolina Historical Review* 5 (1928), p. 20; Howell M. Henry, *The Police Control of the Slaves in South Carolina* (Emory, Va., 1914), pp. 28–34; Edgar J. McManus, *A History of Negro Slavery in New York* (Syracuse, 1966), pp. 79–99; Ralph B. Flanders, *Plantation Slavery in Georgia* (Chapel Hill, N.C., 1933), pp. 23–31.

8. Aptheker, *Slave Revolts,* pp. 18–23; Benjamin Quarles, *The Negro in the American Revolution* (Chapel Hill, N.C., 1961), pp. 111–9; John S. Lofton, *Insurrection in South Carolina: The Turbulent World of Denmark Vesey* (Yellow Springs, Ohio, 1964), p. 32; Report of Secretary of War Henry Knox, 1789, *American State Papers, Military Affairs,* 7 vols. (Washington, 1832–1860), 1:5.

9. *Articles of Confederation* (1781), art. II, VI; Mary S. Locke, *Antislavery in America from the Introduction of African Slaves to the Prohibition of the Slave Trade* (Magnolia, Mass., 1965), pp. 112–29.

2 / The Law
of Black Suppression

There was little doubt of the need for a stronger central government as the delegates to the Constitutional Convention met in Philadelphia in May 1787. Debtor disturbances, among them Shays's Rebellion, a revolt of impoverished farmers against taxation and the judiciary, which had threatened a federal arsenal at Springfield, Massachusetts, had stressed emphatically the weakness of the central government under the Articles of Confederation. The government had been helpless; it lacked an effective national military organization and the authority to interfere in the domestic affairs of the states. Convention delegates insisted that the new government provide a means for suppressing disorders which were designed to subvert the execution of laws and the judicial process. State militia organizations could not be depended upon to end rebellions, particularly if the militiamen sympathized with the aims of the rebels, as they did in Shays's Rebellion. The delegates wanted both a stable militia and a stable national standing army, providing the states could prevent uninvited national interference. Without too much difficulty, they agreed that the national government should guarantee each state a republican (representative) form of government and should protect the states from domestic violence upon a request from the state legislature, or the governor when the legislature was not in session.

In the debate on the military clauses of the Constitution which would empower Congress to provide the militia to quell internal disorders, no one explicitly stated that the national military power might be used to suppress slave revolts. The precedents for slave control as a local responsibility were well established. However, while debating the proposal to prohibit the slave trade, Rufus King of Massachusetts introduced the relationship between slavery and the use of national military forces. King felt that importing additional slaves would make national defense more difficult and costly. He believed it unjust not only that the North was obligated to defend the South in the event of slave revolts while the South was free to import more slaves, but that southerners were bitterly opposed to the levying of export taxes which would compensate the federal treasury for this additional defensive burden. Since theirs was an agricultural exporting economy, southerners were generally opposed to export taxes. John Rutledge of South Carolina did not believe the South would encourage the slave trade or, in an unconscious contradiction, that slave insurrections would occur as a result of further importations. Rutledge suggested that if the North's disapproval of the slave trade was based on military considerations, the South should be willing to exempt northern states from obligation to protect the South from slave rebellion. No other southerner agreed with him, and there is no evidence that northerners endorsed his proposal or tried to convince others to accept it. The Constitution as finally drafted, in conformity to southern wishes, forbade Congress from prohibiting the slave trade before 1808 or levying a tariff on exports from any states.[1]

In the debate over apportionment of representation, Gouverneur Morris of New York opposed counting slaves as only three-fifths of a person both for taxation and representation.

The southern states, he commented, " . . . are not to be re-strained from importing fresh supplies of wretched Africans, at once to increase the danger of attack, and the difficulty of defense." While gaining nothing from the Three-Fifths Com-promise, northern states bound "themselves to march their militia for the defense of the Southern States; for their defense against those very slaves of whom they [Northern opponents of slavery] complain." [2] The convention ignored Morris and ac-cepted the compromise formula.

The Fugitive Slave Clause of the Constitution was also adopted with little debate. Some opposition arose over the pro-posal to make the governor of the state responsible for insuring the return of fugitive slaves. James Wilson of Pennsylvania felt that the responsibility would be too burdensome for the gov-ernor, and possibly too costly, if military force became necessary. The proposal finally adopted does not specifically give the re-sponsibility to any governmental official, but ultimately, the rendition of fugitive slaves falls on the president under his duty to enforce the Constitution and laws.[3]

When the military clauses of the Constitution were considered by the state ratifying conventions, the same issues, the need to protect states' rights and to insure state control over the move-ment and disposition of state militias, received earnest debate. The slavery issue was brought into the debate in the Virginia convention by George Nicholas, who pointed out the additional security for slavery provided in the Constitution. Along with the power of the state to use its militia to control the slaves, "it will be the duty of the general government to aid when the strength of the union is called for." [4] The Fugitive Slave Clause was scarcely noticed by northern delegates to the ratifying con-ventions, but in the South, it was used as a definite selling point. James Madison particularly emphasized its usefulness in Virginia, as did some of the Federalists in the North Carolina convention. These debates lend credence to the view that the southern states would not have ratified the Constitution without the proslavery compromises. The Fugitive Slave Clause and the commitment of the national government to protect slavery, but not interfere with it, were indispensable parts of the Constitution.[5]

The military system provided by the Constitutional Convention and ratified by the states was entirely consonant with the principles of federalism developed during the American colonial and revolutionary experience. The language in the Constitution was vague enough so that Congress, in drafting enabling legislation, could use its own discretion to fill in the substance. The military clauses as stated in the Constitution, provided that the states would keep order within their own borders, but if invasion occurred, the national government was responsible for defense. If overpowering rebellion occurred, the state government could request federal aid, but the national government could not intervene at will. However, Congress had the power to utilize the militia or regular forces to enforce federal laws. The maintenance of internal security and slave control primarily remained a local responsibility but the national government was explicitly bound to insure the return of fugitive slaves and to support state governments in suppressing domestic violence which could include slave insurrections.[6]

In the First Congress on 29 September 1789, a bill was passed to implement the military clauses of the Constitution; the act recognized the small military contingents established under the Articles of Confederation and authorized the president to call militiamen into service to protect the frontier from Indian raids. In the Second Congress, a bill was passed on 2 May 1792 which provided that the state militias could be called out to execute the laws of the Union, suppress insurrections, and repel invasions. This additional legislation, which gave the president the power to federalize the state militias when the United States was endangered or upon a state request for aid in time of domestic violence, was based on the recognition that regular forces were too small to be used for anything except manning seacoast fortifications and protecting the frontier. By 1807, when the regular military forces were increased to ten thousand men, the statute was changed to authorize the president to call out the land and naval forces of the United States or the militia. The House debates on the Militia Act of 1792 consisted largely of controversy over what conditions constitute an insurrection and the possibility of the national government utilizing the military in a tyrannical fashion. Significantly, the act does not say that the president *must* call out the militia but only that "it shall be lawful" for him to do so. This principle was clearly expressed in the act of 1795 which repealed the Militia Act of 1792: the president was given sole discretion, without further consultation or congressional action, to determine when an exigency requiring the use of the military existed.[7]

Congressional interpretation of national responsibility for the suppression of slave disturbances was clearly expressed in debates concerning the abolition issue. Quakers and other reformers initiated an abolition movement in the early days of the Revolution, and their activities persisted throughout the antebellum period. On 8 March 1790, when Congress received a petition against slavery and the slave trade from the Quaker Pennsylvania Society for Promoting the Abolition of Slavery, Representative James Jackson of Georgia insisted that discussion of the slavery issue would cause insurrection in the South. When the discussion continued unabated, Representative William Smith of South Carolina made a lengthy speech in defense of slavery. One argument northerners frequently used was that slavery made the South weaker in case of invasion, and Smith felt this view was erroneous; he believed that blacks might, in fact, make good soldiers and could be used to defend the South. After considerable debate, the House decided to adopt a general statement of its power over slavery under the Constitution without acting on the Quaker petition. As the situation appeared to the House members, the Constitution forbade prohibition of the slave trade until 1808, and Congress had no authority to interfere with slavery in the states.[8]

The proslavery supporters in the First Congress became increasingly sensitive to any discussion of the slavery issue, constantly asserting states' rights and pointing out the danger of fomenting slave revolts as a defense against anything remotely resembling antislavery argument. Even the alleged "kidnapping" of free blacks from Pennsylvania by North Carolinians who insisted they were runaway slaves was to many southerners not a matter of congressional concern, since states' rights might be infringed upon if the national government became involved in the issue. A representative from Pennsylvania brought the subject before the Fourth Congress, after being informed that some free blacks from his state had recently been kidnapped. Smith of South Carolina, who had been willing to make long arguments in defense of slavery, now adamantly opposed any discussion of the kidnapping question because some agitation might promote insurrectionary conditions in the South. The House, evidently impressed by his argument, agreed and resolved that "it is not expedient for this House to interfere with any existing law of the states on the subject." [9]

The Pennsylvania kidnapping issue remained unsettled. Representative John Swanwick of Pennsylvania succeeded in presenting a petition from some blacks in his state who complained that slaves who had been manumitted by Quakers in North Carolina were being forced back into slavery. Smith of South Carolina once again objected, explaining that the plight of the blacks resulted from a North Carolina statute which forbade manumissions and gave any claimant the right to reduce persons, freed in contravention of the statute, to slavery. Some of these freed blacks had escaped to Pennsylvania; persons claiming ownership to the runaways, as provided in the Fugitive Slave Act of 1793, took them back to North Carolina. James Madison of Virginia asserted that this petition did not deserve the time or attention of the House; he believed that if these petitioners were free, they could settle their grievances in the North Carolina courts, but if they were slaves, the Constitution gave them no hope of being heard in Congress. The petition was rejected by a vote of 33–50.[10]

In June 1796, when the crisis brought on by French attacks on American shipping demanded increased military preparation, the possibility of slave uprisings again drew the attention of Congress. A bill was passed authorizing the president to require state governors to hold a total of eighty thousand militiamen in readiness, apportioned according to the number of white inhabitants in each state. In the House, Smith of South Carolina suggested that the bill ought to provide for apportionment in each state based on the total number of whites and three-fifths of the blacks. The southern states would therefore call out more men but, Smith asserted, if war came, the additional men would be needed. Abraham Venable of Virginia found Smith's thinking unclear. He stated that if the South needed more troops for its protection, the Constitution provided that they must be supplied from other states as well; there was no need for the three-fifths formula. Joseph McDowell of North Carolina reminded Smith that if his plan were adopted, with the large number of whites assigned to military duty, those at home would be left defenseless against the blacks. Smith hastily withdrew his proposal. George Thacher of Massachusetts, who consistently attacked the proslavery forces while he was in Congress from 1789 to 1801, could not resist needling Smith by asking him whether he meant that three-fifths of the blacks should be armed and used as soldiers. Smith stammered that he had no such intention. The bill was passed without the three-fifths proposal.[11]

The proslavery tactic of pleading the danger of insurrection as a technique to squelch antislavery arguments had not yet completely served its purpose. In November 1797, when the Quakers presented their annual petition begging for the end of slavery and the slave trade, fear of revolt was again successfully invoked by proslavery congressmen. Nathanial Macon of North Carolina denounced the petition and the petitioners, who were, in his opinion, warmongers "bent on bloodshed" rather than peacemakers.[12] In January 1800, Representative Robert Waln of Pennsylvania presented another petition of free blacks asking for an end to the slave trade, which met the same harsh reception given the Quakers' petition. While debating whether to submit the petition to a committee, Harrison Gray Otis of Massachusetts endeared himself to the proslavery elements by drawing attention to the crude lettering of the petition. He suggested that the petitioners were illiterate and had no notion of what they were signing. The discussion was interrupted by John Rutledge of South Carolina who introduced the issue of the successful slave revolution against the French in Haiti in August 1791. He claimed that emissaries from Haiti had been sent to America to stir up unrest and that, once again, the discussion of abolition and the slavery problem might encourage insurrection. Another representative from South Carolina, Robert Goodloe Harper, added that the petition was just another Quaker petition; apparently, since the previous petitions were rejected, the Quakers had induced unknowing blacks to sign the present one. The House resolved that the petition created disquiet and should therefore not be entertained by the House. George Thacher cast the lone dissenting vote. The proslavery position decrying antislavery agitation was overwhelmingly accepted.[13]

When, in December 1803, the manpower needs of South Carolina's expanding cotton and rice production required her to reopen the foreign slave trade, the possibility of insurrection again became a national issue. Representative David Bard of Pennsylvania proposed that the national government levy a tax on each slave imported. The congressmen from South Carolina defended the state's actions on the basis of state sovereignty. They claimed that the action of South Carolina was an expression of the Tenth Amendment in which powers reserved by the states could not be usurped by the national government; what South Carolina did about the slave trade was of no concern to the national government or any other state. Bard and John Smilie of Pennsylvania then subjected the South Carolinian's argument to a devastating attack. As importation of slaves meant the importation of enemies into the country, Bard asserted that the concern of the other states and the national government was understandable. Smilie was even more explicit. The reopening of the trade, he insisted, would weaken the defense of the entire nation and it was common knowledge that the military power of the nation was constitutionally bound to suppress slave insurrection. The House, unimpressed by Bard and Smilie, postponed consideration of the tax. South Carolina continued the foreign slave trade until Congress exercised its power to prohibit it by the act of March 1807 which went into effect on 1 January 1808. The concern of Bard and Smilie was well founded, for in the four years before importations were made illegal, some 39,075 additional Africans were brought into the already large slaveholding state of South Carolina.[14]

As seen from the Congressional debates, the southern viewpoint in 1804 was that Quakers and other outside agitators were inciting insurrection, and any discussion of opposition to slavery in Congress would create incendiary conditions. Further, slavery was a local practice which the national government had no authority or right to regulate. And yet, if the southern states requested aid for slave insurrections or the return of fugitive slaves, the military force of the nation was constitutionally obliged to comply.

The proof of whether the proslavery theories elaborated in the first congresses could be successfully implemented came when two rebellions involving opposition to federal tax laws compelled the use of national power. In the Whiskey Rebellion of 1794, the governor of Pennsylvania refused to call out the state militia. The federal courts appealed to the president since the laws of the United States were "obstructed by combinations too powerful to be suppressed by the ordinary course of judicial proceedings. . . ." [15] President Washington called fifteen thousand militiamen from Pennsylvania and surrounding states into federal service and issued two proclamations calling for an end to the rebellion. The insurrection petered out with little opposition. Similar action was taken in response to the other instance of local obstruction to a federal law, Fries Rebellion, which erupted in Pennsylvania in 1799: President Adams issued a proclamation of rebellion, asked the governor of Pennsylvania to call out one thousand militiamen, and the affair was promptly suppressed.[16]

The action taken in these rebellions demonstrated that the national government could discharge its responsibilities under the sections of the military act designed to end obstruction to federal law. In view of the concern that Shays's Rebellion and other debtor disturbances had created at the Constitutional Convention, the response of the government was of a kind anticipated by the framers. Still to be tested, however, was the section of the military act designed to end insurrection within a state upon a state request for federal aid. Statements made regarding the use of national power to suppress slave revolts in the convention and the first congresses indicate a clear awareness of the national responsibility in such cases: national military power would be invoked to quell black insurrection and to remand fugitive slaves when, and if, it became necessary.

NOTES

1. *American State Papers, Military Affairs,* 7 vols. (Washington, 1832–1860), 1:5–6; Max Farrand, ed., *Records of the Federal Convention,* 4 vols. (New Haven, 1911), 2:220–2; Henry Wilson, *History of the Rise and Fall of the Slave Power in America,* 3 vols. (Boston, 1875), 1: 47–8. John S. Lofton, *Insurrection in South Carolina: The Turbulent World of Denmark Vesey* (Yellow Springs, Ohio, 1964), p. 54; Ernest M. Lander, "The South Carolinians at the Philadelphia Convention, 1787," *South Carolina Magazine of History* 57 (1956), p. 316.

2. Farrand, *Records,* 2:220–2; *Constitution of the United States,* art. I, sec. 2.

3. Kempes Schnell, "Court Cases Including Slavery: The Application of Anti-slavery Thought to Judicial Controversy, 1830–1860" (unpublished doctoral dissertation, University of Michigan, 1955), p. 156; James Madison, *Journal of the Federal Convention* (Washington, 1893), pp. 460, 631.

4. Jonathan Elliot, ed., *The Debates in the Several State Conventions on the Adoption of the Federal Constitution,* 5 vols. (Philadelphia, 1861), 3:427.

5. Schnell, "Court Cases," p. 157; Farrand, *Records,* 3:84; Elliot, *Debates,* 3:254, 325.

6. *Constitution of the United States,* art. IV, sec. 4, art. I, sec. 8; Andrew C. McLaughlin, "The Background of Federalism," *American Political Science Review* 12 (May 1918), pp. 215–40.

7. The 840 soldiers stationed at Springfield, Massachusetts arsenal and at West Point comprised the small military contingent which was created by a resolution of the Confederation Congress in October 1786 and was continued by act of April 1787. See *American State Papers, Military Affairs,* 1:5, 6; 1 *United States, Statutes at Large* 95 (hereafter cited as *Stat*); 1 *Stat* 222; 1 *Stat* 264 (1792); *see also* 2 *Stat* 443 (1807); 1 *Stat* 424 (1795). *See* Appendix, Title 10:332.

8. *Annals of Congress,* 1st cong., 2nd sess. (1790–1), pp. 1413, 1415, 1456; Herman Ames, *State Documents on Federal Relations* 5, (Philadelphia, 1900), pp. 1–2.

9. *Annals of Congress,* 4th cong., 2nd sess. (1796–7), p. 1895.

10. *Annals of Congress,* 4th cong., 2nd sess. (1796–7), p. 2021; John H.

Franklin, *The Free Negro in North Carolina 1790–1860* (Chapel Hill, N.C., 1943), pp. 22–5; Herbert Aptheker, *A Documentary History of the Negro People in the United States,* 2 vols. (New York, 1968), 1:40–4 contains a copy of the black petition, which may also be found in *Annals of Congress,* 4th cong., 2nd sess. (1796–7), pp. 2015–8.

11. *Annals of Congress,* 5th cong., 1st sess. (1797–9), pp. 292–3.

12. Ibid., p. 661.

13. *Annals of Congress,* 6th cong., 1st sess. (1799–1801), pp. 229, 231, 234, 242, 244–5; Harper and Rutledge were Federalists and anti-French. *See also* Henry Aptheker, *American Negro Slave Revolts* (New York, 1943), p. 44.

14. *Annals of Congress,* 8th cong., 1st sess. (1803–4), pp. 995, 1015; Lofton, *Denmark Vesey,* pp. 104–7.

15. 1 *Stat* 264 (1792). This act had three sections designed both to enforce federal law and suppress insurrections against state governments. Sections 2 and 3 were at issue in the Fries and Whiskey Rebellions; 1 *Stat* 424. *See* Appendix, Title 10:331, 332.

16. Leland D. Baldwin, *Whiskey Rebels: The Story of a Frontier Uprising* (Pittsburg, 1939), pp. 56–60; Bennett Rich, *The Presidents and Civil Disorder* (Washington, 1941), pp. 2–20, 22–6. *See also* Frederick T. Wilson, *Federal Aid in Domestic Disturbances, Senate Document 209,* 57th cong., 2nd sess. (1903), pp. 34–42 (hereafter cited as *Sen. Doc.*)

3 / Defiant Slaves and Defiant States

In the late summer of 1800, Gabriel Prosser, a young slave of Henrico County, Virginia, was executed, along with forty other slaves, for daring to attempt revolt against the slaveholders. Prosser's projected insurrection ushered in a turbulent period of some thirty-five years when, in the crucible of slave rebellion, the congressional interpretation of national military responsibility in a republic was tested. The machinery that had successfully quelled opposition to federal taxing power in the Whiskey and Fries Rebellions was now confronted with racial disturbances *within* a state.

In period of quiescence after the adoption of the Constitution, southern slaveholders continued to rely upon their own resources to control the black population, just as they had done during the colonial period. The systems of patrol and militia duty, already in existence, were legislatively reestablished in the new nation. After the enactment of the national militia law of 1792, patrol remained an integral part of the military, both forces drawing from the same class of males. However, when no warfare or revolt threatened, it was difficult to keep patrol performance at a high degree of efficiency; militiamen performed drill and muster inadequately, if at all. Many instances of drunkenness, improper conduct, failure to report for duty, and brutality toward innocent slaves and free blacks were reported. But when necessity dictated, the patrol was adept in suppressing rebellion without outside help.[1]

The example of black revolt in Haiti, which began in August 1791, and the influx of terrified French refugees into the seaboard cities of the United States created sufficient fear of insurrection to keep the local patrols and militia in a state of readiness. Congressmen and local officials in the South continued to make persistent references to the Haitian revolution and its incendiary effects. As reported plots were an everyday occurrence, residents in areas with large slave populations feared the necessity of sending militiamen to defend the western frontiers. Local patrols had sufficient reason to be assiduous in their duties.[2]

Gabriel Prosser attempted to execute his plot in this atmosphere of crisis. The planned revolt appeared to be a well-organized project involving about one thousand blacks in the vicinity of Richmond. The slaves gathered on 30 August 1800 but disbanded because a violent storm and flood made military operations impossible. During the next month, many blacks, including Prosser, were arrested. Although the plot failed, the reaction it engendered is significant. Governor James Monroe and other public officials in Virginia had heard rumors of the revolt, and on the day of the disturbance, two faithful slaves reported the plan to their masters. Local and state government officials were sufficiently aroused by the prospect to ask for aid. Monroe requested and received the use of the federal armory at Manchester. Although federal intervention was unnecessary, the plot being aborted and the leaders captured before any slaveholders were killed, the immediate federal response to Madison's request established a precedent.[3]

A heightened uneasiness persisted after Prosser's plot, and the continuous rumors of slave conspiracies in the next few years led many states to enact more stringent measures to control both slaves and free blacks. Although free blacks had no discernible connection with Prosser's plot, southerners believed that the social events at which they were present furnished the occasion for planning the rebellion. Southern legislatures passed laws strengthening local militia and patrol units; they also restricted the internal slave trade, fearing that slaveholders might attempt to sell insurrectionary blacks to their unsuspecting neighbors in other states. Virginia's House of Delegates, directing its enmity toward free blacks, authorized Governor Monroe to discuss with President Thomas Jefferson the possibility of purchasing lands where such "unsettling" persons could be sent. Jefferson was sympathetic to their proposal yet refused to spend federal money for the purpose. Although he did suggest that Virginia buy land in the Northwest Territory, he indicated that this area would some day be joined to the Union. Jefferson thought the difficulty would lie in finding an area in which free blacks would not only be welcomed but slaveholders also assured that the blacks would not instigate and support slave revolt anywhere in the United States. The colonization effort was abandoned. However, in 1806, the Virginia legislature passed an act which required free blacks who were manumitted to leave the state. Many free blacks left the Lower South to resettle in the Upper South and Midwest. States in these areas began enacting legislation to prevent the entry of free blacks within their borders. As the number of free blacks in the United States increased from 59,000 in 1790 to 319,000 in 1830, many blacks faced the problem of finding a place to live. Even Massachusetts felt compelled to expel many free blacks.[4]

Although the ever-present rumors abounded, the next large-scale insurrection did not occur until January 1811 in Louisiana. The fear generated by the Haitian revolution and the large population of free Negroes in the area coupled to accentuate the tension. Further aggravation was caused by a dispute between a group of free Negroes and the territorial governor over efforts to disband a Negro militia organization which had been in existence since about 1736. When news reached the city that 400 to 500 slaves had revolted in the parishes at the Andry plantation outside New Orleans, it caused an uproar. Since the territorial militia was inefficient due to lack of training and interest, General Wade Hampton, who had control of military forces in the territory, hastily assembled two companies of the most efficient volunteers he could find, along with a company of regular army troops, and put down the disturbance. About 660 soldiers reportedly took part in the engagement. The free Negro militia ingratiated themselves with the white community by offering to assist in military operations against the slaves. Eighty-two of the Andry rebels were killed or executed soon after capture. The governor's letter books indicate continued reliance on federal forces; troop movements in the area were planned to maintain the mobility required to suppress possible uprisings.[5]

Following the Andry revolt, southern state governments continued to tighten restrictions governing the activities of free blacks, refusing passage to some, expelling others, and emancipating loyal slaves who informed on alleged insurrectionaries. Renewed interest in colonization led to the organization of the American Colonization Society in 1817 with some prominent southerners as members. Opposition developed rapidly. Some abolitionists criticized the society on the grounds that no native American should be expelled from his country; others argued that if the colonizers were sincere, they would only colonize slaves and not free blacks; some proslavery interests regarded it as an emancipationist tool. In addition to restrictive legislation directed at blacks and southern interest in colonization, southern state legislatures enacted measures to suppress abolitionist literature and discussion which might incite the slaves to rebel. Nevertheless, the southern states found little real comfort in their legislative programs; the slave problem required their sustained activity in order to maintain the will of the national government to insure slave control.[6]

The debates over the admission of Missouri to the Union beginning in 1819 provided the southerners with reassuring evidence of the will of Congress to defend the slave system. James Tallmadge of New York explained that he had not suggested free soil in Alabama because free blacks would then be too near slaves in adjoining states, thereby increasing the likelihood of rebellion, but he thought a boundary for slavery expansion should be set at Missouri. State legislatures responded to Tallmadge's proposal with a spate of resolutions. The northern legislative position essentially hinged on the unfairness of increasing proslavery representation in Congress under the terms of the Three-fifths Compromise. Considerable discussion also emphasized the position that extended enslavement of blacks would increase the possibility of internal disorder. Proslavery legislatures stood firmly on the Louisiana Purchase treaty which insured the right to property of persons in the area; they also believed that continued opposition to slavery in Missouri would create bitterness and distrust in the South as well as slave discontent.[7]

In the congressional debates, the battle lines closely conformed to the resolutions passed in the states. Representative William Plumer of New Hampshire most clearly expressed the concern of northerners in a lengthy speech in February 1820. He succinctly noted that the Constitution was established to provide for the common defense and to insure domestic tranquility; constitutionally, slavery was a domestic institution which the national government could not touch unless an insurrection compelled state officials to request federal aid. It seemed altogether reasonable to Plumer that since this burden of protection was placed upon the entire Union, Congress should act to reduce the likelihood of insurrection which necessitated the use of federal troops and money by preventing the expansion of slavery. Plumer further noted that the slave states had always been a great burden to the rest of the nation; in times of war, southern militiamen were needed at home to "awe" the slaves. Representative Charles Rich of Vermont and other northern congressmen advanced much the same argument. Representative Harrison Gray Otis of Massachusetts, although opposing the further extension of the system, expressed a view which was gaining great favor with proslavery spokesmen: slavery was a beneficial institution, not only to the South, but to the entire country; there were strong economic ties between the two sections and a slave revolt would be economically disastrous to the nation, in addition to placing the lives of northerners in jeopardy. Said Otis, "All considerate persons in every section of the Union should unite with one accord with their masters in putting down every species of revolt and insurrection, as pregnant with dreadful consequences to the whole section." [8]

During the Missouri Compromise debates, the ideas and proposals presented may have encouraged rebellion against the institution of slavery. There is evidence that Denmark Vesey, who planned an insurrection in Charleston, South Carolina in the summer of 1822, seized on such antislavery discussion to convince his associates that attempted revolt might bring outside help. Vesey, a literate free black, plotted the only large-scale city revolt during the history of slavery in the United States. His plot is a landmark in black American history in that it was led by a free black who was willing to risk his life to free others; all too often slaves were emancipated for informing on alleged insurrectionaries, and free blacks seemed more concerned about maintaining what semblance of privilege they had than in improving the circumstances of the enslaved blacks. The nine thousand men under Vesey were prepared to enter Charleston and begin a general massacre of not only whites but also those blacks who did not join the revolt. Success would enable the rebels to move to Haiti where further plans would be made. However, the plot was discovered before fruition, again through the disloyalty of slaves who informed their masters. Vesey and five of his lieutenants were captured, tried by a jury of two judges and three white citizens, and hanged on 2 July 1822. The investigation continued and eventually thirty-five blacks were hanged and forty-two sent into exile. Another four white men were convicted of collusion with the insurrectionaries; it was alleged they had hoped to acquire loot if Vesey's plot succeeded. They were sentenced to short prison terms and assessed fines. The controversy which developed between the governor of South Carolina and the city court over the handling of the trials led to the publication of detailed histories by both sides which remain the chief source of information concerning these events and the continuing debate over the magnitude and nature of the plot.[9]

In regard to the military response to Vesey's plot, there remains considerable evidence of willingness on the part of the national government to supply military aid. Extensive military preparations had been made by state authorities when they were informed of the existence of a plot, although they did not deem their resources adequate. During July, after many of the supposed insurgents were captured and when trials and continued investigations were at their height, Governor Thomas Bennett wrote to Secretary of War John C. Calhoun, later to become the chief theoretician of the proslavery forces, describing the insurrectionary situation and requesting additional federal troops. Bennett pointed out that the nearest fort held a large quantity of powder which the insurgents might seize and that only five men manned this garrison. Immediately, Calhoun ordered a company of artillery from St. Augustine, Florida to Charleston and instructed the commander to cooperate with the governor in suppressing the disturbance. The troops arrived in Charleston on 15 August. Governor Bennett later asked for additional forces to frighten blacks in the area. Since the South Carolina legislature was not in session, the governor was acting within the Constitution and statutes by asking for aid on his own authority. However, his request should have been directed not to the Secretary of War, but to the president, who under the statute had nondelegable authority to decide whether the disturbance warranted federal intervention. The apparent concern for strict conformity to the statutes was obviously lacking in the military response to both the Vesey and Prosser plots.[10]

The South Carolina legislature reacted frantically in the aftermath of the Vesey plot. Measures were passed to prevent the return of free blacks who had left the state, to imprison black seamen whose vessels entered harbors of the state until time of departure, and to execute persons who aided projected or actual insurrections. The enforcement of the Black Seaman's Act, which overstepped the bounds of state police power, brought immediate protest from the masters of vessels whose sailors were imprisoned. In the test case of *Elkison v. Deliesilline,* which was decided in 1823, federal judge William Johnson, a citizen of South Carolina, held the law invalid. Johnson felt that the act conflicted with both an 1815 convention with England which provided for mutual free ingress and egress of naval personnel and with the exclusive power of Congress to regulate foreign commerce. Nonetheless, South Carolina, joined by other southern states that had passed similar legislation, continued to enforce the law despite the court decision, asserting that state sovereignty and powers reserved under the Tenth Amendment to the Constitution supported her position. Protests from the British government and resolutions of condemnation from northern states brought no response from the southerners. President Monroe used no federal troops to enforce this decision of the district court or to uphold the supremacy of national authority and its treaty-making power under the Constitution. Secretary of State John Quincy Adams requested that the legislature repeal the act in question, while suggesting to the British government that under the federal system, indirect measures were sometimes effective and reassured the British that if violations continued, the national government would intervene. The violations continued; the president and Congress did nothing.[11]

Little additional legislation was passed in other areas of the South in response to the Vesey conspiracy. The southern states now relied on tightening enforcement measures already on the statute books and increasing the alertness of the patrols. When Secretary of War James Barbour sent a circular letter to state governors requesting information on military preparedness in July 1826 considerable concern about slave insurrection was reported. The lieutenant governor of Mississippi felt that volunteers who could respond quickly would be much more effective than the militia should a slave revolt occur, adding that his state was especially sensitive to this problem because of a large population of slaves. The adjutant general of Virginia believed that some means of insuring a speedy response from the militia might alleviate the problem. In summarizing the reports for Congress, Barbour stated that since the presence of large numbers of slaves kept the South perpetually on guard, great reliance for military defense would continue to be placed on the regular army. Nevertheless, he believed that the planters of the Lower South should be required to raise sufficient militia, including artillery and cavalry, to aid the regulars in manning the forts in the area and "to keep the black population in check." [12]

In 1831, "unusual uneasiness" again prevailed in the South. Rumors of revolts and insurrections were rampant. Military units were increasingly wary and kept the black population under careful surveillance. In Louisiana, officials informed the War Department that a major revolt threatened and requested that additional troops be sent to the area; troops in the vicinity were put on alert. Along the eastern seaboard, army units were moved from northern states into the South to prevent suspected insurrection.[13] The rumors were partly fulfilled in Southampton, Virginia in August 1831, when Nat Turner instigated a revolt with approximately seventy slaves. State military volunteers with the aid of federal troops, moved in to suppress the rebellion. The mayor of Norfolk sent notes requesting aid to the commander of Fortress Monroe and to the naval vessels, *Warren* and *Natchez* of the West India Squadron, stationed off Norfolk. Three companies of artillery with a field piece, a marine guard, and a detachment of seamen from each ship left for Southampton on the steamer *Hampton*. Disembarking at Suffolk and marching twenty-five miles, they stopped overnight and arrived the next day at Jerusalem where they joined the commander of the state militia, General Richard Eppes. According to the military report, the presence of the troops reassured a small group of white women and children gathered there. Although the regular troops had no opportunity to engage in actual conflict with any insurrectionaries, their commander thought that the "celerity" with which they acted and the "demonstration made by them during the march across country will undoubtedly have a lasting and salutary effect on the future conduct of that deluded people [blacks] against whom they were intended to act." The commander of the naval yard at Norfolk issued seven hundred stands of arms and twelve thousand rounds of ammunition to local white citizens. Approximately sixty-five white persons were killed. The rebels, with the exception of their leader, were all killed or captured within ten days after the outbreak of the disturbance. Nat Turner, who was not captured until 30 October, was executed after confessing on 11 November; eventually, eighteen of his companions were executed.[14]

On the heels of the revolt, fear mounted in other communities and local officials requested aid from army officers. Arms and ammunition were issued from the federal arsenal at Fortress Monroe to the citizens of Hampton, Virginia. The authorities at New Bern, North Carolina requested and received a detachment of army troops from the same fort to quell rumors and fear of disorder. These requests for aid were handled in an informal manner without regard to constitutional statutes. When Colonel James House at Fortress Monroe, Commodore J. D. Elliott, who commanded the West India Squadron, and Commander Lewis Warrington at the Norfolk navy yard reported their actions during the Turner disturbances to the Navy and War Departments, they received assurance that the president gave his "entire approbation" to the "promptitude" with which they had acted.[15]

A comparison of the manner in which the federal government exercised its military responsibility in several instances reveals some striking differences. When federal law was violated and federal courts defied in the Whiskey and Fries Rebellion, the president acted scrupulously and carefully within the limitation of the statute before invoking the use of troops. The federal government deferred action when South Carolina defied the federal courts in the Black Seaman's Controversy. In rumored or actual slave revolts, however, troops were utilized without the least thought of statutory requirements for invoking aid, yet the president gave his stamp of approval to prompt quasilegal military action. This legal variation might be explained on the grounds that federal revenue was a sufficiently important motive for military enforcement, but apparently the legal status of black seamen was not. In the cases of black insurrection, the president and War Department may not have believed that protocol should interfere with the national enforcement of the proslavery compromises of the Constitution. In any event, the Constitution proved to be a firm protector of the institution of slavery. Federal troops were sent even when they were not needed; in New Bern, North Carolina after the Turner revolt, the captain commanding the regular troops reported that some of the "principal citizens" admitted that federal aid was unnecessary, that troops had been requested precipitously, and that their continued presence would only make the citizens less vigilant when they finally left. The captain asserted, however, that if the local citizens were asked, many of them would demand a permanent federal garrison of troops as additional protection.[16]

The 1832 crisis in South Carolina offers another convenient vantage point from which to consider the uneven application of federal military power. In the Black Seaman's Controversy in 1823, South Carolina had demonstrated that a federal court decision and treaty could be successfully ignored; they now proposed to nullify a federal tariff law. South Carolina's increasing sensitivity on the antislavery issue, coupled with an economic decline in the 1820s, stimulated efforts to find a convincing formulation of the state sovereignty position which had been used to defend slavery since the first congresses. The philosophy found its fullest expression in the works of John C. Calhoun. Calhoun insisted that slaveholders were the real defenders of the Constitution, while those who challenged their interpretations were its enemies. Thus, in opposing the unwanted high tariffs, the public officials of South Carolina draped themselves in a constitutional theory of strict constructionalism and state sovereignty to evade a distasteful federal law, while they invoked broad constructionalism and national responsibility in order to demand federal aid to suppress black revolts. Ironically, Calhoun, who as secretary of war had dispatched federal troops to aid white South Carolinians after Vesey's Plot in 1822, worked out an elaborate theory to support insurrection by white South Carolinians against that same federal government.[17]

Although Andrew Jackson and Secretary of War Lewis Cass had congratulated the military commanders involved for their "promptitude" in dispatching unneeded federal troops at the time of the Turner Revolt, they vacillated when confronted with South Carolina's nullification of the federal law. Jackson responded to South Carolina's announced intention to defy enforcement of federal tariff collection by issuing a proclamation on 10 December 1832 which asserted that the law would be enforced. However, the president also ordered Cass to inform General Winfield Scott, who commanded the troops in South Carolina, to consult with the local district attorney and collector of customs, but to stand by for further instructions. South Carolina called out twelve thousand volunteers to resist federal law enforcement. Meanwhile, Jackson announced that he would take no positive action until he saw certified copies of the Nullification Acts, which had been passed by a special state convention. On 6 January 1833, in response to Jackson's request for further authority, Congress passed the Force Bill, which extended the jurisdiction of federal courts in revenue cases and empowered the use of any additional forces necessary to uphold the laws. At the same time, Congress passed an act reducing tariff rates. On 15 March, the South Carolina convention repealed the state ordinance nullifying the tariff law, and yet three days later, in an expression of defiance, the convention nullified the Force Bill. No confrontation occurred because no attempt was made to enforce the law. In effect, South Carolina had again successfully defied the national government.[18]

Jackson's dilatory policy could be attributed to a belief that federal military law did not provide for cases of state defiance, which was the position of the governor and legislature of South Carolina. However, a careful reading of the statutes indicates no distinction between insurrections *in* a state and insurrections *of* a state. The military provisions of the Force Bill added nothing to presidential authority; the only real amendment was a provision relieving the president of the necessity of issuing a dispersal proclamation before using the army and navy. Jackson's sympathy with slaveholders, as he was one, clashed with his nationalistic and assertive tendencies, and he felt that avoiding bloodshed among white South Carolinians was more important than law enforcement. His interpretation of presidential power in such cases was evidently shared by some members of Congress. In the debates on the Force Bill, Senator Theodore Frelinghuysen of New Jersey, who was on the committee that drafted the bill, explained that the president did not have the power to intervene under existing statutes, but that he was given that power in the Force Bill.[19]

While expressing the interest of his state in the continuance of the protective tariff during the House debates on the Force Bill and the 1833 lowering of the tariff, Tristam Burges, from the manufacturing state of Rhode Island, gave his opinion of the connection between nullification, military responsibility, and slavery. He stated that South Carolina proposed to take up arms for the glorious purpose of making slaves more valuable by rendering the product of their labor more valuable. He did not see why northern states should aid them in this endeavor. Instead, southerners should support northern manufacturing by paying the tariff. If manufacturing declined, the cities would decline, the population would become more dispersed, and the militia would be scattered and not easily gathered in an emergency. Regular troops might have to be recalled from the South, where they were primarily located to provide slaveholders with protection, and distributed more equitably around the country. (At this time, the approximately seven thousand men in the regular army were stationed largely in the South and West.) Burges further asserted that he saw no specific language delineating national responsibility for the suppression of slave insurrection in the Constitution; however, the Constitution had been consistently interpreted that way and northerners had not generally objected since they were deeply concerned about the safety of southerners. Burges indicated that he did not mind providing protection for southerners so long as they paid for it, and he felt a tariff beneficial to northern industry would be sufficient payment. Nullification made it possible to support the economic power of slavery on the one hand and to avoid payment for protection of the system on the other. Burges' effort was wasted. By 1832, it was well established in opinion, law, and precedent that the entire nation was responsible for the military protection of slavery and slaveholders.[20]

In the period from 1800 to 1833, the military arm of the United States proved its reliability to the southern slavery interests in the Prosser, Andry, Vesey, and Turner revolts. Yet, in the confrontations with South Carolina in the Black Seaman's Controversy and the Nullification Crisis, the national government merely demonstrated its hesitancy to act. The contradiction in response is obvious. Although the blame for this contradiction might be placed on the desire to prevent bloodshed or the need to confine the defiance to South Carolina, the most likely explanation is the powerlessness and extralegal status of black people. Blacks were nonpersons whose condition, whether slave or free, was of no constitutional concern to the national government. On the other hand, the perpetuation of the slave system and the protection of white people against slave revolt had become a constitutional responsibility of the government. It was more politic to change the law or ignore the plight of those damaged by failure to enforce a federal court order than to antagonize white southerners. During this thirty-year period, the proslavery provisions of the Constitution were reinforced by a body of tradition and practice; federal responsibility for the defense of slavery became more deeply entrenched in national policy, perhaps even beyond the possibility of reversal.

NOTES

1. Howell M. Henry, *Control of Slaves in South Carolina* (Emory, Va., 1914), pp. 36–8; Ralph B. Flanders, *Plantation Slavery in Georgia* (Chapel Hill, N.C., 1933), pp. 276–9; Joe G. Taylor, *Negro Slavery in Louisiana* (Baton Rouge, 1963), pp. 170–1, 204; Orville W. Taylor, *Negro Slavery in Arkansas* (Durham, N.C., 1958); James Sellers, *Slavery in Alabama* (Birmingham, 1950), p. 247.

2. Correspondence between Secretary of War Henry Knox and Captain Thomas Holt, commanding at New London, Virginia, 17 October 1793, General Accounting Office Record Group (hereafter cited as R.G.) 217, 3rd Auditor's Report, National Archives; Henry Aptheker, *American Negro Slave Revolts* (New York, 1943), pp. 209–19, *passim;* F. Roy Johnson, *The Nat Turner Slave Insurrection* (Murfreesboro, N.C., 1966), pp. 35–8; Roland McConnell, *Negro Troops of Antebellum Louisiana* (New Orleans, 1968), pp. 45–6; John S. Lofton, *Insurrection in South Carolina: The Turbulent World of Denmark Vesey* (Yellow Springs, Ohio, 1943), pp. 72–4; John H. Franklin, *Free Negro in North Carolina 1790–1860* (Chapel Hill, N.C., 1943), pp. 60–2.

3. Aptheker, *Slave Revolts*, pp. 219–23.

4. Ibid., pp. 234–9; Henry, *Control of Slaves,* pp. 35–9; John Russell, *The Free Negro in Virginia 1619–1865* (Baltimore, 1913), pp. 66–7, 96–7; Henry Ames, *State Documents on Federal Relations 5 American State Papers, Military Affairs* (Philadelphia, 1900), 2:464–7; *Annals of*

Congress, 9th cong., 2nd sess. (1804–5), pp. 994–1000; Leon Litwack, *North of Slavery; The Negro in the Free States, 1789–1861* (Chicago, 1960), p. 16; Aptheker, *Slave Revolts,* p. 226; John Hope Franklin, *From Slavery to Freedom* (New York, 1969), p. 217.

5. McConnell, *Negro Troops,* pp. 48–9; Aptheker, in *Slave Revolts,* pp. 249–51, says that sixteen more were executed in New Orleans shortly afterward. Dunbar Rowland, ed., *Official Letter Books of W. C. C. Claiborne, 1801–1816,* 6 vols. (Jackson, Miss., 1917), 6:17, 20; *Constitution of the United States,* art. IV.

6. Lofton, *Denmark Vesey,* pp. 81–2, 94–5, 125–6; Aptheker, *Slave Revolts,* pp. 268–72; Franklin, *Free Negro in North Carolina,* p. 193; Ames, *State Documents,* pp. 3, 11–12, 18–19; Litwack, *North of Slavery,* pp. 20–9.

7. Ames, *State Documents,* pp. 4–10.

8. *Annals of Congress,* 16th cong., 1st sess. (1820), pp. 1398, 1415, 1427, 16th cong., 2nd sess. (1820–1), p. 98; Samuel E. Morison, in *Harrison Gray Otis, 1765–1848: the Urbane Federalist* (Boston, 1969), pp. 424–32, puts Otis in perhaps a more favorable light but does not contradict the view that he accepted federal responsibility for the suppression of slave revolts.

9. James Hamilton, *Negro Plot on Account of the Late Intended Insurrection Among a Portion of the Blacks of the City of Charleston, South Carolina* (Boston, 1822); Lionel Parker and Parker Thomas, *An Official Report of the Trials of Sundry Negroes Charged with an Attempt to Raise an Insurrection in the State of South Carolina* (Charleston, 1822); Lofton, *Denmark Vesey,* chap. 12; Richard Wade, "The Vesey Plot; A Reconsideration," *The Journal of Southern History,* 30 (May 1964), pp. 143–61.

10. Thomas Bennett to John C. Calhoun, 15 July 1822, Register of Letters Received, file no. 30B (16), War Records Branch, National Archives, 30 July 1822; Calhoun to Colonel A. Eustis, 22 July 1822, file no. 55B (16), item 324, R.G. 107, National Archives; Calhoun to Major James Bankhead, 22 July 1822, item 446/408, R.G. 107, National Archives; *see also* Lofton, *Denmark Vesey,* pp. 172–3 and *Sen. Doc.* 209, 57th cong., 2nd sess. (1903), pp. 32–3, 50.

11. *Elkison v. Deliesilline,* 8 *Federal Cases* 493 (1823) (hereafter cited as *Fed. Cases*); Philip Hamer, "Great Britain, the United States and the Negro Seaman Acts, 1822–48," *The Journal of Southern History* 1 (1935), pp. 3–28; *Annals of Congress,* 17th cong., 2nd sess. (1822–3), p. 1055; Ames, *State Documents,* pp. 12, 45; *Constitution of the United States,* Sixth Amendment.

12. *American State Paper,* Military Affairs, 7 vols. (Washington, 1832–1860), 3:393, 414–5, 443, 1823.

13. Aptheker, *Slave Revolts,* pp. 290–310; *Sen. Doc.* 209 (1903), p. 56.

14. Aptheker, *Slave Revolts,* pp. 293–309; *Richmond Enquirer,* 2, 3, 6, and 16 September 1831; *Sen. Doc.* 209 (1903), pp. 261–2; Aptheker believes that troops helped to massacre blacks but does not say whether they were federal or state forces, *see Slave Revolts,* pp. 300–1.

15. *Richmond Enquirer,* 16 September 1831; *see also Sen. Doc.* 209 (1903), app. p. 262.

16. *Sen. Doc.* 209 (1903), app., pp. 263–4; The Virginia legislature responded with a brief flurry of interest over whether slavery ought to be maintained. The legislature did nothing tangible except to conclude that slavery could not be abolished unless compensation was paid to owners which no one apparently was willing to do, *see* Theodore M. Whitfield, *Slavery Agitation in Virginia 1829–33* (Baltimore, 1930).

17. Lofton, *Denmark Vesey,* pp. 211–37. William Freehling, *Prelude to Civil War, The Nullification Crisis in South Carolina* (New York, 1965), *passim.* Chapter 2 indicates that the economic decline was not all pervasive and that some proponents of nullification were prospering.

18. Bennett Rich, *The Presidents and Civil Disorder* (Washington, 1941), pp. 45–50; Freehling, in *Prelude to Civil War,* pp. 280–96, sets out the facts but concludes that the Nullifiers lost. I maintain that, legally and philosophically, since Jackson refused to enforce federal law, the law as it stood was successfully defied.

19. *Annals of Congress,* 22nd cong., 2nd sess. (1832–3), pp. 132–3.

20. *Register of Debates in Congress,* 23rd cong., 2nd sess. (1833–4), pp. 1394–5; Francis B. Heitman, *Historical Register and Dictionary of the United States Army* (Washington, 1903), p. 626; *House Document* 2 22nd cong., 2nd sess. (1832), p. 19 (hereafter cited as *House Doc.*).

4 / The Seminole War as a Black Freedom Movement: Phase One

In 1839, a pamphlet published by William Jay, son of the first Chief Justice of the United States, reviewed the federal government's legal and financial support of the institution of slavery from 1789. Among the instances chronicled by Jay were the ruthless suppression of slave insurrection and the relentless offensives against the Seminole Indians in the name of the Fugitive Slave Act even to the point of disregarding the territorial rights of foreign powers. Jay, like most abolitionists, was particularly incensed by the warfare waged against the Seminole Indians and the blacks residing among them because of southern proslavery interests and threats of secession. In words which support the repeated assertion that abolitionists were worse disunionists than southerners, Jay maintained that separation would be a good solution to the dissension; at least slavery would no longer have federal protection. For then, "should the slaves attempt to revolt the masters would be left to struggle with them unaided by the

fleets and armies of the whole Republic." As an additional consequence, fugitive slaves would be free as soon as they crossed the
southern boundary of the North.[1]

A review of the events cited by Jay will offer some basis for
determining the validity of his position. The fugitive slave problem on the southeastern frontier dated back to the colonial
period. Very early, slaves who escaped from the vicinity of South
Carolina sought sanctuary in nearby Spanish Florida, hoping to
avoid capture by living among the Seminole Indians. Since there
were no Spanish claimants to their persons, their chances for
maintaining their freedom were relatively high. They were evidently easily integrated into the Indian community. Quite natu-
rally, this refuge for runaways was a provocation as well as a
threat to southern slave interests.

When the colony of Georgia was established in 1733, South
Carolina at first approved the idea of forbidding slavery in the
new colony, thinking it would act as a buffer between South
Carolina and Spanish Florida. But when slaves began fleeing to
Georgia as well, South Carolinians changed their minds and encouraged the introduction of slavery in Georgia. The colonial
anxiety was not unwarranted as records reveal that by 1736, there
were sufficient numbers of runaway blacks and their descendants
to establish settlements in Florida. The problem was compounded
by the Spanish crown's refusal to grant British requests for extradition of the runaways, to the consternation of the British and
the southern colonies.[2]

The Seminole component of the problem emerged in 1750.
That year, many Creek Indians left Georgia because of tribal
dissatisfactions and migrated to Florida. Their numbers were
augmented from time to time by additional Creeks who disagreed
with tribal decisions or who were opposed to tribal treaties made
with the United States. One large group emigrated in 1814 because of opposition to the terms of the Treaty of Fort Jackson
made by some Creek leaders with the American government.
These emigrant Creeks became known in their language as *Seminoles,* which means *runaways.* Under Spanish colonial policy,
these exiles were incorporated into the Spanish population and
could acquire title to land and claim the protection of Spanish

laws. Some of these Seminoles formed fast friendships with blacks in Florida and, in a few cases, acquired title to blacks under Spanish law in order to ward off attempts by slavecatchers to return the former slaves to Georgia.

The Spanish government defended Indian–black interests against Georgian claimants but not from altruistic motives. Spain, fearing territorial incursions, regarded Florida as a buffer between the British colonies and her colonies to the south. In order to avoid the possibility of Indian attack on Spanish settlers in East Florida and to enlist the aid of Indians in the colony's defense if necessary, Spain sought to appease the Indians. Although the Spanish did not encourage slaves to flee to Florida, they feared offending the Indians by remanding the fugitives to their alleged masters. Spain enjoyed disconcerting the Americans, but avoided a confrontation.[3]

Under Spanish administration, the Indians and blacks in Florida prospered. Spanish administration of that territory, interrupted briefly by the cession of East and West Florida to Great Britain at the end of the Seven Year's War in 1763, was tolerant and unobtrusive. In the colonial period, the British stationed a few regular troops in South Carolina, largely to prevent slave rebellion; during the Seven Years War, the number of troops was increased. The British military did not pursue or in any way molest the blacks in Florida during the colonial period or during the British control of Florida from 1763 to 1783. Their garrisons were too weak and torn by strife between military and civilian officials to suppress or capture the fugitives and Indians, even if that had been their policy. Their presence, however, did act as a deterrent by reducing the number of slaves escaping to Florida from Georgia and South Carolina until the Revolution. During the Revolution, the British encouraged the flight of slaves and welcomed their support.[4]

The movement toward American independence left the problem of the treatment and disposition of the Florida Indians and blacks in the hands of the colonists. Georgians and South Carolinians expected the Continental Congress to afford them at least as much protection against the escape of slaves as the British had; Georgia's Council of Safety informed the Continental Congress in 1775 that a large force of troops would have to be sent to prevent slaves from accepting the British invitation to join those fugitives already in Florida. The two colonies continued to be a defensive problem throughout the war. In March 1779, Congress noted that South Carolina was unable to deploy troops effectively in the national crisis because they were needed to control her slaves. Although Congress was sympathetic to southern requests for aid, it also indicated that the army could not be expected to keep slaves from running away to the British; other military matters of colonial defense were more critical at this time.[5]

When Spain reacquired Florida in the peace settlement after the Revolution, the Georgians were disturbed. They were well acquainted with the Spanish position on the extradition of claimed fugitives, and they felt this issue was too central to their existence to dismiss or allow any compromise. Believing that the situation required immediate action, the government of Georgia planned to circumvent claims by Spain and obtain support from the American government under the Articles of Confederation. They asserted that after the peace settlement in 1783, the government of Georgia had made a treaty with the Creek Indians providing for the return of all slaves resident among the Creeks to Georgia claimants and, by logical extension, the return of the blacks residing among the Seminoles, who were merely runaway Creeks. Georgia demanded national enforcement of the alleged treaty in the face of several inconsistencies: the Creek denials that such a treaty had ever been made; the difficulty of establishing the slave status of persons who had lived free in Florida for a generation or who were born in Florida; and the fact that Georgia could not even produce a copy of the treaty.

When the Georgian claim was presented to Congress for action, Congress pointed out that under the Articles of Confederation, treaties could only be made by authority of Congress. In 1785, therefore, Congress appointed commissioners to negotiate with the Creek nation. When only two of the one hundred settlements comprising the Creek nation sent representatives to the meeting, the federal commissioners would not negotiate. The representatives from Georgia, however, proceeded to treat with the Creeks despite the legal prohibition against state treaty-making.[6]

The ensuing illegal treaty bound the entire Creek nation to return all slaves resident among them, and all fugitive slaves who sought refuge in the future, to Georgia claimants. The treaty was, of course, invalid on both sides, and frontier hostilities continued between Creeks and Georgians. Georgia was unable to repossess slaves living among the Creeks, who were slaveholders themselves, or to force the Creek nation to assume the extralegal responsibility of recapturing blacks in Florida. Georgia was therefore happy to be among the first states to ratify the new Constitution with its proslavery compromises. Clearly, they believed that the Fugitive Slave Clause and the military clauses of the Constitution would insure the suppression of Indians and the return of fugitives from Florida.[7]

There can be little doubt of the influence of the Fugitive Slave Clause and the military enforcement power of the national government on Georgia's haste to ratify the Constitution. On 4 January 1789, General Anthony Wayne of Georgia wrote to a delegate, James Wilson of Pennsylvania, requesting him to support prompt congressional approval for the establishment of a military district on the southern frontier similar to that established under the control of General Arthur St. Clair in the Northwest Territory. Wayne stated that the situation in Georgia, "from the depredations of the Indians . . . [and] the insidious protection afforded by the Spanish to our runaway Negroes" was so alarming "as to threaten the state with ruin and depopulation" unless timely aid was given by Congress.[8] On 25 December 1789, Wayne also wrote to Henry Knox, the new Secretary of War, urging immediate strong military occupation along the southern frontier before the Spanish gained increased influence among the Indians. He suggested that troops sent to Georgia be stationed so as to prevent fugitive slaves from "taking protection under the Spaniards. . . ."[9]

One of the first treaties made by President Washington supported the claims of the Georgia slaveholders. The 7 August 1790 treaty with the Creek Indians in Georgia reasserted the demands made in the earlier invalid treaties: the Creeks were bound to return black fugitives to their masters, even if these fugitives were living in Florida among the Seminoles. Promptly denouncing this indirect effort to interfere with their affairs, the Seminoles in Florida made it clear that Creeks from Georgia bent on enforcing the treaty could anticipate trouble. Further, Spanish authorities in Florida announced that resident blacks as well as Seminoles were under their territorial jurisdiction, and no subjects of the Spanish crown would be extradited to slavery. Impediments to enforcement also increased when even the southernmost Creek tribes rejected the idea that the treaty applied to the Seminoles. Temporarily thwarted, the Georgians sought new ways around these obstacles in their effort to maintain the system of slavery.[10]

Undaunted, President Washington appointed another commission to make a new treaty which all parties would accept as binding. The treaty, negotiated in 1796, again bound the Creeks to return fugitive slaves and implied that the Creeks were also acting for the Seminoles. The reasoning behind the continued insistence on that fiction is obvious: if the Creeks claimed that the Seminoles were really Creeks, then an argument could be made for Creek jurisdiction over the "Creeks" in Florida, Spanish sovereignty notwithstanding. A further argument could be made that failure to abide by the treaty gave the United States, as one of the high contracting parties, the right to take military action against the recalcitrants, even in Spanish territory. In a secret article, the treaty provided for payment of fifteen hundred dollars annually to the Creeks forever, for twelve hundred dollars annually to their principal chief, and one hundred dollars to six other chiefs for assiduous performance of the treaty obligation. In effect, a national bounty was promised for the capture of fugitive blacks.[11]

Despite the treaty, little progress was made in subduing the hostile Indians and blacks in Florida. Impatient with the unwillingness of the president to invade the Spanish possession openly, Georgia officials sent the state militia to Creek country to force the Creeks to comply with the treaty. They were repelled by the Creeks and blacks. Georgians, seeing their military efforts fail, thereafter urged the necessity for annexing Florida to the United States so that the vexing problem of Spanish sovereignty would be removed.[12]

In 1811, Congress, sympathetic to Georgia's viewpoint and also interested in American expansion, approved a measure providing for the annexation of Florida. Soon after its passage, an insurrection encouraged by the federal government was incited by a few malcontents in the northeastern part of Spanish territory and in Georgia. American forces took possession of Amelia Island in order to put down the "insurrection." When the Spanish government protested, President Madison, who had connived in the uprising, disavowed any federal connection in this shameful episode.[13]

Frustrated by the failure of the latest tactic, the state of Georgia again sent state troops into Florida in the fall of 1812, this time *to exterminate* the Seminoles and reenslave the refugee blacks. To Georgia's consternation, the southernmost Creeks aided the Seminoles, and together they defeated the militia. It was now obvious that repeated military efforts by a single state were doomed to failure. At that time, the Monroe administration, occupied with the War of 1812 on the northern frontier and with efforts to negotiate the acquisition of Florida from Spain, was reluctant to arouse Spanish and Indian antagonism on the southern frontier.[14]

During the War of 1812, the problem was further compounded by the British invitation to American slaves to join their naval service or to immigrate to the West Indies. A British officer whose forces had been driven out of Pensacola by Andrew Jackson furnished arms to the Indians and blacks in Florida and organized a small military unit. After the Battle of New Orleans, a strong fort was erected on the Appalachiola River by the British. When the British withdrew, the blacks were given possession of the fort with its artillery and military supplies. At that time, Spanish sovereignty was no obstacle to British territorial incursions; Spain was distracted by a revolution and civil war in her Latin American colonies.[15]

Southerners, however, were infuriated at the possession of a fort by persons whom they regarded as potentially destructive to the institution of slavery. Secretary of War William Crawford of Georgia, sympathetic to complaints from his state on this issue, carried on a lively correspondence laying the plans for the destruction of the fort with General Edmund Gaines, who commanded the southern frontier, and Andrew Jackson, who commanded the southwestern military district of the United States. On 16 May 1816, Jackson ordered Gaines to blow up the fort "regardless of the ground on which it stands." Gaines sent a regular army regiment and a contingent of upper Creek allies, together with artillery and the aid of two off-shore naval gunboats, to reduce the fort. Obviously, the fort was demolished without difficulty, and approximately 270 black women and children were killed, reportedly when an early shell hit a magazine of stored ammunition. A few survivors were turned over to Georgia slaveholders who claimed that their ancestors had owned ancestors of the prisoners. Weakly protesting this outrage, the Spanish government made avowals of friendship and blamed the British for erecting the fort in the first place. The naval gunboat commander explained to the Spanish that the United States had the legal right to punish the exiles under authority of treaties made with the Creeks, who had jurisdiction over the exiles. The weakened state of the declining Spanish empire in part explains her lack of real effort to defend her sovereignty; now at best, Spanish protection for the exiles in the face of American appeals to the "immutable laws of self-defense" would prove unreliable.[16]

In the wake of the Appalachiola Fort affair, the Indians and blacks, as well as the American forces on the southern frontier, prepared for increased hostilities. In mid-November 1817, General Gaines and a regular army force of three hundred men attacked a southern Creek settlement at Fowlton near the Georgia–Florida border in order to "punish the Indians" for their failing to adhere to the treaty of 1796. A gunfight ensued in which a number of Creeks were killed. These Creeks had persisted in their opposition to American plans for the Indians and blacks in Florida.[17]

On 30 November 1817, a group of Seminoles and blacks attacked a boat descending the Appachiola River with supplies for the American outpost at Fort Scott in southern Georgia. Thirty-five American soldiers and the wives of six soldiers were killed in the assault; six soldiers and one woman were taken prisoner. The American public was infuriated by this "perfidious" Indian attack. In his message to Congress on 25 March 1818, President Monroe pointed to the "unprovoked" warfare of the Indians and charged that the Seminoles were bound by the 1796 treaty with the Creeks not to commit depredations against Americans. The regular army was authorized to prepare an invasion of Florida to "punish" the Seminoles.[18]

At this point, General Andrew Jackson took personal command of the expedition which was to become known as the First Seminole War. With an army composed of 3,000 volunteers from Georgia and Tennessee, his home state, as well as 1,000 regular troops from Fort Scott, Jackson set out to subdue the Indians and blacks. At the time of the Fort Scott incident, General Gaines estimated that of the 2,400 exiles in Florida, only 400 were black. As Jackson pursued them in Florida, about one-half of the exiles were reported killed, and only a few were enslaved; the others escaped. The most celebrated incident of this campaign was the summary execution of two British subjects, Alexander Arbuthnot and Robert Ambrister, who, according to Jackson, were inciting the Indians to violence.[19]

Jackson, reporting to the War Department on his expedition in May 1818, explained that the campaign was designed to "undeceive" the Seminoles, who thought they would be protected by Spanish sovereignty. In correspondence between Jackson, the governor of Pensacola, and the Spanish military commander at St. Marks, which Jackson enclosed in his report to the War Department, the Spanish insisted that they had no connection with the Seminoles and blacks and that they had not directed raids against any United States citizens. Jackson's response to the Spanish was that they had neglected their duty to prevent such outrages because of impotence and enmity toward the United States. Jackson then took over the Spanish fort at St. Marks, ignoring the defenseless commander's protests, as well as the fort at Barrancas. In his communications with the Spanish and the War Department, Jackson kept insisting that the United States had a right to engage in warfare on Spanish territory. In his view, the

United States' mission and justification dated from the Fort Scott "massacre." No mention was ever made of the 270 deaths at the Appalachiola fort or the punitive expedition against the settlement at Fowlton.[20]

Jackson's defensive position of his actions was necessitated by criticism both in Congress and by the new Secretary of War, John C. Calhoun. Calhoun's criticism was not a result of legal or humanitarian concern, but was a politically motivated effort to tarnish Jackson's reputation. The congressional opposition stemmed from both political motivation and the necessity of displaying to the British some concern for the hanging of two English subjects. Senate and House committee reports on Jackson's expedition circumvented any discussion of the actual conflict over the fugitive slave issue. The house majority stuck to criticism of the summary execution of Arbuthnot and Ambrister, whom Jackson had accused of inciting this "savage and negro [sic] war." It was suggested that under the circumstances civil proceedings might have been preferable to a court martial. However, the Senate report strongly denounced Jackson's disregard of Spanish sovereignty and his circumvention of the war-making power of Congress as delegated in the Constitution.[21]

Jackson replied to their criticisms by summarizing the report he had sent the War Department earlier, with two significant additions: Congress had approved the war by making appropriations for it; additionally, the president as commander-in-chief was the only person who could decide whether he had carried out his orders faithfully, and as the president had in fact approved his conduct, Congress had no grounds for objection. The controversy fizzled on that note, and Jackson, the hero of New Orleans, was now also the savior of Florida.[22]

Justification by the administration for military actions in Florida became less complicated in 1819. The difficulty Spain was experiencing with her rebellious Latin American colonies and the impossibility of gaining English support in any military action against the United States finally led her to cede Florida to the United States in the Adams–Onis Treaty. Florida was now American territory and military power could be legally used to enforce the Fugitive Slave Act of 1793 without further explanation. Since any black person was presumed to be a slave, free blacks found in Florida could be adjudged as slaves who had fled some rightful owner. In order to remain true to the proslavery compromises of the Constitution, the national government was forced to make war upon the Indians and blacks in Florida; there was no solution short of armed confrontation, unless the blacks would surrender. The southern states quickly demanded that blacks be remanded under authority of the Fugitive Slave Act, as well as under the treaties made with the Creek nation which was still regarded as semisovereign. Any treaty-making would, of course, have to be done with the Creeks so long as the Seminoles refused to make any agreement affecting the rights of blacks living in Florida.[23]

In 1821, Secretary of War Calhoun appointed commissioners to make an additional treaty with the Creeks containing the same clause which provided for the rendition of blacks. The commissioners were ordered to negotiate for the benefit of Georgia, whose officials had traditionally insisted on this clause and had sent observers to insure and protect her interests. When one of the federal commissioners remonstrated against the Georgians dictating the terms of the treaty, Calhoun replaced him with one of the Georgian observers. The Creeks candidly told the commissioners that, while they could return black people within their nation, they could not be responsible for the Seminoles who were not under their jurisdiction. The commissioners insisted on the opposite view, reminding the Creeks that this was the settled construction accepted by the United States government since the treaty of 1796. In the resulting Treaty of Indian Springs, the Creeks ceded about five million acres of land to the United States for which they were to receive $200,000. The United States also agreed to reimburse parties who claimed to have slaves among the Creeks, thus gaining title to the slaves. Everyone was apparently satisfied: Georgians subsequently received $109,000 for slaves and other property lost; the Creeks received payment for their land; and the United States government became a slaveholder with title to those elusive blacks.[24]

But the problem was not solved yet, nor the last blood shed. Fugitive slaves continued to seek asylum in Florida, even after the First Seminole War. In 1822, a congressional committee was appointed to explore solutions to the problem. One of the committee's first moves was to ask Andrew Jackson, as an expert on Indian matters, for advice. Jackson responded helpfully with a suggestion that the Seminoles be forced to reunite with the Creeks and return to Creek country and that runaway slaves be remanded to Georgia claimants.[25]

Meanwhile, President Monroe decided that the Creeks were right in their protestations that the Seminoles were a separate tribe. Therefore, he sent commissioners to negotiate with the Seminoles in September 1823. Even though the majority of the Seminoles distrusted the Americans, the Camp Moultrie Treaty was made with a few of their members. The provisions of the treaty provided that the United States government protect the Seminoles from all persons whatsoever and prevent white persons from intruding on their lands. In return, those Seminoles present promised to prohibit fugitive slaves from joining their ranks and to apprehend and return them to their masters upon request. No claims were made to blacks resident in Florida at the time of the treaty. In addition, the Indians were to retreat to their own district in the south of Florida, an area with the least salubrious climate and poorest soil in the territory. The Indians voluntarily removed to the lands set aside for them.[26]

The presidential election of 1825 dropped the problem into the hands of John Quincy Adams. As secretary of state, Adams had approved Jackson's conduct in Florida and had shown more interest in the acquisition of Florida from Spain than sympathy for the Seminoles and blacks. During his administration as president, the Bureau of Indian Affairs handled the problem in conformity with the interests of slaveholders. In 1825, the bureau directed its agents to take any black identified by a slaveholder as a runaway slave to St. Augustine where the dispute would be decided by a federal judge as provided in the Fugitive Slave Act. However, the agents were given the authority to judge the validity of any counterclaims made for the same black by the Seminoles. If the agent felt the Indian making the claim was truthful, the Indian was permitted to keep the black until the judge decided the issue; if the agent did not believe the Seminole, he could ignore his claim. The alleged slave had nothing to say in the matter. The only evidence that would be permitted to rebut the presumption of slave status and immediate enslavement was the possession of manumission papers. No recent runaway or any person descended from those who had fled since 1660 could possibly produce such papers.[27]

With this mandate, slaveholders claiming blacks as their property now entered Florida in large numbers. Contrary to the law, some agents surrendered blacks without a court decision, and regular army troops at Fort King in Florida were assigned to aid in the arrest of fugitives. The poorly supported and reckless claims of slavecatchers, even to blacks for whom the Seminoles could prove title, as well as the incursions of whites into Indian areas supposedly protected under the treaty of 1823, led to an increasingly tense situation.[28] Consequently, in May 1828, Colonel George Brooke, who commanded the United States Army in Florida, and the federal district judge at St. Augustine ordered Indian agents to cease giving slaves claimed by Indians to slaveholders until title was established by the court. This policy was designed to decrease friction with the Indians, not to protect blacks who were defenseless without the possession of "free papers." The national government faced an impossible dilemma: on the one hand, it had to enforce the Fugitive Slave Act which would allow slaveholders to enslave practically every black in Florida; on the other hand, it was bound to abide by the Indian treaty which insured no penetration of Indian territory. Failure to keep white persons off Indian land could precipitate war.[29]

After rejecting one solution to the Florida difficulties—leaving the Indians and blacks in peace—the national government adopted the policy of "removing" the Indians west of the Mississippi, an action which would leave the way open for settlement of Florida by slaveholders. The Indian Removal Act of May 1830 authorized the president to negotiate with the tribes east of the Mississippi, offering to pay them for their land in the east and granting them land west of the Mississippi River to which perpetual title would be attached. The act itself did not dictate coercion, but it was federal law which the president was expected to uphold even if military force became necessary.[30]

Andrew Jackson, who assumed the presidency in 1829, was ill-suited to handle the Indian problem. He had successfully "punished" the Indians during his expedition of 1818 and had shown his lack of concern for Indian interests when he refused to enforce a Supreme Court decision favorable to the Cherokees in 1832. The Indian Removal Act, however, promulgated a policy he favored, and he stood ready to enforce it. The first step in its enforcement was the 1833 Treaty of Payne's Landing made with the Seminoles, which provided that eight chiefs go west to approve the land set aside for them, accompanied by Abraham, one of the blacks among them, to act as interpreter. If the chiefs found the country suitable and believed reuniting with the Creeks feasible, they would agree to further articles of the treaty providing for removal westward. Other articles of the treaty provided for an exchange of land based on the provisions in the Indian Removal Act and the United States' liquidation of slaveholders' claims to blacks among the Seminoles, so that the blacks could join them in the move beyond the Mississippi. While in the West, the chiefs were induced to sign an additional treaty on 28 March 1833 in which they expressed satisfaction with the area set aside for them and agreed to permanently move westward on lands separate from the Creeks.[31]

When the Seminole chiefs returned, they told the Indian agents that they would report on conditions in the West to their people and decide whether to move. To this, the agents replied that when the chiefs agreed to move, they had bound the entire Seminole nation and also indicated that the Creeks had advised the War Department that the Seminoles should now be reunited with them and be placed under Creek jurisdiction in the West. The Creeks had also asserted that since the United States acquired title to any slaves among the Seminoles in 1821 by agreeing to pay Georgia claimants, these "slaves" would become the property of the Creeks when they moved west. This assertion was a crushing blow to the hopes of the Seminoles and the blacks. If they went west, all blacks would again be in danger of enslavement, now by Creeks! Further, as far as the national government was concerned, the Camp Moultrie Treaty, setting aside land for the Seminoles in Florida, was void; the Seminoles had no alternative—they must go west.[32]

The Seminoles and blacks tried to obtain a change in policy from the War Department through the intercession of their agent. The Indian agent bluntly told the commissioner on Indian affairs that the reason the Seminoles were so slow in preparing for the move west was that they knew the blacks would be reenslaved by the Creeks. They were also sure that if they remained in Florida, white people would reenslave the blacks unless the government gave them separate land and protection. Meanwhile, slaveholders petitioned Jackson to accelerate the process of Indian removal from Florida, because the slave system could not be firmly established if free blacks and Indians remained in the territory. Estimates of the number of Seminoles and blacks involved vary, but most authorities agree that there were approximately two thousand. The War Department replied to the Seminole agent and white petitioners that the removal policy would be carried out as speedily as possible. The Seminoles and blacks prepared for war.[33]

NOTES

1. William Jay, *Miscellaneous Writings* (Boston, 1853), pp. 245, 249, 311-9.

2. Herbert Aptheker, "Maroons Within the Present Limits of the United States," *The Journal of Negro History* 24 (1939), pp. 172-3; Kenneth Porter, "Negroes and the Seminole War, 1817, 1818," *The Journal of Negro History* 36 (1941), pp. 249-80.

3. *American State Papers, Military Affairs,* 7 vols. (Washington, 1832-1860), 1:748-9.

4. Herbert Osgood, *The American Colonies in the Eighteenth Century,* 4 vols. (New York, 1958), 2:218; John W. Shy, *Toward Lexington: The Role of the British Army in the Coming of the Revolution* (Princeton, 1965), pp. 12, 33, *passim;* Charles Mowat, *East Florida as a British Province, 1763-84* (Berkeley, 1934), pp. 113-4, 120-1.

5. Peter Force, ed., *American Archives,* consisting of a collection of *Authentick Records, State Papers, Debates, and Letters and Other Notices of Publick Affairs,* 9 vols. (Washington, 1837–53), 5th ser., p. 1; Worthington C. Ford, ed., *Journals of the Continental Congress,* 33 vols. (Washington, 1904–36), 13:385; Aptheker, *American Negro Slave Revolts* (New York, 1943), p. 22.

6. *American State Papers, Indian Affairs,* 2:15, 5:25; *Articles of Confederation,* art. IX.

7. Loc. cit.; *Constitution of the United States,* art. IV, sec. 2 and 4, art. VI, art. I, sec. 8; art. II, sec. 3.

8. Anthony Wayne to Henry Knox, 25 December 1789, MS, Clements Library, University of Michigan, Ann Arbor, Michigan.

9. Anthony Wayne to James Wilson, 4 July 1789, MS, Clements Library.

10. *Annals of Congress,* 1st. cong., 1st sess. (1789–91), pp. 1068–74; *American State Papers, Indian Affairs,* 1:73–4, 304–5, 320, 336, 387, 792; Laurence Foster, *Negro–Indian Relationships in the Southeast* (Philadelphia, 1935), p. 23.

11. *American State Papers, Indian Affairs,* 1:586–7.

12. Ibid., p. 813.

13. Rembert W. Patrick, *Florida Fiasco: Rampant Rebels on the Georgia-Florida Border, 1810–15* (Athens, Georgia, 1954), p. 170 ff.

14. Ibid., pp. 199–207.

15. *House Exec. Doc.* 119, 15th cong., 2nd sess. (March 1819) contains letters and reports to and from the War Department describing the events leading up to the destruction of the fort.

16. Loc. cit.; *see also American State Papers, Indian Affairs,* 1:714, 748, et. seq.; *Sen. Doc.* 172, 15th cong., 1st sess. (24 March 1818). Cf. James Parton, *Life of Andrew Jackson* 3 vols. (1860), 2:402, who asserts that the Spanish wanted the fort destroyed. There is a letter written under threat of attack from the commander of Pensacola to Jackson, which indicates that the commander agreed with Jackson's viewpoint about the fort.

17. *House Exec. Doc.* 173, 15th cong., 2nd sess. (March 1819); *American State Papers, Military Affairs,* 1:681–2, 712, 714, 764.

18. *American State Papers, Military Affairs,* 1:680, 687, 700, 739; *American State Papers, Indian Affairs* 2:4, 16; *Sen. Doc.* 173, 15th cong., 1st sess. (25 March 1818).

19. *American State Papers, Military Affairs,* 1:690–1, 700–8, 735–40; 754–7.

20. *Sen. Doc.* 35, 15th cong., 2nd sess. (November 1818), contains letters to and from Jackson, Gaines, and the War Department.

21. *House Doc.* 100 (24 February 1819); *Sen. Doc.* 82 (12 January 1819).

22. Loc. cit.; *American State Papers, Military Affairs,* 1:735, 754–5.

23. Fugitive Slave Act of 1793, 1 *Stat* 302 (1793); *Constitution of the United States,* Fugitive Slave Clause, art. 14, sec. 2.

24. *American State Papers, Indian Affairs,* 2:248–9, 253, 429, 665.

25. Ibid., 2:69–71, 433–4, 439, 440.

26. Loc. cit.

27. *House Exec. Doc.* 271, 24th cong., 1st sess. (December 1835), contains documents, letters, and reports on Seminole difficulties.

28. Loc. cit.

29. *House Doc.* 17, 19th cong., 2nd sess. (December 1826), contains letters transmitted from War Department relative to Seminole Affairs; *House Doc.* 82 (January 1825), contains letters from Indian agents concerning condition of Indians and blacks.

30. 4 *Stat* 411–12 (1830); *Constitution,* art. II, sec. 2, art. VI.

31. *Sen. Doc.* 142, 24th cong., 1st sess. (December 1835), contains letters and papers tracing the origin and evolution of Seminole hostilities. The cases involving the Cherokees were *Cherokee Nation v. Georgia,* 5 Peters 1 (hereafter cited as Pet.) (1831); *Worcester v. Georgia,* 6 Pet. 515 (1832).

32. Loc. cit.; Treaty of Indian Springs, 1821, supra.; *American State Papers, Indian Affairs,* 2:248–9, 253, 429, 665.

33. Loc. cit.; *American State Papers, Military Affairs,* 6:466, 478.

5 | The Seminole War as a Black Freedom Movement: Phase Two

The old lines of battle in the Seminole War were redrawn: the government remained committed to the removal of the Seminoles and the reenslavement of the blacks; the Indians and blacks insisted upon their right to remain free and in Florida. The Second Seminole War began late in 1835, when Wiley Thompson, an Indian agent, arrested and consigned to slavery the part Negro wife of Osceola, a Seminole chief. Apparently, when Osceola protested too vigorously in June of 1835, Thompson confined him to jail for six days. Upon his release, Osceola vowed retribution; on 28 December, Thompson was slain by the Seminoles in retaliation. The incensed Indians and blacks also successfully ambushed a regiment of American reinforcements en route to Fort King, Florida. Seminoles and blacks then stormed through Florida, attacking settlements and creating great fear among the white inhabitants. Pressure for action mounted in Washington, but the prolonged failure of the Americans to change their perspective, or to accurately define the issues, allowed this protracted war to continue for almost another decade, ending not in victory for either side, but in dismal confusion.[1]

Congress, at least publicly, exhibited a singular lack of understanding of the causes and nature of the Seminole War. Jacksonian Democrats, such as Senator Thomas Hart Benton of Missouri, defended the administration and the enormous war expenditures and lent their support to Democratic generals, such as Thomas Jesup. The anti-Jacksonians, Whigs or the Federal Party, attacked the administration for expenditures in a war against a "ragtag band of naked savages," yet praised Whig generals, such as Winfield Scott and Zachary Taylor, who were "hampered" by the inefficiency of Jacksonian war departments. The United States was hopelessly mired in an endless war where regular army tactics did not work and critics made the most of it. Discussion about the war in Congress mainly concerned requests for appropriations. That the nation must expand into Florida and make it safe for slavery was not questioned. Since the nation's military power was pledged to defend and support slavery, there was no point in discussions hostile to slavery interests. Proslavery advocates were already sensitive enough after the slave revolts, the Nullification Crisis, the Missouri controversy, and the fight over abolitionist petitions in Congress. Both Democrats and Whigs wanted to gloss over sectional differences and cement party loyalties, not divide the country. Consequently, Congress approved the policy of not discussing antislavery petitions by adopting a series of "Gag Resolutions," which postponed indefinitely the entertainment of the sticky issue. Little mention was ever made of the real reason for the Seminole intransigence—the fear that the Florida blacks would be enslaved. Congress refused to acknowledge that the war would have been unnecessary if some assurances had been given the Seminoles that the blacks would be left alone.

When the war appropriation bill came up in January 1836, Daniel Webster, reflecting the general tenor of the Senate, said that he knew nothing about the war except what he read in the public gazettes. He had deduced that the cause of the conflict was the attempt to remove the Indians. Henry Clay chimed in that he knew nothing either. In reply, Benton explained that the killing of white people by the runaway blacks was a partial cause of the war. In his opinion, the loss of so many lives resulted from abolitionist agitation. When succeeding administrations were asked about the aims of the war, the standard reply was that the immutable laws of self-defense, as well as the Fugitive Slave Act and the preservation of the institution of slavery in Georgia, South Carolina, and Florida, dictated the use of American military might against the Indians and blacks. National policy was to remove or exterminate the Indians and blacks in Florida even though the current conflict centered on the failure of the Indians to uphold treaties which were fraudulently obtained by the United States.[2]

Soon after the hostilities recommenced, General Winfield Scott was given command of the army in Florida. As the war dragged on with little success, he was severely criticized. Jackson, comparing Scott's failure with his own success in 1818, removed him from command in 1837. At this time, the army had captured about 124 women and children, but not one warrior.[3] General Thomas Jesup, one of Scott's critics, replaced him. Jesup succeeded in obtaining a surrender from the Indians on 6 March 1837. The agreement provided that the Indians and blacks were to migrate together to the West under the protection of the United States Army. The army was reduced in size, and the exiles and Seminoles began peaceably moving westward.[4]

The war was almost immediately resumed, however, when Jesup failed to keep his agreement. He had met resistance when the slaveholders in Florida and Georgia, insisting that the blacks were their property, refused to permit the blacks to migrate; in addition, Osceola had been captured when he came in to parley under a flag of truce in October 1837. Jesup, although properly criticized in the press for his violation of the laws of war in capturing Osceola, regarded this violation as a necessary step in concluding the war. There was considerable legal authority, however, for the slaveholders' insistence that blacks not be taken west. Jesup could not legally permit property to be transferred unless there was some judicial determination of the rights of the parties concerned. The army, under the Constitution, was pledged to protect slaveholders in the use and enjoyment of their property. The 1832 Treaty of Payne's Landing had supposedly solved that problem for Jesup by providing payment from the federal treasury to liquidate any claims to blacks living among the Seminoles. Claimants of slaves were to file with the United States' government, both for blacks residing among the Indians at the time of the Treaty of Payne's Landing and, by extension, for any others who joined the Indians while they were in the process of moving westward. However, the slaveholders did not accept this solution. At first, they wanted to restrict any operation of the treaty to those residing among the Indians when the treaty was made. Later, they wanted to overturn the treaty provisions altogether by saying one could not tell one group of blacks from another and, in any case, all blacks should remain in slavery. General Jesup and the War Department promptly yielded to the slaveholders' demands and delivered claimed blacks to the claimants rather than permitting all blacks to go west with the Seminoles as promised. The war was supposedly waged to enforce the Treaty of Payne's Landing and also the surrender agreement of March 1837. Officers and men were detailed to take blacks who joined the Seminoles for transportation westward to places where claimants could conveniently reenslave them.[5]

When the Seminoles and blacks responded to this perfidy by refusing to cooperate in their removal, Jesup renewed warfare. In the summer and fall of 1837, Jesup, desperate for success, made an agreement with the Creeks and the Florida militia, granting them ownership of any unclaimed black exiles they captured. This agreement had the approval of the War Department. Consequently, the Creeks gained title to some ninety captured blacks; the Florida militia claimed varying interests in other blacks. On 6 September 1837, Jesup ordered payment to the Creeks for the value of their ninety blacks, detaining the blacks at Fort Pike, Louisiana, until the government decided what to do with them. The secretary of war approved his action on 7 October 1837. Subsequently, the Creeks refused reimbursement, stating that they preferred possessing the slaves. The War Department then persuaded a Georgia slaveholder to offer the Creeks fifteen thousand dollars for the ninety blacks, which the

Creeks accepted after some debate. Meanwhile, the ninety slaves had inadvertently been moved to a fort west of the Mississippi. When the Georgia slaveholder sent an agent armed with a War Department order to claim the slaves, the commanding general refused to comply because he lacked sufficient forces to control what he feared would be a violent Indian reaction. Now the Seminoles and blacks were in disarray; some blacks had been sent west and others had been reenslaved; still others remained hidden in Florida, hoping for a change in national policy.[6]

Meanwhile, in conjunction with an administration request for an additional appropriation for the war in September 1837, Secretary of War Joel Poinsett circulated a letter he had written to Silas Wright, chairman of the Senate Finance Committee, explaining the administration's position on the war. Congress was also referred to a five-volume War Department preparation which contained correspondence and reports on the topic of Indian removal. Poinsett's letter indicated that since the Seminoles had agreed to move west and then unexplainedly failed to comply, the government was solely attempting to carry out the removal policy enacted by Congress and to protect Floridians from violent outrages. Thirty-five administration critics would not permit the matter to rest there. On 19 September 1837, Representative Henry Wise of Virginia proposed that a select committee be appointed to inquire into the causes, the corruption, and the expenditures of the war. The House spent the next session trying to decide whether such a committee was necessary. Critics and defenders alike, however, assumed that the only problems were the savage fighting ability of the Indians and the insalubrious climate and swampy terrain of Florida.[7]

In an effort to capture the blacks and Seminoles remaining in Florida, the government now invoked the aid of the Cherokees, who were convinced that the best policy for the Seminoles was to go west to avoid annihilation. When several Seminole chiefs, who came under a flag of truce to parley with the Americans and Cherokees, were taken prisoner and sent west, the strategy failed. The Seminoles resolved not to submit to the United States or move without guarantees of protection for the blacks.[8]

Since Jesup did not want to fail in Florida as ignobly as General Scott had, as early as July 1837, he hinted to the War Department that it might be necessary to permit the remaining Seminoles to stay in the southern part of Florida. In 1838, his policy in shambles and his army disgruntled, Jesup was ready to give up military efforts against the Seminoles. He met with some Seminole chiefs to see if they would accept terms permitting their people to remain in the Everglades. The Seminoles found this solution acceptable. Jesup wrote to Poinsett, a South Carolina slaveholder and a good Jacksonian, asking for approval of the policy. Poinsett replied that the Treaty of Payne's Landing, made under the authority of the Removal Act of 1830, was the law of the land and its execution was the constitutional duty of the president. Poinsett's position had been reversed from his attitude during the nullification controversy in which he counseled Jackson to have patience with South Carolina in the face of her violation of federal law. He chose to ignore the terms of the surrender agreement made by General Jesup in March 1837, stating that it was not a treaty and thus not the supreme law of the land. Administratively overruled, Jesup capitulated and continued to capture as many blacks as possible for reenslavement. Before the end of Jesup's command in Florida, some nine hundred Seminoles and three hundred blacks had been removed. To compound the military problem, the Seminoles were assigned to Creek lands in the West and, not surprisingly, they refused to live with the Creeks. The Cherokees, conscience-stricken as a result of their efforts to persuade the Seminoles to surrender, gave them temporary use of part of their territory.[9]

By 1838, the costs of the war approached twenty million dollars, and the Whigs were still making political capital out of this fact. In response, on May 31, Representative Hopkins Turney, a Democrat from Tennessee, asserted that Indian removal was a beneficial policy and that the Whigs were aligning themselves with abolitionists, who were Indian and Negro lovers, by criticizing the policy. Further, opponents of removal were the same people who under the garb of religion "strained every nerve for the nefarious purpose of exciting the slaves of the South to insurrection and bloodshed." Wise of Virginia said that he failed to see why the Indians could not remain in peace in Florida until they gradually became extinct. In addition, Indian agents had told him that the Indians had not really approved the Treaty of Payne's Landing, thus making the entire program of removal fraudulent. Charles Downing, delegate from the territory of Florida, jumped to attack Wise, maintaining that Indian agents had obtained their information from Indians and blacks. Since white men had told Congress that the treaty was valid, he declared that the word of the whites should be believed in preference to that of the blacks and Indians. Wise retreated.[10]

In the Senate on 8 June 1838, Samuel Southard of New Jersey attacked the administration's position, insisting that the war was being pursued to enforce an invalid and fraudulent treaty. Benton was well prepared for the defense on this occasion. He outlined the entire history of American–Seminole relations since 1831 from the administrative point of view. He concluded that the Seminoles had independently decided to go west because game was exhausted and white settlers were approaching their land. Further, Benton felt that the real motive for the delay in removal was the "desire for blood and pillage" on the part of the Indians but still more "on the part of the five hundred runaway Negroes mixed up among them." These Indians and blacks, he continued, believed they could raid white settlements forever and run back to hide in the swamps; consequently, the American military establishment proposed to "undeceive" them of that notion. Benton read from the Treaty of Payne's Landing, skipping over Article VI, which provided for the liquidation of slaveholder's claims to blacks so that they could peacefully go west with the Seminoles. Next, he chronicled the bloody deeds of the Seminoles and exiles, making no mention of the injustices they had suffered. Anyone who defended the Seminoles, according to Benton, was indulging in "mawkish sentimentality on behalf of yellow and black men," whose leaders ought to be summarily executed as Jackson had executed Arbuthnot and Ambrister during the First Seminole War. Benton optimistically predicted an early end to the war since the Indians and blacks were surrendering or being killed in encouraging numbers. The war, however, was to continue for another three years.[11]

When the new Congress met in December 1839, Poinsett reported that the Indians were still hostile and their number not significantly lessened, despite Benton's sanguine prediction of the year before. The administration, anxious to end the war before the next election campaign, introduced an armed settler bill for the settlement of Florida. Speaking in favor of the bill, Benton reversed his previous position and explained that the Indians could no longer be caught and removed, since there had been no real battles in Florida for two years, only massacres and assassinations. Regular army tactics were apparently doomed to failure. However, he believed that placing ten thousand armed settlers in Florida who would receive land grants for their service when the war was over might prove to be an effective strategy. These settlers were to live in stockades, receive government supplies, and have a small number of regular army personnel stationed among them. When the Indians were forced to come out of hiding, the settlers would exterminate them. The Whigs were opposed to the proposal. William C. Preston, Whig senator from South Carolina, insisted that the government clear all the Indians and blacks out of Florida before settlement proceeded. As the settlement in Florida would consist primarily of plantations with slaves, slavery could not exist in an area where Indians and blacks could entice slaves away from their masters. Senator Robert Strange of North Carolina, although asserting he was an administration supporter, agreed with Preston and proposed that bloodhounds be used against the Indians and blacks. Preston suggested that the administration put General Zachary Taylor, a Whig, in charge of a riding squadron to search and destroy the enemy. Benton attempted to reply to the critics by saying that Florida should be settled by yeoman farmers who wanted to work their own land, since large slaveholdings would make the area even less defensible. He believed that the government recognized that it must change its policy since the old policy had not worked. Florida must be settled promptly, he continued, and Whigs were opposed to a policy which would facilitate this because they thought the state would vote Democratic. According to Benton, Whigs and the abolitionists who wanted Florida to remain a haven for runaways were in agreement. Despite the administration's efforts, the armed settler bill failed to pass, and the war continued as before.[12]

When Zachary Taylor succeeded Jesup in May 1838, he would not temporize or attempt reconciliation in Florida and again began a course of action aimed at moving every Indian and black westward. However, he would have nothing to do with efforts to reenslave blacks. Despite this change of attitude, the Indians refused to trust the Americans. American military efforts were a fiasco. Finally, President Van Buren and Secretary of War Poinsett, in desperation, decided to make a new treaty giving the Seminoles land in Florida—the same suggestion previously proposed by General Jesup and Indian agents which had been rejected. At this time, however, the Jacksonians were suffering increasing criticism for their inability to end the war. An agreement was made with the Indians on 18 May 1839 that they and the blacks could remain in southern Florida, and the war was declared at an end.[13]

Some blacks and their Indian friends were unconvinced and refused to believe that the whites would leave them in peace. They decided to ignore the government's demands for their surrender and organized resettlement. They had been deceived too often by promises from the military. Stymied, the army and militia of Florida now began hunting the Indians and blacks in order to force their surrender. Bloodhounds were brought in from Cuba to aid in the hunt, but this technique proved ineffective. In the early spring of 1840, after almost two years in Florida, Zachary Taylor was granted his request to be relieved of his station.

The remarkable Indians and blacks were not only capable of evading the army but were able to attack white settlements at will. At this point, the regular army had about five thousand troops in Florida, although many of these were incapacitated by recurring tropical fevers and the oppressive heat. The expenditures for the war became an issue in the presidential campaign of 1840, partially contributing to Van Buren's defeat. The American public, including many members of Congress, knew little of the black problem as it related to the war; however, they were aware that the war was very costly. In desperation, the War Department brought several Seminoles back from the West to tell those in Florida of the glories of removal, but this action only further infuriated the Indians and blacks, who by this time were determined to fight to the finish.[14]

When the Taylor administration took office, Colonel William Worth was assigned to take command in Florida on 19 May 1841. Worth was ordered to reduce expenditures and find some means of bringing the war to a close. The regular army had become increasingly discontented with its role in the war over the last ten years. They were assailed by slaveholders for their failure to prevent the escape of slaves and to return all blacks in Florida to slavery. Further, the people of Georgia and Florida successfully undermined any workable agreements or solutions the army made with the enemy. The army payroll was swollen with payments to Floridians as commissary workers and contractors and with the expense of rations supplied to Floridians driven from their homes.[15]

Colonel Worth adopted a policy that Jesup had dishonestly tried earlier, which involved holding a chief hostage in order to entice the Indians and blacks out of hiding. Worth told the chief to send five of his braves to explain the new removal policy to his people. The government guaranteed not to enslave the blacks; yet if the Indians and blacks did not surrender, the chief would be hanged. As a result of this ploy, about two hundred Indians and blacks came out of hiding during July 1841. They were immediately sent west. Claimants of blacks were told to seek compensation from the national government. Thereafter, convinced of the honesty of this policy, Seminoles and exiles readily came forward to emigrate.

Worth cut expenditures by sending people who were on government rations home and discharging civilians on the army payroll. He also relied on regular army troops and refused to utilize the Florida and Georgia militias. In response to this action, the governor of Georgia, as well as the congressional delegate from Florida, protested to President Tyler. Worth responded that the militia was too expensive, seemed more interested in capturing and enslaving blacks than warfare, and intimated that they were a hindrance to efforts to end the war. Secretary of War John Spencer told the protestors that Worth would be advised of their position and would take whatever action was proper.[16]

The war in Florida was finally closed in August 1843. The few hostile Indians remaining in the territory agreed to stay in southern Florida. Most of the Seminoles and blacks had willingly moved west, and at least some of the blacks had evaded the re-enslavement. On 25 January 1845, the government made a treaty with the Seminoles and the Creeks that the blacks and Seminoles would live separately in a part of Creek country with partial autonomy. Any dissension over transactions occurring before the treaty date would be decided by the president of the United States.

Travesty was to compound treachery, for as soon as the blacks moved to Creek lands, attempts were made to enslave them. They fled to Fort Gibson, where the military commander accorded them temporary protection until he could get instructions from Washington. President Polk was disconcerted by the incident, and upon finding a written basis for the blacks' claim in the surrender agreement made with General Jesup in March 1837, he wrote Jesup, requesting an interpretation of this document. Jesup replied that the agreement made them free from all claims. Polk also wished to have a supporting opinion from the attorney general. However, there was some difficulty because the Attorney General was Nathan Clifford of Maine, who might take too favorable a view of the black claim for freedom. Therefore, Polk waited to secure an opinion until after Clifford left to become minister to Mexico in 1848. John Mason of Virginia, who was given an interim appointment by the president, wrote an opinion on this matter, before being replaced by Isaac Toucey of Connecticut. Mason's opinion was that the blacks were entitled to their freedom, but that the executive arm could not use the military power of the United States to protect them. The blacks saw the handwriting on the wall; after twenty years of fighting for their freedom, they fled to Mexico in September 1850.[17]

Relentlessly, slaveholders continued to pursue their claims to blacks who had been transported west, still insisting that any black found in Indian Territory was a slave. Although, in August 1838, Attorney General Benjamin Butler had prepared an opinion for the secretary of war indicating that the Constitution and laws obliged the president to use military power to remand fugitive slaves found only in a *state* and not in Indian Territory, this did not settle the issue. In February 1854, Caleb Cushing, attorney general under Franklin Pierce, decided that Butler was mistaken. Cushing's opinion had been solicited when a Mississippian requested military aid to claim a group of blacks who were allegedly living among the Choctaws. Cushing explained that when Article IV, Section 4 of the Constitution required the national government to protect the states against domestic violence, it included territories by extension; therefore, Article IV, Section 2 meant persons held to labor in a territory as well as a state. Further, the Fugitive Slave Act specifically provided for the rendition of runaways in the northwestern and southwestern territories. Since these were the only territories possessed by the United States at the time, the provision should be extended to territory acquired thereafter. Another argument he advanced was that Indian Territory was south of the Missouri compromise line, which was to be the northern boundary for slavery in the Louisiana Purchase territory; and in slave areas, all black people were presumed to be slaves unless proven to the contrary. Finally and most importantly, Cushing stated that the Act of Congress of 30 June 1834, granted the commissioner of Indian affairs the authority to remove anyone from Indian territory who was there contrary to law and gave the president the power to use military force for compliance. Fugitive slaves did not belong in Indian Territory; therefore, claimants could call upon the president to use the army to remand them if necessary.[18]

Although it is possible to discount Cushing's opinion as inapplicable to the blacks among the Seminoles since it specifically referred to the Choctaws and, on the additional basis, that the Treaty of Payne's Landing laid a legal basis for the presence of blacks among the Seminoles, the blacks who remained in Indian Territory were obviously in danger. The terms of the treaty, which had not withstood claims by the Creeks nor changed administration policy, offered them little support. The exiles who fled to Mexico in 1850 were wise to do so.[19]

The history of the United States in its relations with the Seminoles and blacks during the First and Second Seminole Wars clearly illustrates the use of military power to support the institution of slavery at any cost. The Indians and blacks could not be left in Florida even when it meant violating Spanish sovereignty. Blacks were not permitted to move peaceably westward because slaveholders were not willing to allow even one black person to obtain his freedom. There was no niche or corner of safety for the free black in a slave society. If even one little enclave of Indians and blacks remained unmolested, it posed a threat to the institution of slavery; the Indian removal policy was therefore thought necessary. The enforcement of that policy was the major concern of the federal army for twenty years, and by the end of the war, military costs alone were well over twenty million dollars. As William Jay said in 1839, it was a war which had the primary objective of saving Florida for slavery.

NOTES

1. John K. Mahon, *History of the Second Seminole War, 1835–42* (Gainesville, Florida, 1967), pp. 96, 98, 103–6; Kenneth Porter, "Relations Between Negroes and Indians Within the Present Limits of the United States," *Journal of Negro History* 17 (July 1932), pp. 287–367.

2. *Congressional Globe,* 24th cong., 1st sess. (1835–6), pp. 290–1.

3. *Sen. Doc.* 224, 26th cong., 1st sess. (December 1839), pp. 38–41, 47, 48, 347–50.

4. *House Doc.* 225, 24th cong., 2nd sess. (December 1836), *House Doc.* 78, 25th cong., 2nd sess. (December 1837), pp. 76–7; *American State Papers, Military Affairs,* 6:561, 7:724, 834.

5. *House Doc.* 225, 25th cong., 3rd sess. (December 1838), pp. 2, 7, 13; Joshua A. Giddings, *The Exiles of Florida: Or, the Crimes Committed by Our Government Against the Maroons, Who Fled from South Carolina and Other Slave States* (Columbus, Ohio, 1858), p. 148. An abolitionist, Giddings set out to prove that slavery was the cause of the Seminole hostilities. He was biased but there is much useful source

material in his book and much validity to his point of view; Mahon, *Second Seminole War,* p. 216.

6. *House Doc.* 225, 25th cong., 3rd sess. (December 1838), pp. 30–9.

7. *Register of Debates in Congress,* 25th cong., 1st sess. (1837), pp. 640–4, 667, 702–3, 738, 764, 770–1, 1290–6, 1326, 1682; *Sen. Doc.* 512, 23rd cong., 1st sess. (1837).

8. Loc. cit., Grant Foreman, ed., "Report of the Cherokee Deputies in Florida, February 17, 1838, to John Ross, Esq.," *Chronicles of Oklahoma,* 9 (1931), pp. 423–38.

9. *House Doc.* 78, 25th cong., 2nd sess., pp. 33, 35.

10. *Congressional Globe,* 25th cong., 2nd sess. (1836), pp. 357–8, and app., pp. 453, 478, 536–8, 559, 566, 574–8, 1480.

11. Charles Kappler, *Indian Affairs, Laws and Treaties,* 2 vols. (2nd ed., Washington, 1904), published as *Sen. Doc.* 319, 58th cong., 2nd sess., 2:249, 290; *Congressional Globe,* 25th cong., 2nd sess. (1838), app., pp. 353–4.

12. *Congressional Globe,* 26th cong., 1st sess. (1839–40), and app., pp. 73, 75, 79, 84, 98, 99. In August 1842, Benton's efforts succeeded and Congress enacted an Armed Settler's Bill. By this time, the Seminoles and blacks had largely been exterminated or removed. The bill did encourage settlement in Florida, however, since under its provisions a head of a family could acquire 160 acres of land at no cost. *See* James Covington, "The Armed Occupation Act of 1842," *Florida Historical Quarterly* 40 (1961), pp. 41–52.

13. *House Doc.* 225, 25th cong., 3rd sess. (1838), p. 30; John T. Sprague, "Macomb's Mission to the Seminoles: John T. Sprague's Journal Kept During April and May, 1839," Frank F. White, ed., *Florida Historical Quarterly* 35 (1956), pp. 130–93.

14. *House Doc.* 225, 25th cong., 3rd sess. (1838) pp. 1–99, *passim;* James W. Covington, "Cuban Bloodhounds and the Seminoles," *Florida Historical Quarterly* 33 (1954), pp. 111–9.

15. *House Doc.* 262, 27th cong., 2nd sess. (1842), pp. 27, 34–5.

16. Loc. cit.; *House Doc.* 200, 27th cong., 2nd sess. (1842), pp. 10, 41, 53, 63.

17. *Opinions of the Attorney General* 4 (1848), pp. 720–9; *House Doc.* 15, 33rd cong., 2nd sess. (1854) and *House Doc.* 58, 34th cong., 1st sess. (1855), contain letters and reports gathered by the War Department

explaining the Creek–Seminole difficulties and the flight by Seminoles and blacks to Mexico.

18. *Opinions of the Attorney General* 3 (1838), pp. 370–1. *Opinions of the Attorney General* 6 (1854), pp. 302–12.

19. *House Doc.* 15, 33rd cong., 2nd sess. (1854–5), includes army report of 16 October 1854 which indicates that a group of Seminoles and approximately 60 blacks were living near Eagle Pass in Mexico on a plane of "perfect harmony and equality."

6 Abolition and the Abrogation of Civil Liberties

The national proslavery policies demonstrated in the Seminole Wars found further reinforcement during the pre-Civil War period as federal troops were consistently used to suppress the increasingly active abolitionist movement. At the same time, constitutional military power was withheld when protection was needed for antislavery activists in the exercise of their civil liberties. Abolitionists in both the North and South were left to the mercy of local officials who usually refused protection. The national government felt no legal obligation to protect anti-slavery activists and, in truth, reacted indifferently to attacks upon them. In fact, the Supreme Court, in *Barron v. Baltimore* (1833), reinforced the legal position of the proslavery forces by asserting that Congress could not interfere with the exercise of the freedoms included in the Bill of Rights, since no such prohibition applied to the states; the national government could not intervene if a state chose to prohibit free speech. The consequences of this decision, combined with federal obligation to prosecute those who interfered with the rendition of fugitive slaves, made the federal government the enemy of abolitionists, who were left legally defenseless.[1]

Had the national government been sympathetic to the antislavery cause, there was sufficient legal and constitutional authority to protect abolitionists from physical violence. When the mechanisms of law and order within a state failed to prevent or suppress disturbances, the national government was obligated to intervene. In instances of slave revolts or plots, national power was utilized, often without even consulting the president or state officials; civil authorities were happy to ratify federal action after the fact. In cases of abolitionist activity, local officials did not want antiabolitionist mobs suppressed, indeed suppressionist mobs were often led by prominent judges, militia officers, lawyers, merchants, and planters. The "Doughface," or southern dominated, administrations of the period were no more interested in protecting abolitionists than were the local governments. Consistent with the current constitutional practices and interpretations, southern states passed laws prohibiting discussion of antislavery doctrines and the circulation of abolitionist literature, again using the overworn rationale that such activity "stirredup" slave rebellions.[2] Tyranny, terror, and mob violence were used to coerce antislavery activists. Suspected abolitionists were tarred, feathered, and run out of town; antislavery literature was burned.[3]

Abolitionists and antislavery supporters were generally received no better in the North than they were in the South. Northern states did not enact legislation prohibiting discussion of slavery, but mob violence often awaited antislavery spokesmen. As in the South, mobs attacking the abolitionists were often led by the leading citizens in the community, and police officials made little effort to interfere. For example, in 1829, antiabolitionist and antiblack mobs roamed through Cincinnati's black area wreaking destruction and devastation. In July 1834, rioting against abolitionists in New York City resulted in mass destruction of the black section. The mayor of New York did call up the militia, but when the violence subsided, he blamed the disturbance on abolitionists. Ironically, the defenseless black community suffered the misdirected violence generated by abolitionism. Further, in Philadelphia in 1838, the members of the local antislavery society received threats that their meeting would be disrupted, and fearing violence, they asked the mayor for protection. No protection was given; the police stood by as fires and rioting terrorized the city. Finally, blacks and abolitionists were subjected to so much injustice and violence that a reaction formed; some northerners feared that all freedom of expression might ultimately be endangered. As a result of this change in temper, as well as a decline in abolitionist activity, blacks and abolitionists were much safer in the North after 1840.[4]

Civil liberties were also denied antislavery spokesmen attempting to exercise their freedom of the press. Indignant mobs often vandalized the presses and ran abolitionist editors out of town. Northerners who generally professed a belief in editorial freedom recanted when it came to the publication of literature attacking slavery. Mesmerized by fears of disunion, they were reluctant to impinge, judge, or interfere with the South's peculiar institution. Also, many northerners who had proslavery leanings or who were genuinely neutral saw no benefit in discussions of such an explosive issue. The publication and circulation of abolitionist literature grew in spite of public pressure. In 1835, southern legislatures asked northern states to pass legislation suppressing abolitionist publications. Most northern legislatures seemed to favor the requests but found it difficult, within the framework of existing state constitutions, to draft legislation which would suppress only the abolitionists. The contradictions in public sentiment were expressed in a violent episode involving Elijah Lovejoy, an antislavery publisher, who founded a press in Alton, Illinois in November 1837. The attorney general of Illinois called public meetings in an effort to find a way to shut down Lovejoy's press. When the meetings became volatile, the mayor of the city attempted to pacify the aroused citizens, but he admitted that civil authority could not disperse them. As a result, Lovejoy was killed and twelve of his supporters were tried in January 1838 on the strange charge of organizing to use force in an effort to protect Lovejoy's press, an action which was de-

scribed as an "unlawful defense of property." They were acquitted, but so were several mob members who had been charged
with inciting to riot. The absence of military protection for the
abolitionists in Alton lends credence to legal indifference that
bound the country at this time. In the aftermath of the Turner
Revolt, the mayor of Norfolk had called for military assistance
and received it; the mayor of Alton could have asked for the dispatch of federal troops to keep order. He did not; in fact, he
incorrectly claimed that Lovejoy and his associates, in asserting
their civil rights, had created the disorder.[5]

The Fugitive Slave Act of 1850 generated a wave of violence
inundating those who persisted in helping slaves to gain freedom.
The distinctive authority of this new act made both national
and state governments responsible for the capture and return of
runaway slaves. The act further stipulated that those who har-
bored or aided runaways or interfered with the legal processes
were subject to imprisonment or fines. Marshals could summon
bystanders and citizens as a "posse comitatus" and even regular
troops and the militia to enforce the act. Since the Fugitive Slave
Act of 1793 had no such stringent provisions, the new act was
obviously designed to close the legal loopholes which had allowed citizens who aided fugitives to evade punishment.

The federal government worked vigorously to enforce the new
act and to suppress attempted violations. On 15 February 1851,
Frederic Wilkins, alias Shadrach, a waiter in a coffee house in
Boston, was arrested on a federal warrant which alleged that he
was a fugitive slave. Public reaction was voluble in its opposition
to the federal government. In response, President Fillmore issued
a proclamation asking citizens to cease interfering with law enforcement officers. At the same time, Secretary of War Charles M.
Conrad ordered the commanding officer of the troops in Boston
to make troops available if the marshal needed aid. In defiance,
antislavery advocates, most of whom were black, forced their way
into the courtroom and liberated Shadrach from the custody of
the marshal, and later arranged for his safe escape to Canada. In
the aftermath, several persons were arrested; five were tried and
acquitted for violating the Fugitive Slave Act.[6]

Its authority challenged, Congress held hearings on the problems associated with enforcing the Fugitive Slave Act; both houses entertained a resolution which supported the president's authority to use the military to enforce the act when civil authority proved inadequate. It was manifest that the president already had sufficient statutory authority to dispatch troops in instances of opposition to federal law, but Congress wanted to substantiate its position in an effort to pacify southerners who were leaning toward secession. However, some southerners, concerned with providing a legal basis for secession, upheld the theory that the national government could not coerce a state to comply to federal law. They were unwilling to support the resolution which gave the president the military responsibility to enforce the act. They wanted *state* authorities to enforce the Fugitive Slave Act to avoid establishing new precedents for national intervention in state affairs. Jefferson Davis of Mississippi, for example, refused to vote for the resolution, arguing that if Massachusetts did not want to enforce the Fugitive Slave Act, she could do what all states were free to do, "take the extreme medicine, secession." Despite the southern opposition, both houses passed the resolution. The effects of its passage was felt almost immediately when a second fugitive slave was captured in Massachusetts on 3 April 1851. The slave was placed on board a vessel bound for Georgia which was heavily defended by militiamen, marines, and regular army troops. A group of blacks attempted rescue, but the armed forces present were too formidable.[7]

In 1851, the enforcement of the Fugitive Slave Act precipitated violence in Christiana, Pennsylvania. Christiana's large population of free blacks and fugitive slaves formed a league of mutual protection against southern slavecatchers who were continually kidnapping blacks to return them to alleged owners. On this occasion, Edward Gorsuch and his son, along with a marshal from Philadelphia and a few other people, arrived in Christiana with a warrant to claim a fugitive slave. The alleged fugitive was sheltered at the home of William Parker, one of the black leaders of the league. When the slavecatchers' demand that the slave be brought out of the house was answered with a warning shot, some member of the Gorsuch party fired twice into the house. By this time, a crowd of blacks had gathered and a riot ensued. Gorsuch was wounded and his son killed. The alleged fugitive, along with Parker and the other black participants, managed to escape. Immediately, city authorities organized a civil posse, and with the aid of forty-five marines, they arrested thirty-five blacks and two Quakers, Castner Hanway and Elijah Lewis. They were charged with resisting the Fugitive Slave Act. At Hanway's trial, the counsel for the government, concurring with President Fillmore's position, maintained that those who resisted the Fugitive Slave Act were opposing the Fugitive Slave Clause of the Constitution and were therefore guilty of treason. However, the charge of treason is fallacious, because the Constitution defines treason as the act of levying war against the United States or giving aid and comfort to its enemies. Hanway was possibly guilty of violating federal law, but was not guilty of treason. He was acquitted, and all charges against the remaining defendants were dropped.[8]

Disturbances broke out in Boston again in May 1854, when Anthony Burns was ordered remanded to his master in Virginia as a fugitive slave. Bostonians, black and white, could no longer countenance the incarceration and reenslavement of persons who had lived among them for years. A belligerent crowd of some fifty thousand gathered around the court house. A disorganized attack was mounted and repulsed. To control the crisis, fifty federal artillerymen, along with two pieces of artillery, as well as a detachment of federal marines and the state militia called out by the governor, were sent to reinforce the marshal. The federal troop commander dispatched his troops on the authority of a letter received in February 1851, the occasion of the Shadrach incident. The United States marshal also wanted General Winfield Scott to deploy troops for support, but Scott refused to comply until he received orders from the president. Although a few prominent antislavery spokesmen were arrested, they were subsequently acquitted on a technicality. However, Burns was successfully transferred to a federal revenue cutter and returned to Virginia under the escort of several naval vessels. An indication of the continued tension in Boston in the aftermath of this incident is the fact that troops were quartered in the city until 2 June.[9]

In 1854, when another alleged fugitive, Joshua Glover, was arrested in Racine, Wisconsin and taken to Milwaukee, his plight aroused a local abolitionist group in Milwaukee who assisted in his escape from jail. Action taken by local officials was thwarted when their request for troops to aid in Glover's recapture was refused by the commanding officer at Fort Brady on the grounds that he wished to await confirming orders from Washington. The commander was not inclined to use regular army troops in pursuit of alleged fugitives, particularly at the discretion of local officials. Since the fugitive had escaped to Canada, the affair was closed before orders came from Washington.[10]

In the midst of the antiabolitionist riots and the disorders caused by the enforcement of the Fugitive Slave Act, the specter of secession hounded the halls of Congress. The congressional proslavery compromises had brought only temporary appeasement. When the great battles over whether to receive and debate abolitionists petitions began in 1836, proslavery forces successfully introduced a series of Gag Resolutions, making it virtually impossible to discuss the slavery issue in Congress. Antislavery advocates regarded the petition strategy as a means of adding civil libertarians to their forces, and they succeeded. However, Congress was placed in the awkward position of denying the right of petition on the grounds that slavery was a domestic concern, which applied not only to slavery in the states, but also to the District of Columbia where Congress had the constitutional duty of governing. On 7 January 1836, Thomas Hart Benton, who had so vigorously supported federal action against the Seminoles and blacks in Florida, attacked abolitionists for sending petitions to Congress, contending that these petitions made slaves think that they had allies ready to come to their aid if they rebelled. Senator John Tyler of Virginia asserted that his state could put down any insurrection occurring in daylight without aid, yet feared the possibility of midnight assassinations. He concluded by stating that Virginia asked only for the disavowal from other states of any intention to interfere with slavery. Silas

Wright, senator from New York, assured southerners of the North's intention to quell, not promote, insurrection. At this point, John C. Calhoun of South Carolina stated that all discussion was unnecessary since it was common knowledge that there were men in the North "who were ready to second any insurrectionary movement of the blacks." [11] In his opinion, the petition struggle only gave comfort to these agitators. This southern diversionary tactic was effectively used to maintain "the Gag" in Congress for eight years.[12]

The proslavery forces in the national government gathered momentum in the 1840s and 1850s. Texas was annexed and the Mexican War fought in part to provide territory for slavery expansion. Along with a more effective fugitive slave law, the Compromise of 1850 promised no interference with slaves in the District of Columbia. The Supreme Court, in the critical *Dred Scott v. Sandford* decision (1857), affirmed the southern claim that slave property was guaranteed in all the territories and that the federal government lacked the power to prevent its extension. Since 1790, Congress had quailed before southern rantings about slave insurrections and disunion. "Doughface" presidents and secretaries of war used the statutes to dispatch troops in defense of proslavery interests and to withhold them from providing protection to antislavery activists.[13]

The incident at Harper's Ferry was the last of a series of domestic disorders to occur before the Civil War. When John Brown and twenty-one armed followers, including five blacks, took possession of the army arsenal at Harper's Ferry, Virginia in October 1859, fears of revolution were aggravated among southerners and sympathetic northern allies. But the slaves did not "rise up" as Brown had dreamed, and the "invasion" was suppressed by local militia, along with a detachment of marines under Lieutenant Colonel Robert E. Lee. A detachment of eleven officers and one hundred and forty-two men were also sent from Fortress Monroe, and President Buchanan issued a statutory proclamation declaring a state of rebellion. Although this affray was clearly of little military significance, it provided the southerners with comforting evidence of the continued governmental willingness to respond swifty when the South was threatened. Congressional reaction was predictable; the Democrats responded to the Brown affair by blaming "Black Republicans," antislavery Republicans, who then denied complicity; the southerners blamed abolitionists and northern antislavery supporters, who praised Brown but denied any intention to incite a rebellion.[14]

The Harper's Ferry episode culminated a tradition dating from 1790 in which national military power was used to defend slavery and suppress those who would attack or subvert it. The North had stood by the proslavery compromises in the Constitution. Many abolitionists' heads had been bloodied and civil liberties abused without benefit of federal protection. The approaching Civil War revealed no federal intention to alter protocol or withdraw that protection. It was southern secession that precipitated emancipation and an end to federal support of slavery. The South left federal protection out of the fear of losing slavery; the federal government did not abandon the institution of slavery.

NOTES

1. See Chapter 2 supra for information on how the doctrine was already established before the intensified abolition movement of the 1830s; *Barron v. Baltimore,* 7 Pet. 243 (1833).

2. 1 *Stat* 424 (1795), 2 *Stat* 443 (1807).

3. Howell M. Henry, *Police Control of Slaves in South Carolina* (Emory, Va., 1914), pp. 154–64; Russell Nye, *Fettered Freedom; Civil Liberties and the Slavery Controversy 1830–1860* (E. Lansing, Mich., 1963) pp. 177–92, 217–8. *See also* Leonard Richards, *"Gentlemen of Property and Standing": Anti-Abolition Mobs in Jacksonian America* (New York, 1970).

4. Schnell, "Court Cases," pp. 24–32 and notes there cited. *See* W. E. B. DuBois, *The Philadelphia Negro* (New York, 1967), pp. 27–31 and notes cited for other early urban riots; Richards, *Gentlemen of Property,* pp. 159–65.

5. Merton Dillon, *Elijah P. Lovejoy: Abolitionist Editor* (Urbana, Ill., 1961), pp. 159–70; Schnell, "Court Cases," pp. 33–4, 42–3.

6. Letters from Conrad to Commanding Officer at Fort Independence, February 17, 1851, R.G. 109, National Archives, Sec. of War, Letters Sent: *Sen. Doc.* 209 (1903), p. 75; Marion Gleason McDougall, *Fugitive Slaves, 1619–1865* (Boston, 1891, reprinting, 1967), p. 48; there were some fugitive slave riots under the 1793 Fugitive Act also. In 1833, for example, two fugitives in Michigan, Thornton Blackburn and his wife, evaded a slavecatcher in an interesting fashion. Mrs. Blackburn fled to Canada after a woman visitor exchanged clothes with her and took her place in jail. Mr. Blackburn joined her after escaping just outside the jail while a crowd of approximately five hundred blacks pushed the sheriff back. Arthur Kooker, "The Antislavery movement in Michigan, 1796–1840: A Study in Humanitarianism on an American Frontier" (doctoral thesis, University of Michigan, 1940), p. 63.

7. Dunbar Rowland, ed., *Jefferson Davis Constitutionalist, His Letters, Papers and Speeches*, 10 vols. (Jackson, Miss., 1923), 1:29; *Congressional Globe*, 31st cong., 2nd sess. (1851–2), p. 828.

8. Schnell, "Court Cases," pp. 284–8. Benjamin Quarles, *Black Abolitionists* (New York, 1969), pp. 211–2); McDougall, Fugitive Slaves, p. 51.

9. Henry Wilson, *History of the Rise and Fall of Slave Power in America*, 3 vols. (Boston, 1875), 2:435–44; *see also* letters and papers collected in *House Doc.* 30, 44th cong., 2nd sess. (1876), pp. 89–91, *Sen. Doc.* 209 (1903), pp. 76–7.

10. Loc. cit.; Hazel Wolf, *On Freedom's Altar; The Martyr Complex in the Abolitionist Movement* (Madison, Wis., 1952), p. 106; *Ableman V. Booth* 21 Howard 506 (1859), concerning trial of newspaper editor who aided Glover's escape; *Sen. Doc.* 209 (1903), p. 78; *Liberator*, 7, 24, April 1854.

11. *Register of Debates in Congress*, 24th cong., 1st sess. (1835–6), pp. 86, 89–90, 207, 711, 723, 730.

12. Nye, *Fettered Freedom*, chap. 2, *passim*.

13. 9 *Stat* 462 ff. (1850); *Sen. Journal*, 31st cong., 1st sess. (1850), pp. 118 ff.; *Dred Scott v. Sandford*, 19 Howard 393 (1852).

14. *Senate Committee Report* 278, 36th cong., 1st sess. (1859). There are numerous works available on John Brown and the Harper's Ferry incident; *see*, for example, W. E. B. DuBois, *John Brown* (Philadelphia, 1909); Sen. Doc. 209 (1903), p. 101.

7 / Controlling Blacks During the Civil War

Despite the federal government's support of the pro-slavery compromises of the Constitution before 1860, the South seceded from the Union after the election of Abraham Lincoln. The southern conviction that the Republicans were bitter enemies of slavery precipitated this decision. John Brown's raid and the sympathetic reaction in the North, as well as a series of insurrection scares in 1860, blamed in part on northern agitators, accelerated the southern secessionist course. Upon leaving Congress to return to Louisiana in 1861, John Slidell of Louisiana articulated southern apprehension concerning slavery by predicting that if Lincoln were inaugurated with southern assent, a general slave revolt would occur. Slidell stated that the slaves, believing Lincoln meant to free them, would rebel against being held in bondage illegally. Jefferson Davis of Mississippi emphasized in his farewell message that slaves never revolted unless there was some outside inducement, citing the example that if the United States elected to use military force against southern planters, it would leave the slaves free to revolt. He was sure that the national government would not wish to be responsible for a bloody slave uprising. In another attempt to explain secession, South Carolina submitted a resolution which listed the following grievances: the incitement of slaves to revolt by northern agitators, the conviction that the Republicans would abolish slavery, and the belief that the federal government would become the enemy of the South rather than its protector. The Mississippi resolution of 30 November 1860 was an echo of the others. In short, the southern states believed that Republicans would refuse to enforce the proslavery compromises of the Constitution and would use federal troops to destroy, rather than protect, the system of slavery.[1]

Secession became a reality in 1860 when federal fortresses and military depots were seized by the Confederacy. When President Lincoln's attempt to provision Fort Sumter in South Carolina failed because the Confederates fired on the supply boat, Lincoln issued a call for 75,000 army troops from the states in April 1861. The army called up by Lincoln was to be used to repossess federal property confiscated by southern insurgents, but the troops were instructed not to interfere with peaceful southerners or their property. On 31 May 1861, Lincoln called for an additional 83,000 men, one-half to serve as volunteers for three years unless discharged sooner, the remainder to bolster the strength of the regular army and navy. Despite the obvious implication of this manpower increase, the army still was not intended to interfere with the property of peaceful southerners, even if the property consisted of human beings.[2]

When Congress met in July 1861, the statute of 1795, providing for enforcement of Article IV, Section 4 of the Constitution, was amended to meet the exigencies of total insurrection of a state. This amendment gave the president the power to declare a state(s) in rebellion and to prohibit commerce between citizens of the United States and the citizens of a rebellious state(s). Under the authority of this statute, Lincoln issued a proclamation on 16 August 1861 declaring the seceded states in rebellion since 15 July 1861. As the war was territorial, a civil war, between the federal government and the Confederacy, Congress had to authorize or enact necessary legislation. By amending the 1795 statute, Congress affirmed the steps Lincoln had taken before they met and enlarged his powers to deal with the continuing emergency.[3]

Having seceded because of their fear of "Black" Republican hostility toward slavery, southerners expected no aid from national troops if their slaves rebelled nor assistance in recovering fugitive blacks who sought refuge with the Union Army. However, the Lincoln administration, fearing disaffection in slave-owning border states and uncertain of the nature of its powers during a massive civil disturbance, adopted a conservative policy. Southern protestations to the contrary, the 1860 platform of the Republican party had supported state control of domestic institutions and had denounced raids, such as John Brown's, as unconscionable interference in state affairs. Southern fears were not allayed even when Lincoln, in his first inaugural address, declared that he would not interfere with slave property in the states as it was clear that the Constitution forbade such interference. Further, even though the moral sensibilities of many northerners were offended by the Fugitive Slave Act of 1850, it too would be enforced. Lincoln, and the Union, in effect, guaranteed to support the proslavery compromises of the Constitution.[4]

During the first year of the war, that promise was kept. The intention of the national government not to engage in emancipation of the slaves became apparent immediately as more and more blacks came under Union authority wherever northern troops advanced. In the spring of 1861, General Benjamin F. Butler permitted fugitive slaves and black refugees to remain in his camp at Fortress Monroe in Virginia, declaring that since they had helped erect Confederate defenses, they were contraband of war. Initially, the War Department accepted this legalistic definition of slave status. As increasing numbers of displaced blacks, most of whom had not worked on Confederate defenses, came to Butler's camp, the general permitted them to stay and used many of them as laborers. The War Department did not give explicit approval to Butler's disposition of these additional blacks. Many of the slaves who came to Fortress Monroe had, in fact, been abandoned by their masters when the Union Army advanced.[5]

After federal troops gained control of the Sea Island district of South Carolina in November 1861, numerous blacks deserted by the masters, as well as fugitive slaves, were employed and maintained by the Union Army. Legal problems created by the disposition of blacks in Virginia and South Carolina were rare, principally because no masters came to claim the slaves. If claims had been made, there is evidence to indicate that the army would have been happy to reconsign the slaves and have them off army rations and payroll. Some Union commanders even continued to uphold the antebellum policy of protecting resident slaveholders from slave revolts. In Louisiana in the fall and winter of 1862, General Butler and General Nathaniel Banks dispatched Union troops to suppress slave uprisings reported by local plantation owners. On several occasions, slaveholders expressed fears of slave rebellion to Union commanders and were assured that the army would control the slaves. The preservation of the Union, not the emancipation of the slaves, was still the primary objective of the Lincoln administration. In territory subjugated by the Union Army, slavery was protected and enforced, just as it had been before the war. A legal issue was raised, however, in areas where slaves of loyal Unionist masters fled and sought protection from federal troops. Policy was inconsistent in Missouri and Kentucky; some commanders permitted fugitive slaves to remain within their lines and others excluded them. In November 1861, General Charles Halleck, Commander of the Military Department of the West, ordered his men to send fugitive slaves already within their lines back to their masters and to receive no others.[6]

Congress, attempting to clarify the issue early in 1861, reaffirmed that slavery in the states was a domestic institution and not within the ambit of federal legislation. As the war progressed, this position became less and less tenable and was eventually discarded. On 6 August 1861, responding to reports that slaves were being used on Confederate defenses, Congress passed the first Confiscation Act. The act freed forever slaves used by rebels to aid or abet the insurrection of the states. The passage of the act was opposed strenuously by congressmen from border slave states but was carried over their opposition.[7] Congress further attempted to clarify federal policy regarding fugitive slaves by passing the Confiscation Act of July 1862, which forbade officers to surrender slaves to rebel claimants and declared slaves of disloyal masters who came within Union lines free forever. The proslavery compromise of the Constitution which required the rendition of fugitive slaves was abrogated. Still, enemies of the act maintained, with some justification, that the act was unconstitutional, since it violated the Fugitive Slave Clause of the Constitution, which had not been amended. In response, supporters of the act declared that the exigencies of war dictated its promulgation. While northern abolitionists had been unable to obtain repeal of the Fugitive Slave Act with the South in the Union, abrogation of the act came quickly with the South in rebellion.[8]

Very early, Union generals in the field were given authority to determine whether slaves belonged to rebels and could offer them freedom on the basis of that determination. Some Union generals, such as David Hunter and John C. Fremont, attempted to move faster than either Congress or the administration by declaring slavery abolished in all areas of their commands, but their orders were countermanded by Lincoln. Late in the summer of 1862, the administration was still not completely ready to change the legal status of blacks or redefine its own position.

With the passage of the Confiscation Act of July 1862, Congress had anticipated President Lincoln in establishing abolition as a war aim. By September 1862, however, Lincoln was finally convinced that the emancipation of slaves in disloyal states was necessary to win the war. But as a tactician and politician, he made a final effort by issuing his Preliminary Emancipation Proclamation, which declared that slaves in those areas in rebellion on 1 January 1863 would be freed. The South had four months in which to decide to surrender and retain slavery or to continue fighting with the knowledge that losing the war would mean the complete destruction of slavery as an institution. The alternative must, of course, be considered from the southern point of view: Southerners believed that even if they did surrender, slavery would inevitably be extinguished and that the South would never regain a place of power and prominence in national affairs. Lincoln explicitly reinterpreted the Domestic Violence Clause of the Constitution in the Emancipation Proclamation, by declaring that the military and naval authorities would "recognize and maintain" the freedom of slaves in the disloyal states and would "do no act or acts to repress such persons [slaves], or any of them, in any effort they may make for their actual freedom." [9] The passage of the Thirteenth Amendment in February 1865, and its ratification the following December, was the final blow to slavery and ended the necessity for protection of slaveholders by federal troops. Slavery was abolished not only in disloyal states, but throughout the Union. The Constitution no longer was a pro-slavery document.[10]

While Union policy was evolving toward abolition of slavery, the South was left to cope with its blacks, unaided, for the most part, by federal power. Delegates from the seven Confederate states—Alabama, South Carolina, Florida, Georgia, Louisiana, Mississippi, and Texas—met in Montgomery in February 1861 to frame a government for the Confederacy with the awareness that provisions had to be made to deal with domestic slave violence. Faced with the problems of waging war against the Union, they had the additional task of controlling a large black population. The constitution they adopted was similar to the United States Constitution; however, property in black slaves was expressly recognized. The Confederate government pledged to protect each Confederate state against domestic violence, which technically meant that troops would be provided to suppress slave revolts if local patrols proved inadequate. In actuality, with a war in progress and a limited number of men available, each state and community was left to its own devices. The new Confederacy, conceived in the chaos of impending war, was severely challenged; external pressures, internal dissension, and the continuing problem of slave control made forging unified national policy difficult.[11]

In the first year of the war, many slaveholders reacted to the threat of Union troops disturbing their slaves by simply moving the slaves behind Confederate lines. Initially, this strategy was effective; however, during the latter stages of the war when Union troops were stationed throughout the South, it became impractical. Some planters devised horror stories about the evil "Yankees" in order to frighten the slaves and discourage them from escaping behind Union lines. However, slaves defected in increasing numbers throughout the war.[12]

The threat of widespread slave insurrection demanded more attention than the flight of fugitive slaves to the Union armies. The mobilization of large numbers of white males for the war effort increased apprehension among the population at home. State legislatures responded by tightening restrictions and supervision of slave activities. Patrol duty was made a more regular function with increased fines for the failure to perform such duty, and laws requiring white male supervision of slaves on plantations were stringently enforced. In 1861, the Louisiana legislature increased the fine for permitting slaves to live on plantations without supervision from fifty cents to one hundred dollars a head. The conscription law passed by the Confederate Congress provided an exemption of one adult white male for every twenty adult slaves on a plantation. The "Twenty Negro Law," as it was called, was a source of great irritation and controversy throughout the war. Those southerners who possessed no slaves regarded it as a subterfuge whereby the wealthy could escape military service and complained that some thirty thousand persons evaded the draft in accordance with the provisions of this law. Supporters of the exemption maintained that someone had to remain at home to provide protection against the slaves who might rebel or flee to the Union army if they were unattended.[13]

Additional legislation for slave control was passed by state legislatures during the war; for example, a Texas statute of 1863 provided that a white person convicted of selling, giving, or lending dangerous weapons to slaves would be confined at hard labor in the penitentiary for two to five years. An Alabama law increased the fine for furnishing liquor to slaves from fifty dollars to five hundred dollars, or imprisonment for one to five years. Designed to prevent slaves from wandering about at liberty, a

Mississippi act increased the penalty for permitting slaves to sell their own free time, with part payment to the master, from fifty to five hundred dollars and sixty days in jail.[14]

At the beginning of the war, patrol and legislative enactments were rigidly enforced. The situation gradually deteriorated. As the war went badly for the Confederate states, old men and boys were pressed into patrol service to replace the young adult males who were drafted. However, when the militia was called up, old men and boys were drafted as well. Slaves took advantage of the opportunities afforded to rebel. In New Orleans in May 1861, disturbances among the slave population were suppressed by the militia. In October, a Confederate officer wrote to his superior that slaves were in a rebellious mood and that the military must be wary lest the blacks mount a successful revolt. Real or imagined reports of slave plots and rebellions were recorded throughout the Lower South during the war.[15] However, no significant slave revolt took place in the Confederacy as the war progressed. Many discontented slaves simply fled to the Union lines. Fortuitously, the advancing Union forces operated as a safety valve. The repressive measures adopted in the South after the Emancipation Proclamation were rapidly dissipated. There were, however, continuing efforts to insulate slaves from the knowledge of Lincoln's intention to free them.[16]

As the war continued, the position of southerners became more precarious. Many intransigent southerners never yielded the notion that the war itself was of no importance if the slave system was not maintained. Even in 1865, with defeat almost imminent, the conscription of slaves was seriously considered, yet the preservation of the slave system had a greater priority than the war effort. Some Confederate congressmen claimed that granting freedom to slaves who fought for the Confederacy would subvert their basic contention that slavery was the natural condition for blacks and make victory irrelevant. Rather than compromise in any way on the slavery issue, the South preferred to lose the war. When the Confederate Congress was finally driven to provide for recruitment of slaves in March 1865, no promise of freedom was given; individual states were to decide what reward to give their slaves when the war ended.[17]

Left to their own devices, the Confederates dealt poorly with the management problem of their enormous hostile slave population. The Confederate Constitution provided for assistance from the central government when rebellion occurred, but the central government lacked the resources to provide it. The Confederates considered the large numbers of blacks who defected to the Union to fight against their former masters as criminals. The Confederates threatened these freedmen, and the Confederate army massacred them when they could; but in actuality, there was nothing they could do. Whatever view one takes of the causes of the Civil War, the Confederacy, its resources exhausted, lost the institution of slavery while fighting a war to maintain and extend it.

NOTES

1. James Blaine, *Twenty Years in Congress: From Lincoln to Garfield* (Norwich, Conn., 1884–6), 1:253; Dunbar Rowland, ed., *Jefferson Davis Constitutionalist, His Letters, Papers and Speeches*, 10 vols. (Jackson, Miss., 1923), 5:33; *South Carolina, Declaration of Causes of Secession,* Frank Moore, ed., *The Rebellion Record*, 11 vols. (New York, 1861–8), 1:3 ff.

2. James Richardson, *Messages and Papers,* 6:1–61.

3. 12 *Stat* 329 (1861); 12 *Stat* 331 (1861); 12 *Stat* 333 (1861); *The Prize Cases,* 4 Miller 878, 2 Black 667 (1863).

4. Richardson, *Messages and Papers,* 6:5 ff.

5. Moore, *The Rebellion Record,* 2:437; U.S. War Department, *The War of the Rebellion: A Compilation of the Official Records of the Union and Confederate Armies*, 128 vols. (Washington, 1880–1901), (hereafter cited as *O.R.*) ser. I, 2:52–3, 649–52.

6. *House Exec. Doc.* 72, 37th cong., 3rd sess., pp. 1–6; *O.R.*, ser. II, 1:778, 808–9, 812; ser. I, 3:370; ser. III, 1:243; ser. I, 17:470, 5:301–2, 20:439–42, 14:33–4, 15:618–9; ser. III, 2:43; Bell Wiley, *Southern Negroes, 1861–65* (New Haven, Conn., 1938), pp. 183–90; Moore, *The Rebellion Record,* 7:33, 2:437.

7. *Confiscation Act of August 6, 1861*, 12 *Stat* 319 (1862).

8. 12 *Stat* 592 (1862); *Congressional Globe*, 37th cong., 2nd sess. (1862), pp. 3087, 3102–9, 3121–4.

9. 12 *Stat* 1269–79 (1863).

10. *Constitution of the United States, Thirteenth Amendment.*

11. Richardson, *Messages and Papers of the Confederacy*, 2 vols. (Nashville, Tenn., 1906), 1:37 ff.; *Confederate Constitution*, art. I, sec. 9, art. IV, sec. 4, same language as in art. IV, sec. 4 of the *Constitution of the United States*.

12. Wiley, *Southern Negroes*, pp. 5–6; *O.R.* ser. I, lx:477, 24:681; John W. DeForest, *A Volunteer's Adventures: A Union Captain's Record of the Civil War*, James Croushore, ed. (New Haven, Conn., 1946), pp. 26–7.

13. "Journal of the Confederate Congress," *Southern Historical Society Papers*, new series. X whole no. 65, 48 (1941), pp. 1958–9; Albert Moore, *Conscription and Conflict in the Confederacy* (New York, 1924), pp. 68, 70, 74; *Laws of Florida* (1861) reg. sess. 34.

14. *Acts of Louisiana* (1861–2), reg. sess. 130; *Public Acts of Georgia* (1862), p. 40; *General Laws of Texas* (1861–62), 9th leg., p. 80.

15. Moore, *Conscription*, pp. 70, 74; *General Laws of Texas* (1863), extra sess., p. 15; *Laws of Mississippi* (1861), called sess., p. 30; Wiley, *Southern Negroes*, pp. 35–7.

16. Aptheker, in *Slave Revolts*, pp. 362–5, believes there were frequent disruptions; despite his viewpoint, it is true that no general rebellion occurred.

17. *O.R.*, ser. IV, 3:1161; "Journal of the Confederate Congress," 7:542, 4:526, 528.

8 The Bottom
Remains on the Bottom

The war was finally over. With the adoption of the Thirteenth Amendment in December 1865, blacks were at last free from oppression—or so it seemed. Their bright hopes were short-lived. The efforts of the Republican congressional radicals to make freedom for slaves a reality through legislation could not override the established prejudices and suppressive doctrines in order to institute effective reform. Acting under its power to enforce the Thirteenth Amendment, Congress passed the Civil Rights Act of 1866, which remained dormant and unenforced until it was resurrected by the Supreme Court in 1968. According to this statute, black people were citizens of the United States and thus entitled to the same rights within the various states as whites, including the right "to sue, be parties, and give evidence; to inherit, purchase, lease, sell, hold, and convey real and personal property" and the right to "full and equal benefit of all laws and proceedings for the security of persons and property, as is enjoyed by white persons." The act provided that federal courts and officials could invoke army aid for its enforcement. As doubts were spread about the law's constitutionality, Congress passed the Fourteenth Amendment, which reinforced the language of the act by affirming the citizenship of blacks. It also forbade infringement of their privileges and immunities, deprivation of their lives, liberty, or property by the states, without due process of law, and state discrimination in general against black people. Significantly, section five of the amendment allowed Congress to provide military aid, if necessary, to enforce its provisions. Although the language of the amendment guaranteed protection of the rights of "persons," its framers indicated the specific intention to remove all disabilities imposed upon blacks because of their color or previous condition of servitude. Thus, by adopting the Thirteenth and Fourteenth Amendments, the guarantee of the right to vote in the Fifteenth Amendment enacted in February of 1869, in addition to the guarantees in the 1866 Civil Rights Act, the radical Republicans believed that they had created a lasting foundation for effectively removing the stigma of servitude from the blacks. Blaming the proslavery compromises of the Constitution for perpetuating slavery, they thought the removal of those compromises would settle the issues arising out of the servitude of blacks. Even preceding events had proven how mistaken they were.[1]

In the aftermath of the war in 1865, the military faced the practical problem of administering the government in southern cities and towns under what was known as Presidential Reconstruction. The army, including the remnants of some one hundred eighty thousand black soldiers who had served the Union during the war, went about the business of occupying, policing, and cleaning the cities, distributing food to the hungry and destitute, and in some areas, setting up schools run by army chaplains. President Johnson delineated the army's role by issuing a proclamation of amnesty on 29 May 1865, which appointed Unionist provisional governors in the southern states and ordered the military to assist the states in organizing elections and registering voters so that peacetime conditions could be restored.[2]

Although the Union army was ordered to work with the provisional governments, areas of conflict quickly developed. In many southern states, former Confederates requested permission to form militia units to prevent the outrages which they said were being committed against the white populace by the freedmen. The army opposed the formation of these units, believing that former Confederates could not be trusted and that those former rebels who were in fact assaulting and murdering Unionists would be the first to join. The army preferred to keep order without the aid of unreliable military units. However, the provisional governors opposed the army opinion, partly on the grounds that the army could not keep order with such a large number of black troops, whom the white population resented. The southerners, who before the war had used the excuse of threatened slave revolt to gain federal military protection, now complained of alleged plots among the freedmen and black soldiers in order to obtain white militia units. In some cases, President Johnson superseded the decisions of his military commanders and permitted the formation of the white militia units, but he reassured the army by giving them authority to control the militia if they failed to conform to federal law or began attacking black and white Republicans.[3]

The army's relations with the black population during Presidential Reconstruction were no more pleasant than they had been before the war. Officially, the army served as the military arm of the Freedmen's Bureau, set up by Congress in March 1865 to protect the interests of former slaves and destitute whites. Army commanders affected commitment to the principle that blacks and whites were equal before the law, while permitting local authorities almost unlimited latitude in handling the black population unless overt prejudice in law enforcement was demonstrated. The army was receptive to suggestions from white citizens that blacks should be incarcerated for supposedly pillaging and looting indiscriminately. Some generals ordered blacks to remain on the same plantations where they had toiled in slavery; others issued orders declaring that blacks found idle would be imprisoned. For the military, white southerners, and the Freedman's Bureau alike, black vagrancy and idleness were the primary evils that Reconstruction should prevent. Issues involving social equality for blacks revealed that army commanders were as prejudiced as southern white society; some officers opposed integration even in schools set up by the Freedmen's Bureau. In addition, many high-ranking commanders asserted openly that blacks should not be permitted to vote because they lacked the intelligence to exercise the franchise, a view which embraced former slaves as well as the thousands of blacks who had been free before the war.[4] When the state legislatures elected under Johnson's plan of reconstruction met, they enacted even more restrictive codes than the orders issued by the army or the Freedmen's Bureau regulations. Known as the Black Codes, these statutes were designed to insure that while whites might work or remain unemployed as they saw fit, the freedmen would be kept to the plow lest they plot mischief.[5]

In an effort to alleviate some of the problems of Reconstruction, when Congress met in December 1865, it established the Joint Committee of Fifteen on Reconstruction, which was an expression of disenchantment with Presidential Reconstruction. Congress passed a new Freedmen's Bureau bill which extended federal jurisdiction and protection to cover cases involving blacks in which local authorities could not be expected to act fairly and placed all officers and agents of the bureau under military protection. The same session passed the Civil Rights Act of 1866 and the proposed Fourteenth Amendment. Congress also established the size of the regular army at approximately fifty-four thousand men, believing this would be sufficient to carry out Reconstruction policies as well as the policing of the frontier.[6] On 2 April 1866, after vetoing the Freedmen's Bureau Bill and the Civil Rights Act of 1866, both of which were overridden by Congress, President Johnson issued a proclamation declaring that the rebellion of the southern states had been suppressed and peace restored everywhere except in Texas; on 20 August 1866, the president extended the formal cessation of hostilities to include Texas. When the Supreme Court ruled in *Ex Parte Milligan* that military courts did not have jurisdiction over civilians in areas where civilian courts were open, the role of the military in Reconstruction sank into confusion. Congress indicated that during

Reconstruction, the army's role was superior, not subordinate to civilian authority. The War Department continued to issue orders directing the army to prevent opposition to federal law and to cooperate with the Freedmen's Bureau in exercising its duties, yet not to interfere with local civilian authorities unless they acted contrary to federal law or attempted to hinder enforcement of federal authority. Unconvinced of the legality of its authority, the army acted cautiously. In some southern states, local officials regarded the president's proclamation as a license to arrest federal officers for minor municipal offenses and to encourage the white population to demonstrate open hostility to the army.[7]

Southerners, perhaps encouraged by the president's antipathy toward the radical congressional program for black equality, expressed their hostility and contempt for the federal programs. Large numbers of blacks were attacked and murdered in the summer of 1866; scattered rioting erupted throughout the South. In Norfolk, Virginia on 16 April, black citizens gathered outside of town to celebrate the passage of the Civil Rights Act with a parade and speeches. White hecklers appeared and a scuffle broke out. When informed that a white man had been killed, the mayor of the city quickly advised the army that his police force was unable to cope with the situation and asked for federal troops to keep order. That evening, the Twelfth Infantry commander dispersed troops in likely trouble spots about the city, but continuing sniper fire resulted in a number of blacks being killed or wounded. The following day, crowds of whites gathered in the streets boasting of plans to attack and kill all blacks and soldiers in the city when night fell. Reinforcements were called in from Fortress Monroe to patrol the city; no massacre occurred. Local officials feebly explained that the blacks had precipitated the disturbance by celebrating the passage of the Civil Rights Act.[8]

Mob violence in Memphis, which followed the Norfolk incident, dramatically illustrates the intense bitterness toward blacks in the former slaveholding states, and particularly toward those who had served in the Union Army. The Third Regiment of the United States Colored Artillery had been organized with blacks from Tennessee who had sought the protection of the

Union Army. From the time of its organization, the regiment had been stationed in Memphis and had been employed in routine police duties about the city, bringing the men into frequent contact with the white populace. The circumstances were abrasive. Many black soldiers were arrested from time to time by white policemen, and many whites, including some policemen, were arrested by the black soldiers. On 30 April 1866, the black regiment was officially mustered out of the army, and the men used their pay to celebrate. The following night, the local police arrested two boisterous veterans and were conducting them to the police station when their path was blocked by a group of blacks. After an exchange of words, the police fired into the crowd of blacks, wounding one person; the two arrested blacks escaped. When the blacks returned the fire, wounding one policeman, a large crowd of whites gathered to assist the police. This mob and the entire Memphis police force then began roaming the city, shooting, beating, or arresting any black person who could be found. This carnage lasted until midnight when a small detachment of federal troops intervened and the rioters scattered. Anarchy erupted the next day. Parties of mounted whites rode through the black sections, setting fires to churches, schools, and houses, and beating all who resisted. The violence lasted for four days. At the time, there were only about one hundred and fifty troops stationed in the city after the mustering out of the black soldiers, and they were unable to maintain order. Major General George Stoneham, commander of the troops in the area, tried to contact the mayor to obtain permission to use the police to aid in quelling the disturbance but was informed that the mayor was unavailable for consultation; the police, in fact, formed the hard core of the mob. Subsequently, Stoneham declared martial law, brought in all available troops, and suppressed the disorder. Forty-six blacks and two whites were killed; ninety-one houses, twelve schools, and four churches were burned in the black neighborhoods, the value of property destroyed being estimated at one hundred thousand dollars. A subsequent military investigation placed the blame squarely on city officials. General Ulysses Grant suggested that legal proceedings be brought against the city for damages suffered by the blacks.[9] United States

Attorney General James Speed opposed the suggestion, however, asserting that since civilian courts were open in Memphis, and the riot was not a violation of the laws of the United States, those who had suffered damages must look to local authorities for redress, an opinion which was quite proper in light of the Supreme Court decision in *Ex Parte Milligan*. Speed was asserting that the blacks who had been attacked under the auspices of the authorities of the city of Memphis had to ask those same authorities for compensation. Before the war, slavery was a matter for local control; after the war, black protection was a matter of local discretion. In the light of Speed's opinion, the Thirteenth Amendment could not be interpreted to offer federal protection, and although the Civil Rights Act of 1866 provided federal protection for the property and persons of blacks, it did not provide monetary compensation for the losses suffered by blacks when sufficient protection was not provided.[10]

Repetition of the violence in Memphis began in August 1866 in New Orleans when several related events culminated in a racial explosion. The reelection of John T. Monroe, who had been mayor of the city in 1862 when Union forces took control from the Confederates, initiated the hostilities. Monroe was an irreconcilable opponent of national policy and a recognized leader of the rebel portion of the white population. Major General Phillip Sheridan, Union Commander of the Department of the Gulf, who tried to keep Monroe and his comrades under close surveillance, left for Texas in late July. However, 30 July 1866 was the date set for the proposed reassembling of the Convention of 1864, which had framed the constitution under which Louisiana operated and was adjourned subject to the call of its chairman. The delegates to the convention had been Unionists, and when the chairman pro tempore issued a call to reconvene, former rebels opposed the meeting. Mayor Monroe unabashedly announced his intention to prevent a meeting of this extinct Unionist body and to arrest the members if they did attempt to assemble. The mainstream of white opinion seemed to support Monroe; some suggested undermining the assembly by ridicule, while others considered the possibility of forcibly concluding the convention.

On 25 July, Mayor Monroe wrote Major General Absalom Baird, commander of the troops in the city, that the convention was calculated to disturb the public peace and that his duty as mayor was to prevent such assemblies. Baird replied that members of the convention had neither asked, nor obtained military approval, but that he felt citizens should be protected in their right of peaceful assembly. However, if the mayor envisioned the need for troops to avoid a disturbance, he had only to ask, and Baird would provide them. Two days before the convention was to meet, the mayor and the lieutenant governor of the state visited Baird and informed him of their decision to have the sheriff arrest the members of the convention upon grand jury indictments. Baird objected and requested that they wait until he received orders from the War Department; he immediately dispatched a telegram to the War Department, not knowing that the lieutenant governor had already telegraphed the president, informing him that large meetings of black and white Unionists were denouncing the president and insisting that blacks should arm themselves. This purely fictional information partially explains the president's curious response to the lieutenant governor in which he informed him that if the civil authorities arrested members of the convention, they could expect assistance from the military. Johnson also gave the state attorney general permission to call upon General Phillip Sheridan for federal troops to aid in suppressing the convention. Having received no instructions from the War Department, Baird ordered four companies of soldiers to stand alert on Canal Street.

At noon on 30 July, about twenty-five delegates gathered at the convention site, but since twenty-five did not constitute a quorum, they decided to recess for an hour. In the galleries and halls of the building were about twenty black men, women, and children who came to watch the proceedings. An hour later, a procession of black men, a few armed with pistols, canes, and clubs, marched up the street toward the convention heralding an American flag. A scuffle which broke out between the marchers and a group of armed white observers quickly ended; the white men then pursued the procession to the convention hall where rocks and brickbats were thrown by both sides. The marchers entered the building, except for a small group which remained outside. A new scuffle with the police began, and when someone fired a shot, the police reacted by indiscriminately firing into the building. The mayor then ordered the police to launch an intensive attack upon the convention. As soon as the convention supporters inside the building waved a white flag, the firing stopped and the police rushed into the building. Convention delegates were beaten, stabbed, and shot promiscuously by the police. In some instances, delegates were driven outside where they were encircled and shot by the police and an aroused white citizenry. The mob, charged with success, then moved through the city, attacking and beating any black person they encountered. Although it is not known precisely how many persons were killed and injured, army medical staff records report thirty-seven blacks found dead, forty-eight severely wounded, and ninety-nine slightly wounded. Many wounded persons were treated and hidden by their families, while still other wounded men fled the city. The federal troops, who did not arrive on the scene until 2:30 P.M., immediately declared a state of martial law, but were ordered by the War Department, upon presidential instruction, to permit the sheriff to arrest members of the convention. Those arrested by the military were subsequently released without trial. The grand jury exculpated the local authorities and placed the blame for the disturbances on the convention delegates. In an exhaustive report to President Johnson, the lieutenant governor, the state attorney general, and the mayor claimed that they had done their utmost to circumvent trouble but that their efforts had been to no avail. In December 1866, a committee appointed by the House of Representatives visited New Orleans, and after a thorough investigation of the affair, reported in February 1867 that the conditions in the city required the establishment of a provisional government. This report gave impetus to the passage of the Military Reconstruction Act which had been under debate during the Thirty-ninth Congress.[11]

On 2 March 1867, Congress enacted the Military Reconstruction Act, which provided for the displacement of civil authority by military governments in the South. These new governments would protect all people in their persons and their property, suppress insurrection and riot, and supervise all elections until the states framed new constitutions and formally approved the Fourteenth Amendment to the Constitution. The states would then be readmitted to the Union. Along with its amendments of 23 March and 19 July, the Military Reconstruction Act became the basis of congressional reconstruction in the South. Dissatisfied with the progress of presidential reconstruction, Congress now legally provided for direct military control over political activity so that the southern states would reconstruct and comply to Congress and to the constitutional reforms resulting from the Civil War.[12] When Military Reconstruction began, one of the first acts of General Sheridan was to relieve Mayor Monroe of his office, as well as other New Orleans city officials responsible for the July 1866 violence. General Sheridan was subsequently relieved of this command by President Johnson, who still controlled military appointments, much to the chagrin of the Congress. It was a small victory for the president over an antagonistic Congress.[13]

Despite the fact that federal military force was used to protect blacks during Military Reconstruction, cessation of open violence against blacks was not achieved in the South. In Mobile, Alabama in May 1867, rioting broke out at a public meeting held by Republicans at which Congressman William Kelley of Pennsylvania was a leading speaker. During his address, some shots were fired, two men were killed, and several wounded. As the mayor and the police had made no attempt to interfere, the mayor was removed from office and a Unionist was appointed to replace him. Two months later in Franklin, Tennessee, gunfire was exchanged between discharged black soldiers and groups of former Confederates; one person was killed and approximately fifty were wounded. Troops arrived in the city the next day to keep order.[14]

Even after southern states returned to the Union, the military was still required to keep order. Once a state was admitted to the Union, federal commanders expected to operate according to Article IV, Section 4 of the Constitution, in which the national government guaranteed each state a republican form of government and protection against domestic violence. When army officials received requests for aid from state and local authorities, they were usually told by the War Department that local commanders must act on their own discretion when deciding upon the advisability of rendering aid, a delegation of responsibility which was contrary to all constitutional and statutory provisions. Local commanders, acting on their own authority, attempted to keep order according to their interpretations of their duties. Some of the new Republican governments organized state militias for protection against, not only former rebels, but also against other Unionist factions who were eager to gain power when, and if, the present governments collapsed. The provisional militias which had been established by the provisional governors under Presidential Reconstruction and later outlawed by the radicals in an act of Congress passed on the same day of the first Reconstruction Act were largely composed of former rebels who opposed the Union Army and all Unionists in the South. When the southern states were readmitted to the Union, the radicals saw the necessity of providing loyal militias to support the newly created radical governments, so a new act was passed allowing the formation of militia units, but only in those states that Congress or the radical governors decided were in need of them. Although large numbers of blacks were enrolled in these units, they were not exclusively constituted of blacks; however, blacks did join the militias freely, because the Republican party was the party of freedom and the pay was equivalent to that of soldiers of the same rank in the regular army. These militia units, reinforced by the presence of regular army units, were used to maintain the Republican governments in the face of continued hostility from unreconstructed southerners and political conservatives who very often formed their own enforcement units such as the Ku Klux Klan. A number of clashes occurred throughout the South between these opposing groups, and one, at Laurens, South Carolina in October 1870, resulted in the death of thirteen people and the wounding of many others.[15]

Congress responded to reports of violence and clashes between Ku Klux Klan and state militia units by passing an act on 20 April 1871 which prohibited persons from traveling in disguises on the roads and highways or attempting to overthrow governments by force. Infringements of this act would be considered violations of the Equal Protection Clause of the Fourteenth

Amendment, and the army was made responsible for the enforcement of the act. The efforts to suppress extralegal vigilante groups did not relieve black people or white Unionists of their fears since encounters with Klan members characteristically occurred on back roads.[16]

In order for Republicans to maintain political control in a state, it was absolutely necessary that blacks and Unionists counter the votes of white Democrats by being allowed to vote without intimidation. This meant, of course, that white vigilante groups would have to be suppressed by unified Republican state governments, but in many states, the Republicans were rent by internal strife. It was to the advantage of the unreconstructed southerners to see the radical governments divide into factions and hasten their own destruction by engaging in constant war, as they did in South Carolina, Louisiana, and Arkansas. The federal government would be called upon to provide aid according to its constitutional duty, but in each case, the problem really consisted of deciding which Republican faction was in fact the legal government. President Grant was beset by this problem again and again during the 1870s. Federal troops would be sent into an area to settle the dispute and then withdrawn. Thereafter, local militias organized by claimants to office would fight at the bidding of the state governor. Additionally, according to one historian, radical governors did not make use of Union militias to protect black and white Unionists from white terrorists as extensively as they should have, because of their fears of a race war between whites and blacks. By not exercising their military power, they often lost office to the conservatives. When northern public opinion cooled to the idea of enforcing the guarantees of the Reconstruction amendments in the South, when white vigilante groups succeeded in murdering and intimidating blacks so that militia units were practically useless, and when the radical Republican regimes were rendered ineffective by internal friction and tension, the movement for racial political equality was stymied. Military Reconstruction was a failure. The army supervised the elections of 1867 and 1868 and was called in from time to time thereafter to settle scattered disputes. However, most southerners were unreconstructed and, short of continuing military surveillance which the North was unwilling to provide, freedom was a dangerous condition for blacks as well as white Unionists. Conservative southerners needed only staying power, biding their time until the North became weary of the "infernal nigger question." They also successfully exploited northern hypocrisy and resentment to defuse the radical Military Reconstruction.[17]

The compromise settlement resolving the Tilden–Hayes election in 1877 was inevitable; this bargain assured the southerners that the army would not be called upon for civil duty in the South, which was a reconciliation made by the white population at the expense of the blacks. The provisions of the Reconstruction Amendments to the Constitution and statutes were relegated to oblivion. Although the military had delivered the black vote to the Republican party for a short time, it had done little to protect black persons from injuries committed by angry and bigoted whites. The Thirteenth and Fourteenth Amendments left the Domestic Violence Clause of the Constitution virtually untouched; there was no will to invoke the Constitution to aid the blacks. Federal troops still had to be requested by local authorities; and local authorities were bent on suppressing, not protecting, the black people of America.

NOTES

1. Thirteenth, Fourteenth, and Fifteenth Amendments; *Constitution of the United States*, 14 *Stat* 27 (Civil Rights Act of 1866). James Sefton, *The United States Army and Reconstruction 1865–77* (Baton Rouge, 1967), pp. 8, 9.

2. James Richardson, *Messages and Papers of the Presidents*, 6:310–4.

3. *Sen. Doc.* 26, 39th cong., 1st sess. (1866), p. 231; Sefton, *Army and Reconstruction*, pp. 25–8.

4. *Sen. Doc.* 6, 39th cong., 2nd sess. (1867), pp. 170–230; *House Doc.* 70, 39th cong., 1st sess. (1866); *see* Theodore Wilson, *Black Codes of the South* (Tuscaloosa, Ala., 1965), pp. 81–95, and Sefton, *Army and*

Reconstruction, p. 43, fn. 49, for similarity between codes, army orders, and bureau regulations.

5. *O.R.,* ser. I, 47:427, 461; Sefton, *Army and Reconstruction,* pp. 42–5.

6. *House Report* 30, 39th cong., 1st sess. (1866), p. 123; Benjamin B. Kendrick, *The Journal of the Joint Committee of Fifteen on Reconstruction* (New York, 1914), pp. vii–xxii.

7. *Ex Parte Milligan,* 4 Wallace 2 (1866); Richardson, *Messages and Papers,* 6:431–2, 438; Sefton, *Army and Reconstruction,* p. 80.

8. *House Doc.* 72, 39th cong., 2nd sess., Letter of Secretary of War, 21 January 1867; *Sen. Doc.* 209, 57th cong., 2nd sess. (1903), pp. 108–9.

9. *House Report* 101, 39th cong., 1st sess. (1866), p. 36; *Sen. Doc.* 209 (1903), pp. 110–1; Sefton, *Army and Reconstruction,* p. 82.

10. *Opinions of the Attorney General* 11 (1866), pp. 531–2.

11. *House Doc.* 68, 39th cong., 2nd sess., pp. 43, 151–3, 166 et seq.; *House Report* 16, 39th cong., 2nd sess. (1866), *Sen. Doc.* 209 (1903), pp. 42, 130; Sefton, *Army and Reconstruction,* pp. 84–8.

12. 14 *Stat* 428 (1867); 15 *Stat* 2 (1867); 15 Stat 14 (1867).

13. *House Report* 16, 39th cong., 2nd sess. (1867), *Sen. Doc.* 209 (1903), p. 142 ff.

14. *Sen. Doc.* 14, 40th cong., 1st sess. (1868), p. 131: *Sen. Doc.* 209 (1903), pp. 113–4.

15. 14 *Stat* 485 (1868); Otis Singletary, *The Negro Militia and Reconstruction* (Austin, 1957), pp. 9, 24, 129; *Sen. Doc.* 209 (1903), p. 119.

16. 17 *Stat* 13 (1871); *The Ku Klux Conspiracy: Testimony Taken by the Joint Select Committee to Inquire into the Condition of Affairs in the Late Insurrected States,* 42nd cong., 2nd sess., *House Report* 22; and *Testimony as to the Denial of the Elective Franchise in South Carolina at the Elections of 1875 and 1876, Sen. Misc. Doc.* 48, 44th cong., 2nd sess. (1876), as well as other house and senate reports written during Reconstruction which describe in detail the violence of the period.

17. Singletary, *Negro Militia,* pp. 145–6. There were also election riots and violence against blacks in the North during Reconstruction; for example, in Philadelphia in 1871, there was so much disorder associated with efforts to prevent blacks from voting—several blacks were killed—that the marines were called in to keep order, *see* W. E. B. DuBois, *The Philadelphia Negro* (New York, 1967), pp. 38–40 and notes there cited; *see* Conclusions in Sefton, *Army and Reconstruction,* pp. 251, 253–4.

9 / Changing Modes of Oppression: 1877–1900

During Reconstruction, the aspirations of the nation concerning black people were in part realized in law, but not in action. Before the promises made to the blacks came to fruition, a spirit of compromise and reconciliation between the North and South gripped white America. The Compromise of 1877, resulting from the Hayes–Tilden election, left the freedman in the custody of conservative southern Democrats, commonly known as the Redeemers, who pledged to protect the black man in the exercise of his constitutional rights. Despite these pledges, a new period of black oppression began. Initially, southern whites attempted to manipulate the black vote to their purposes; failing, they turned to repression and disfranchisement, using a multitude of theoretically legal tactics. Northern whites tolerated this repression and, in fact, adopted these policies when expedient. Despite the oppression, some black people attempted to exercise their right to vote and to make economic progress without the forty acres and a mule it was rumored the Union would give them. They expected the national government to provide them with some protection against intimidation and violence, but no assistance was forthcoming. Federal-state relations were unchanged by the Civil War. As segregation and violence became commonplace, the national government expressed no willingness to enforce a new racial order. Between 1877 and 1900, the Constitution and statutes drafted by the Republicans were circumvented or utilized to maintain the racial status quo.

When Rutherford Hayes became the next Republican president of the United States in 1877, there were 24,140 officers and men in the regular army. From 1877 to 1900, there were never more than 29,000 troops enrolled in the army, except during the Spanish–American War when a temporary expansion occurred. These soldiers were expected to police the frontier and control the Indians, as well as man other garrisons and fortifications throughout the country; the War Department repeatedly informed Congress that the military force was inadequate for the tasks but to no avail. At this point, it was as if the nation was reasserting its historic distaste for a standing army, believing it to be inconsistent with democracy. During this period in the South, the area of major racial disturbances, there were no more than 2,500 scattered troops. Another 2,500 troops were stationed along the Atlantic seaboard, and the remainder of the regular army was on duty in the West. The militias, those antiquated, quasisocial institutions, along with all their local prejudices and sympathies, were still the principal force available to quell racial disturbances.[1]

Almost immediately after his election, President Hayes indicated awareness that racial violence might be a continuing problem but that he intended to wait until the 1878 elections to see what action, if any, was necessary. The presence of significant military problems in 1877, as well as the agreement with the southern Democrats that they would be left alone to deal with the blacks, may account for Hayes' unwillingness to commit the small regular army to duty in those states derelict in their constitutional responsibilities. However, Hayes was compelled to use federal troops when, in the summer of 1877, railroad companies, pleading poor economic conditions, reduced the wages of their employees by ten percent. A nationwide railroad strike resulted. Strikers attacked the strikebreakers sent in to replace them. In most cases, members of the state militias sympathized with the strikers and thus failed to break the strike. In the ensuing panic, various governors appealed to Hayes for regular troops to restore order; for about six days, one-half of the army was tied up with policing duty in West Virginia, Maryland, Pennsylvania, Indiana, and Illinois. Hayes was very careful to respond only to those requests which exactly met the conditions required by the statutes passed under Article IV, Section 4 of the Constitution: the state had to exhaust all of its resources, leaving the disorder still uncontained, and the governor had to make a formal request indicating the existence of an insurrection. The regular troops successfully ended the Great Strike within a few days.[2]

During the 1878 political campaigns, white southerners quickly defaulted on their pledge to protect blacks in the exercise of the right to vote. In Sumter, South Carolina, a riot broke out at a political meeting when the Republicans refused to let Democrats address their rally. Two Bourbon leaders, white conservatives whose ploy at the moment was to use the black vote, narrowly averted a black massacre by their pleas for order. In Williamsburg, South Carolina, the Redeemers disrupted a black meeting and warned a state senator that he would be killed if he did not leave town within ten days. Hayes, however, took no action to end depredations against blacks who wanted to vote. While his party hesitated, believing it could rely upon southern pledges, the election ended their dilemma. The Republicans were soundly defeated in the South, even in places where there were voting black majorities. The whites had not permitted blacks to vote freely; violence, fraud, and intimidation were widespread. Hayes asserted that he had been deceived by the southern promises to maintain order.[3]

Acts of this kind violated the Force Act of 31 May 1870, which was expressly designed to prohibit interference with the voting rights of blacks; interfering or intimidating citizens in the free exercise of their constitutional rights was a federal crime. Violations could also evoke a presidential response under the act of

1871, which provided that unlawful combinations or conspiracies or domestic violence in a state could be suppressed with federal troops if they hindered the execution of the laws and interfered with the right to vote. If the state could not, or would not, provide protection, statutory authority was available if the president chose to assert it.[4]

Attorney General Charles Devens ordered an investigation of the reported violations, and federal marshals arrested a number of people who were later released. James Blaine of Maine demanded and was granted a Senate investigation. The inquiry confirmed commonplace knowledge; black Republicans had been beaten, whipped, and intimidated into either not voting or voting Democratic. Representative Horace Page of California and Senator George Edmunds of Vermont wanted Congress to reaffirm its intention to enforce the Reconstruction amendments and acts; however, Page's proposal was buried in the Judiciary Committee and Edmund's resolution narrowly passed on a strict party vote. Edmund's bill to insure enforcement and compliance to those amendments and acts was tabled. Successful Democratic opposition to these measures rallied on the hoary states-rights' position—states, not federal officials, were responsible for enforcing laws involving crimes against the person. Even though Reconstruction statutes had placed that burden squarely on the national government in the absence of state compliance, that view was unpopular. It was most unlikely that state governments representing the forces that kept blacks from voting would undertake their protection.[5]

At this point, the Democrats in Congress, feeling sufficiently confident and daring, attempted open repeal of the enforcement acts of Reconstruction by attaching riders (resolutions unrelated to the subject of the bill) to appropriation bills. As a matter of party principle, Hayes vetoed the bills; at the same time, he made strong public statements assuring the southerners that troops would not be used at the polls. While party leaders congratulated Hayes for standing on principle, that stand was of no immediate comfort to blacks driven from the polls. In his annual message to Congress in December 1879, Hayes cited the race question as central to the peace and prosperity of the nation and demanded action aimed at resolution of the problem. Diplomatically, he placed the burden of responsibility on the state officials, calling upon them to find solutions.[6]

One form of black response to the fraud and violence in the South was a substantial migration of blacks northward. In 1879, a great exodus of blacks began. Senator William Windom of Minnesota introduced a resolution sympathetically supporting this migration from tyranny and violence; he expressed the hope that blacks would be able to buy lands held by the Northern Pacific Railroad in Dakota and other western territories. Southerners hotly contended that no violence necessitating migration existed; the resolution was not passed. The exodus, aided by some leading Republicans, gained momentum. Even President Hayes became involved when he offered federal protection to boats transporting blacks up the Mississippi after white southerners intimidated the owners with threats to sink all the ships.[7]

When the blacks arrived in Indiana, which had Democratic majorities in 1876, accusations were made by congressional Democrats that it was a Republican effort to colonize the state with black voters who were traditionally Republicans. A congressional investigation found that northern Republicans had welcomed black voters, but discovered no evidence of an organized plan or any support for claims that they had contributed money to this cause. Black people themselves insisted that they left the South because of the crop lien and the convict-leasing systems, poor economic conditions, and the outrages perpetrated against them. The exodus soon slowed to a trickle as word reached the blacks in the South that northern weather was cold and that, in some cases, the atmosphere was as inhospitable to blacks as that in the South; furthermore, the land the blacks could acquire was usually unsuitable for farming, and many migrants were homeless and without a source of income. In Kansas, large bands of black aspirants were refused accommodation in hotels and restaurants. Other tentative efforts to initiate black migration or colonization in the North were not supported by the national government. Migration did not subside because blacks thought their destiny lay in the South; on the contrary, the problem was that most black people did not have the financial resources to migrate, and even if they had, there was no place they could go that promised them a better life.[8]

As the election of 1880 approached, the atmosphere of violence in the South still prevailed. James A. Garfield, the compromise candidate of the Republican party, won the election but failed to develop a southern policy before he was assassinated. He seemed to support federal aid to education for blacks as a solution to the race problem. Chester Arthur, who succeeded Garfield, did not support this policy and, in fact, seemed completely uninterested in the race question.[9] As the off-year elections approached in 1882, outrages in the South increased. On 24 August 1882, Jasper Wright, a black former associate justice of South Carolina's Supreme Court, wrote Attorney General Benjamin Brewster that persons were being murdered at an alarming rate, some in broad daylight. As a basis for federation action, he proposed the Fifth Amendment guarantees that life could not be taken without due process of the law. Instances of violence were not difficult to document. In September 1882, the Greenback candidate for governor of South Carolina in the elections of 1880 was killed in an argument provoked by the charge that he was organizing black voters. At a rally held by blacks in Lancaster, South Carolina, a Democratic representative insisted on speaking in spite of the crowd's protestations. The exasperated blacks finally dragged him out of the meeting. Later that day, whites retaliated by killing four or five blacks and wounding several others. Attorney General Brewster made an attempt to punish the violators by ordering the local district attorney to make arrests. But when the state attorney general defended the alleged criminals and Brewster received no encouragement from the president, he lost interest in the whole problem. Consequently, when blacks wrote Brewster complaining about being prohibited from using public accommodations or being illegally reprimanded or arbitrarily fined, he merely suggested they seek help from state authorities.[10]

As blacks were determined to make the best deal they could under the circumstances, black leaders generally supported President Arthur's policy of forging alliances with independent parties in the South. By not emphasizing the racial issue, the blacks in turn depended on the independents they voted for to protect them. In Virginia, blacks embraced the Readjusters, the William Mahone faction of the Democratic party which supported the repudiation or readjustment of state debts to the national government incurred during the Civil War and Reconstruction. While the Readjusters were in power from 1879 to 1883, black people enjoyed a hiatus from violence. This kind of alliance could work only as long as reactionary Democrats remained divided on some issue other than the racial issue and did not drive blacks out of politics altogether.[11]

This tenuous alliance was in jeopardy when the local elections of 1883 approached in Virginia. In the town of Danville, where the population was slightly more than one-half blacks, blacks had gained a majority on the twelve-man city council, four of nine policemen were black, as were nearly all the justices of the peace. There was no black domination, however, because the mayor, judge, and police chief were whites. In an effort to win the election, whites circulated a broadside alleging that white people were humiliated and unjustly treated in Danville. On 4 November 1883, when a black allegedly jostled a white man on the street, an argument and fight ensued. When the fighting ended, one white and four blacks were dead, and four whites and six blacks were wounded. The ensuing riot lasted for two days. The governor called out the militia, but it arrived too late. It became apparent that blacks were out of politics in Virginia, when only a few blacks voted in the elections, and those who did were Democrats. Although Attorney General Brewster wrote Mahone deploring the mayhem, the Justice Department initiated no action. Congressional committees investigating the riot added nothing to the record. Democrats claimed the incident was exaggerated and that accusations were out of proportion; Republicans maintained that persons elected in such an atmosphere of fraud and violence should not be seated when they came to Congress, but everyone was seated.[12]

The year 1883 became a landmark year in the black struggle, when the Supreme Court declared the Civil Rights Act of 1875, which provided for equal public accommodations, unconstitutional. Black reaction to the decision was not limited to the resolutions of the Civil Rights Congress or the National Convention of Colored Men in Louisville, Kentucky where Frederick Douglass declared that "who would be free, themselves must strike the first blow." In Gause, Texas, blacks rampaged through the city, destroying property. They were reportedly planning a revolt as a result of the Supreme Court's decision. One thousand state militiamen were sent to control the agitators.[13]

In 1884, when Republicans assessed their record after the election of Cleveland, the first Democratic president since Reconstruction, it was evident that Reconstruction had been abandoned and that the federal government was not interested in immigration proposals or any project for blacks that would cost money. Most blacks were illiterate; even those who were educated were oppressed. Those Republicans, who regarded themselves as liberals, believed that blacks should be eliminated from politics because they were uneducated and easily manipulated; on the other hand, they were unwilling to do anything to educate them. The Republican party, and the nation, marked time; no positive economic or social programs for helping blacks were considered or developed and blacks were in no position to help themselves.

The violence that accompanied Cleveland's election was fast becoming a tradition. In Loreauville, Louisiana, twenty Republicans, mostly blacks, entered the city cheering and shouting profanities at the amassed Democrats. Gunfire was exchanged; fourteen to sixteen blacks were killed. In his inaugural address, Cleveland assured concerned citizens he had no intention of initiating a course designed to limit the freedmen in the exercise of their constitutional rights, a position which inspired confidence everywhere but in the black community. Cleveland failed to break tradition and appointed a few blacks to traditional "Negro jobs," such as Registrar of the Deeds in the District of Columbia.[14]

Black protest continued. The unjustified murder of a Charleston black precipitated a mass meeting of blacks. The participants prepared and published a paper for public distribution which forewarned white people that a revolution such as the one in Haiti might occur if something was not done about the oppression of blacks. But, black protest was not restricted to petitioning.

In 1880, when black workers on Louisiana sugar plantations went on strike to demand a wage increase from $.75 to $1.00 a day, the planters broke the strikes by calling up state militiamen who arrested the ringleaders for trespassing. By the fall of 1887, when wages were reduced to $.65 a day as a result of a poor crop in 1886, black workers, who had been unionized by the Kinghts of Labor, went on strike again, this time demanding $1.00 a day with rations and $1.25 without. When Governor Samuel D. McEnery sent ten companies and two batteries of state militiamen to force the strikers to leave their homes on the plantations, a number of shooting incidents occurred, four blacks were killed and four whites wounded. In Thibodeaux where hundreds of evicted blacks had gathered, the violence came to a head. By 21 November, the sugar crop was in danger of being completely lost to the cold, damp weather. Although the governor had withdrawn the militia, a local judge, Taylor Beattie, declared martial law be enforced by troops of white vigilantes. Between the night of 22 November and noon the following day, thirty blacks were killed and hundreds of persons were wounded, of whom only two were whites. The massacre ended the strike. Henry and George Cox, two black artisans and Union leaders, were taken from jail and never seen again. The strike tactic, along with those of petitioning and migration, did not relieve the suffering of blacks and had no apparent effect on the course of national policy.[15]

In the campaign of 1888, Benjamin Harrison ignored the race question and, as a reward, received more white southern votes than any Republican since Reconstruction. Once in office, even black Republicans were rejected when they came to request the traditional jobs and patronage. Harrison recognized that those blacks who did vote would stay with the party since they had no place else to go; their demands could be ignored while he attempted to fuse the party with some groups of white southerners. His efforts failed; white Democrats, solidified by the ever-present race issue, united and withstood Harrison's entreaties. Violence broke out in Barnwell, South Carolina in December 1889 when four blacks accused of participating in the murder of a white man, as well as four other unfortunate blacks confined to the same jail, were lynched by a mob of one hundred white men. Aroused blacks gathered in hostile groups, but by this time, the sheriff had gathered a posse and the governor had mobilized the local militia to prevent black retaliation.[16]

Congress was seemingly oblivious to the violent events which formed the backdrop to their debates in Washington and felt no compunction to assert any influence, legal or otherwise, on behalf of the blacks. And yet, in December 1889, the same Congress debated a southern proposal which involved the colonization of blacks outside the United States. The bill proposed that the government finance an expedition and purchase land for the migrants. When Republicans, black leaders, and newspapers opposed the bill, insisting that it was a matter of national pride and responsibility to provide for black people in this country, the bill was not passed. The inherent contradiction is obvious: an immigration bill was defeated on the grounds that "justice must be done to blacks," when, in actuality, there was no evidence of a national will to provide justice for blacks.[17]

The Republicans made two legislative efforts in 1890 to "give justice to blacks." One attempt was made by Senator Henry Blair of New Hampshire whose aid to education bill would have given federal money to public schools, thereby indirectly benefitting the freedmen. If blacks could be educated, at least their antagonists would be forced to seek reasons other than their ignorance as a basis for unequal treatment. Blair had introduced his bill in 1884 and 1885; finally, it was passed in the Senate and defeated in the House in 1888. It was defeated again in 1890 by forces who expressed fear of federal domination, or who thought that money for public schools would weaken private schools, or who believed that taking money out of the federal treasury would support a demand for a higher tariff.

The other legislative attempt to insure "black justice" was the election bill of Representative Henry Lodge, which provided for federal supervisors to inspect registration books, attend elections, and certify the results. This bill would have invoked a federal presence at elections which might have permitted blacks in the South to vote. Its sponsors cited the fact that thirty to sixty working days of each congressional session were taken up with contested elections, as well as questions related to the black vote in the South, as Republicans tried to overturn the election of Democrats. The act was undoubtedly constitutional; in theory, it greatly resembles the 1965 Voting Rights Act which was upheld in *Katzenbach v. South Carolina* in 1966.[18]

Sponsors of the Lodge Bill thought they could pass it with Harrison's support. Harrison, deciding that his attempts to break the solid South to get support for a high tariff would not work but that he might be able to get some mileage out of the race question, stated in his annual message to Congress in December 1889 that blacks should be protected in all relations to the federal government, as litigant, as juror, as witness, as voter, and as traveler in interstate commerce. Harrison's support was not as expansive as some might have wished, but it offered some encouragement. Despite Harrison's lukewarm statements and confirmation in the House by a strict party-line vote, the Lodge Bill failed to pass in the Senate, after being held over until the next session to make way for a vote on the McKinley Tariff of 1890. Interestingly enough, liberal Republican opponents of the bill insisted that education was the answer to the race problem, and if this was accomplished, suffrage would be permitted by state governments. If their thesis was correct, the failure to provide federal aid to education, and the disinterest of state governments in educating blacks, indicated that the racial problem was becoming accepted as a part of the national scene.[19]

Harrison's administration was plagued by labor troubles which seemed to threaten the very foundation of the national economy and which overshadowed such racial disturbances as the one which occurred in March 1892, when black militants and white police clashed in a small community outside Memphis. Calvin McDowell, black manager of a people's cooperative grocery store, and Theodore Moss, a black postman, became upset when a white man, Cornelius Hurst, came into their community and beat a black youth who Hurst claimed had assaulted one of his children. When other blacks tried to interfere, Hurst began clubbing them. A crowd of black people gathered to devise a plan of retaliation. When a white man tried to disperse them, one of the blacks "shot holes into his clothes." Fear spread through the white community; after some of the whites started leaving town, the local judge issued a warrant for the arrest of the black ringleaders. When twelve deputy sheriffs came to serve warrants for arrest of the black ringleaders, they were ambushed in the grocery store. Four deputy sheriffs were seriously injured. A large posse of white people succeeded in capturing twenty-seven blacks. The next day McDowell, Moss, and Allen Stewart, the so-called "ringleaders," were taken from jail and lynched by a mob of seventy-five whites. No action was taken to prosecute the murderers, either by the state or the national government.[20]

Resolution or action on the race question and its legal problems could hardly be expected from the administration of Grover Cleveland, who, capitalizing in part on the threats implicit in the proposed Lodge Bill and the wave of strikes in the country, defeated Harrison in 1892. In 1893, matters worsened. St. George Tucker of Virginia introduced a bill in the House to repeal all laws relating to supervision of elections. During the Hayes administration, southerners had failed in their attempt to accomplish repeal by adding riders to appropriation bills. In 1894, however, Congress passed, and Cleveland signed into law bills repealing those sections of Reconstruction legislation which related to the protection of voting rights. It was suggested by proponents that such legal protection was no longer necessary and was an insult to the South.[21]

Under Cleveland's administration, labor and racial violence continued. The Pullman controversy in 1894 demonstrated the ability of a president to find constitutional authority for the use of federal troops on presidential initiative, with or without a governor's request, and even as in this case, authority to overrule the governor's specific request that troops not be sent. When Eugene Debs' American Railway Union went on strike, they declared a boycott against Pullman cars; trains were stopped and Pullman cars detached and side-tracked. There is some evidence that the railroad managers had mail cars attached to Pullman cars so that when the strikers detached the Pullman cars, they had to at one point handle the mail cars. Railroad managers then complained that the mails were being interrupted and asked for federal intervention. To keep the mail running, Attorney General Richard Olney ordered thirty-four hundred men, who were hired and paid by the railroad, sworn in as special deputies. When these deputies clashed with the strikers, tumult and the destruction of property followed. On 2 July, the managers obtained a blanket injunction from a federal district court forbidding interference with the operation of the mails and prohibiting the union's refusal to perform normal services. At the same time, the court announced its inability to enforce its orders or to quell the riots and suppress the strike. Cleveland, deciding that this strike was outside the state's jurisdiction and involved the enforcement of federal statutes, sent four companies of federal troops to Chicago. The sporadic disturbances spread from Hammond, Indiana, where regular troops fired upon a mob, into the western states as far as California. In each case, federal troops were ostensibly used to prevent interference of the mail. The rioting and the strike subsided rather quickly after Eugene Debs was arrested on 10 July. Cleveland's ability to find constitutional justification in this instance resulted from his willingness to defend capital from the threat of organized labor.[22] Cleveland was not, however, interested in finding constitutional authority to insure due process of law when racial violence occurred. In that lack of concern, he was no more or less culpable than his predecessors.

However, some white opposition to lawlessness and lynching was developing. In South Carolina, at the state constitutional convention of 1895, a black delegate, Isaiah Reed, introduced a motion authorizing the governor to remove and replace any official who allowed personal harm to come to a prisoner in his custody and provided that the militia be called out in the case of a threatened lynching. The provision would have been a deterrent, because in many cases, lynchings were publicized in the press to insure that the event was well attended! Reed's motion lost. However, a proposal was approved which provided for the removal of sheriffs who were guilty of negligence, permission or connivance in giving up prisoners, and provided punitive damages of two thousand dollars to the families of each person lynched. However, there were no reported cases of damage awards or sheriffs removed from office.[23]

McKinley, who was elected in 1896 as the frank protagonist of the conservative classes, stated in his inaugural address that lynching could not be tolerated and that courts, not mobs, would execute the law. No one disagreed with his rhetoric, but two of the most flagrant incidences of racial violence in the period occurred during his administration. It was a long-standing Republican policy to appoint blacks in the South to minor federal posts to insure their support in the Republican nominating conventions in which blacks were free to function as delegates since the party was anathema to southern whites. Frazier B. Baker was appointed postmaster at Lake City, South Carolina. However, the "democratic white majority" of the community did not want their mail handled by a "nigger." On 21 February 1898, while the United States prepared for the Spanish–American War, a mob of approximately four hundred whites gathered outside Baker's home, set it afire, burned him to death, wounded his wife, a twelve-month old baby, and three other children.[24]

The tragic circumstances surrounding the Baker incident gain magnitude when the records make the fact clear that the government knew about the threats on Baker's life, yet no federal troops or marshals were sent when a federal function was clearly being subverted. If the national government had seemed perfunctory in their response to the threats against Baker, they seemed oblivious to his death. Although Baker's death had failed to arouse the government, it unified the national black community. A mass meeting was held in Chicago, and a series of resolutions adopted. On 21 March, Mrs. Ida Wells-Barnett, a black militant, accompanied by a delegation of Chicago congressmen, went to the White House to have an audience with President McKinley. They stated their case and presented the resolutions which included apprehension of the killer, indemnity for the widow and children, and a national antilynching law. The astute Mrs. Wells-Barnett reportedly told McKinley she believed that Baker's case was clearly within federal jurisdiction and was not a matter for the state court. From her point of view, failure to act would be a dereliction of governmental duty. Four months later, in June 1898, federal agents arrested and charged eleven persons in the Baker case. Although tried in a federal court, none of the defendants were convicted. Two witnesses agreed to testify for the state and were given immunity from prosecution; three were freed on a directed verdict, which means after considering all the facts as the government insisted they occurred, the judge still did not believe there was cause for legal action; the jury was unable to bring in a verdict on the remaining six defendants.[25]

South Carolina was to be the stage for another bloody incident during McKinley's administration. In November of 1898, T. P. Tolbert, a white man, acting on behalf of his brother who was seeking office, stationed himself outside a polling station in Phoenix to take affidavits from blacks who were refused permission to vote. A white Democrat challenged him; a fight broke out and the Democrat was killed and Tolbert was wounded. Subsequently, a white mob formed, and fighting broke out. An uncle and nephew of the candidate were wounded. Blacks fled the melee and organized for retaliation. Later, one group of blacks ambushed a crowd of white reinforcements on the way to join the mob at Phoenix, wounding several men. As the riot gained impetus, whites roamed the area attacking every black they encountered. Eleven blacks were brought to a church near Phoenix and forced to confess; four were killed on the spot and the others were permitted to escape. The next morning, another black who was allegedly part of the ambush party was brought to the same spot and murdered. The South Carolina press blamed the Tolberts for encouraging black people to be "uppity." One Tolbert was arrested and charged with inciting to riot, but was later released; however, a mass meeting of whites resolved that he should move from the community. Thereafter, white terrorists went around killing and assaulting blacks to eliminate subversives and repulse rebellion. Finally, Senator "Pitchfork" Ben Tillman of South Carolina, an arrant racist, informed his constituency that they should kill the Tolberts and stop all that other "devilment" before the federal authorities intervened. Tillman need not have worried; his concern that the national government might intervene to end wholesale attacks on citizens which the state refused to prevent was misplaced. The national government seemingly could find no constitutional means to intercede to protect its black citizens.[26]

The Tolbert incident had not died down before more violence erupted. In November 1898, the black editor of a local black newspaper in Wilmington, North Carolina published a retort to an article written by a local white woman in defense of the lynching of blacks to protect white womanhood. Local whites felt that his reply disparaged the white woman, so they called a meeting in which they decided to expel the editor from the city and destroy his press. Fifteen blacks were called in and given this ultimatum. When the black people of the community conferred and agreed that there was nothing they could do except comply, they mailed a letter to the white citizen's committee indicating their compliance. The deadline expired before the committee received the letter, and four hundred armed whites went to the newspaper office to destroy it. Someone set the building afire. A rumor spread that whites were going to burn and attack the black quarter, so the blacks prepared for an invasion. When the uneasy whites ordered the blacks to stop gathering in groups and ordered one crowd to disperse, the panicked blacks fired at the whites. For two days, terrorism, anarchy, and murder prevailed. Many blacks left the city. Officials dispatched letters requesting immediate federal aid; the replies informed the petitioners that the governor had made no request for federal aid. The state militia, as well as a battalion of naval militia which was in the area, tried to end the riot, but peace and order were not restored until the mobs had vented their rage. Later, conciliatory city authorities tried to persuade blacks hiding in the woods to return to their homes.[27]

Black people protested against this violence at a mass meeting in Cooper Union in New York City by demanding an end to the bloodshed in North and South Carolina and deprecating the inaction of the federal government. In Chicago in 1899, a meeting of the Afro–American Council, composed of America's leading black men, considered proposals for radical action in regard to lynching laws, and for migration as a solution to the race question, as well as the proposals of some black politicians who wanted to defend the administration. The resolutions which were eventually passed declared that blacks had the same right to have their lives and liberties protected as whites. The protestors could not understand how the national government could intervene and go to war to protect Cubans and fail to protect American citizens. To this, the administration responded that it was well established in American legal traditions that war-making was under the jurisdiction of Congress, while citizens must look to the state for protection. Perhaps the best answer to the administration's reply was made by the Massachusetts branch of the Afro–American Society which convened in October 1899 to consider the Phoenix and Wilmington massacres. In an open letter to McKinley, they explained their understanding that, notwithstanding the plea of constitutional inability to intervene in such cases, ". . . where there is a will . . . there is always a way, and where there is no will there is no way. We well know that you lacked the will and, therefore, the way to meet that emergency." [28]

But the debilitated state of law enforcement and the violence that dominated race relations in the United States between 1877 and 1900 could not establish precedence over the concurrent national issues. The Indians, the new industrialism, the labor movement, agrarian reform movements, the silver and tariff issues, the waves of immigrants, and the new role of the United States as an imperialist power captured the attention of the government and citizens alike. In 1900, the black man's position was not markedly improved over his status as a slave. He stood outside the law; his legal attempts to seek justice, as well as his militant enterprises, were frustrated. There was still no enlightened view of how to solve the problem of racial violence within the framework of the Constitution.

NOTES

1. Russell F. Wiegley, *History of the United States Army* (New York, 1967), app., pp. 566–8; U.S. War Department, *Annual Reports of the Secretary of War, 1877–1900* (Washington, 1878–1901).

2. James A. Dacus, *Annals of the Great Strike* (Chicago, 1877); *Sen. Doc.* 209, 57th cong., 2nd sess. (1903), p. 189 ff.

3. Stanley Hirshson, *Farewell to the Bloody Shirt, Northern Republicans and the Southern Negro, 1877–1893* (Bloomington, Ind., 1962), pp. 44–6, 49–50, *passim.*

4. 16 *Stat* 140, partially survives as Section 241, Title 18 of the *United States Code;* 17 *Stat* 13 ff. survives as Section 333, Title 10 of the *United States Code* (see Appendix). The *posse comitatus* act of 1878 forbade the use of regular troops to execute the laws except in cases where Congress authorized their use; this was an exception.

5. *Sen. Report* 855, 45th cong., 1st sess. (1877), 1:xxiv–xxvi; xiv–xvi; *Congressional Record,* 45th cong., 3rd sess. (1878–9), Hirshson, *Farewell to the Bloody Shirt,* pp. 49–51.

6. *Congressional Record,* 46th cong., 1st sess. (1879) pp. 418, 801–7, 837, 504–511, 593–600; Richardson, *Messages and Papers,* 10:4475–87, 4512–13.

7. *Sen. Report* 683, 46th cong., 2nd sess. pt. 2, p. 39; pt. 3, p. 438; Hirshson, *Farewell to the Bloody Shirt,* chap. 3; Herbert Aptheker, ed., *Documentary History of the Negro People in the United States* (New York, 1951), pp. 713–7.

8. Vernon Wharton, *The Negro in Mississippi 1865–90* (Chapel Hill, N.C., 1947), pp. 115–6; Aptheker, *Documentary History,* pp. 724–6, Hirshson, *Farewell to the Bloody Shirt,* p. 77.

9. Richardson, *Messages and Papers,* 10:4598–9; Rayford Logan, *The Betrayal of the Negro* (New York, 1965), pp. 48–51; Hirshson, *Farewell to the Bloody Shirt,* pp. 93–94.

10. Hirshson, *Farewell to the Bloody Shirt,* pp. 100–1; J. J. Wright to Brewster, Justice Department, Letters Received, R. G. 60, 24 August 1882; Brewster to Niles, 28 September 1883, Letterbook P., Letters Sent, National Archives.

11. Aptheker, *Documentary History,* pp. 727–33; *Congressional Record,* 47th cong., 1st sess. (1881–2), pp. 3384–7; Hirshson, *Farewell to the Bloody Shirt,* pp. 117–8; Charles Wynes, *Race Relations in Virginia, 1870–1902* (Charlottesville, Va., 1961), pp. 25–6.

12. Wynes, *Race Relations,* pp. 31–2; Hirshson, *Farewell to the Bloody Shirt,* pp. 119–20; *New York Times,* 4, 5, 6 November 1883. Report of the Special Committee to Inquire into Alleged Election Outrages at Danville, Va., *Sen. Report* 579, 48th cong., 1st sess. (1883), 1:xlii, 2:lxxii. For other incidents, *see* Report of the Special Committee to Inquire into the Mississippi Election of 1883, *Sen. Report* 512, 48th cong., 1st sess. (1883), 1:xxv–xxxvi; 2:lxxiii.

13. *New York Times,* 30 October 1883; Aptheker, *Documentary History,* pp. 658–9, 665.

14. Richardson, *Messages and Papers*, 5:302; *New York Times*, 4 November 1884.

15. George B. Tindall, *South Carolina Negroes, 1877–1900* (Baton Rouge, 1966), p. 246; William I. Hair, *Bourbonism and Agrarian Protest, Louisiana Politics, 1870–1900* (Baton Rouge, 1970), pp. 172–184.

16. Hirshson, *Farewell to the Bloody Shirt*, pp. 166, 182–3; *New York Times*, 29 December 1889, pp. 1, 6; Tindall, *South Carolina Negroes*, pp. 239–40.

17. *Congressional Record*, 51st cong., 1st sess. (1889–90), pp. 155, 157, 802, 628–30, 802–7.

18. Hirshson, *Farewell to the Bloody Shirt*, pp. 192–200; *Congressional Record*, 51st cong., 1st sess. (1889–90), pp. 100, 102, 3760, 6079; *Katzenbach v. Carolina* 383, *U.S.* 301 (1966).

19. Richardson, *Messages and Papers*, 12:5490–1, 5562–4; *Congressional Record*, 51st cong., 1st sess. (1889–90), pp. 6507–8, 6538–44, 6548–52, 6596, 6599–6601, 6688–92, 6772–3, 6940–1, 7792, 8306–7; 2nd sess. (1890–91), pp. 1323–4, 1564, 1739–40. *See also* Vincent P. DeSantis, "Republicans Face the Southern Question, the New Departure Years, 1877–97," *Johns Hopkins Studies in Historical and Political Science* 76 (1959), pp. 198–214.

20. Foster Rhea Dulles, *Labor in America, A History* (New York, 1949), pp. 168–71; *New York Times*, 7 March 1892, p. 1; 9 March, p. 1.

21. 28 *Stat* (1894); Logan, *Betrayal*, note on pp. 61–71.

22. *United States v. Debs*, 64 *Fed. Report* 724 (1894), *In Re Debs* 158 *U.S.* 564 (1895); Dulles, *Labor in America*, pp. 171–82, *Sen. Doc.* 209, 57th cong., 2nd sess. (1903), pp. 347–50.

23. *Journal of the Constitutional Convention of the State of South Carolina* (Columbia, 1895), pp. 122–30; *Constitution of the State of South Carolina*, ratified in state convention, 4 December 1895 (Columbia, 1909), art. VI, sec. 6; Tindall, *South Carolina Negroes*, p. 254.

24. Tindall, *South Carolina Negroes*, pp. 255–6; Aptheker, *Documentary History*, p. 798.

25. Loc. cit.

26. Tindall, *South Carolina Negroes*, pp. 257–8; Appleton's *Annual Cyclopaedia* (1898), p. 700.

27. *New York Times*, 11, 12, 13, 15, 16 November 1898, p. 1.

28. Aptheker, *Documentary History*, pp. 242–7; pp. 788, 790.

10 / Riots, Lynchings, and Federal Quiescence

The turn of the century was an occasion for celebration around the world. Expositions and congresses projected a future wherein man's aspirations for his fellows would be realized through the wonders of technology. The threshold of the century also seemed to mark a quickening in man's social awareness. In the United States, the Progressives worked to cure social ills ranging from impure food and drugs to housing for urban immigrants. A few white Progressives aided in the founding of the National Association for the Advancement of Colored People (NAACP) and the Urban League, but inside the American government, little attention was paid to the race problem. The Republican party platforms of 1900, 1904, and 1908, which contained planks insisting upon the enforcement of the Fifteenth Amendment and the protection of black voters, afforded a basis for reformers to make an issue of black suppression. Despite the pious platform statements and the general air of reform, twelve more years of Republican control only saw the race problem grow in magnitude, statutes on the subject remain unenforced, and the plight of blacks ignored.[1]

Theodore Roosevelt, who succeeded the assassinated McKinley in 1901, seemed interested enough in the racial problem to invite Booker T. Washington to the White House for dinner. A storm of public protest followed. His interest was short-lived; he became less concerned about blacks and even became sympathetic to racist positions. William Howard Taft, who succeeded Roosevelt in 1909, was confident that the southern white man was the black's best friend and assured the South that she need not fear the enforcement of "social equality." He saw no inconsistency between disfranchisement techniques and the Fifteenth Amendment. The federal army in the South, in keeping with the 1877 Compromise, largely ignored instances of racial violence. No president, attorney general, or secretary of war commissioned the military to enforce those extant amendments and statutes which enfranchised and protected the blacks.[2]

From 1901 to 1910, 846 persons were lynched in the United States. Of this number, 92 were white and 754 were black. Ninety percent of the lynchings took place in the South. Congress and the president took no action to prevent lynchings, and state governments did not prosecute the perpetrators, even when the event was publicized at least a day in advance. The president could not bring himself to initiate federal action on the basis of the remaining Reconstruction statutes, and no one in the government seemed to care enough to march a few soldiers into these areas, which would have been sufficient to disperse crowds that sometimes gathered to enjoy the lynchings. Senator "Pitchfork" Ben Tillman of South Carolina offered a convenient rationale for lynching; blacks had deteriorated since the beneficial effects of slavery had been removed and the only way to frighten them into submission was to lynch them. Further, if blacks somehow got elected to political office, they must be mobbed and displaced. The major difference between Tillman and his contemporaries in Congress was that he was candid, while some of them constructed a facade of constitutional theory to justify their inaction or hide their prejudice.[3]

The period of Republican ascendancy was fraught with race riots in the streets, mobbings, and jailhouse disturbances. In Springfield, Ohio in March 1904, fifteen hundred men stormed the city jail to "liberate" Richard Dixon, a black who had allegedly shot and killed a policeman who interceded in a drunken brawl between Dixon and his woman. The mob shot and hanged Dixon and then moved on to burn the black quarter. No attempts were made to put out or control the fire because the mayor feared the mob would not permit it. The local militia gathered at their barracks, but their officers were reluctant to hurt any members of the mob. The mayor finally asked the governor for assistance, whereupon eight companies were sent in and the saloons ordered closed. The militia, which did not arrive until the mob had spent itself, remained in town five days guarding the public fountain. As a punitive measure, the mayor closed black lodging houses and hotels at public insistence. A grand jury was convened which indicted only two men, not for lynching, but for breaking into the jail.[4]

In August 1904, Paul Reed and Will Cato, two blacks convicted of the alleged murder of a white family, were in the Statesboro, Georgia jail protected by a local militia company. The militia was armed only with bayonets and unloaded weapons—they did not want to hurt anyone. A crowd broke into the courthouse, pushed past the soldiers, took the prisoners outside town, and then burned them alive. Obsessed, the mob then embarked on the usual pogrom—attacking innocent blacks. At least four additional black people were killed. Five hundred militiamen were sent to the scene, but to no avail. The terror ended only when the weary throng dissipated itself. A commission appointed by the governor concluded that even a regiment could not have controlled the mob. The governor had not asked for federal aid, and none was offered. A Wall Street broker wrote Theodore Roosevelt, asking him to send troops to arrest the lynchers. Attorney General William H. Moody replied that no federal law had been violated.[5]

W. R. Leaken, an assistant attorney general for the district involved, thought there were federal grounds for a conviction. He wrote Moody for authority to ask a grand jury which was in session for an indictment against the mob leaders. The attorney general responded that an indictment under federal law could be invoked only when a federally protected right was violated. In his view, the Constitution did not protect blacks from murder. Leaken responded by sending Moody a press clipping indicating that the "best people" in the state were disgusted with lynching. Leaken also expressed his belief that the Statesboro case paralleled one in Huntsville, Alabama in September 1904, in which a mob burned a black man, and indictments were brought in federal court. However, the attorney general pointed out the differences between the two cases to Leaken: in Huntsville, when the mob burned the jail, the sheriff let the prisoner out, and the mob captured him outside the jail. The mob leaders were not indicted for murder but for burning the jail and threatening the lives of the other federal prisoners inside.[6] Then, Judge Emory Speer, who was presiding over the jury, wrote the attorney general to ask if Leaken had authority to proceed. He was informed that Leaken had not been given that authority and had, in fact, been reprimanded for his presumptiousness. After the grand jury was discharged, the department had a change of heart and informed Leaken to proceed on his own responsibility, if he so desired. Leaken, angry because now it was too late, wrote a long letter complaining about the department's vacillation. The attorney general explained that the department did not want to issue indictments every time someone was lynched and then be forced to abandon the charges.[7]

The lack of federal response in the Statesboro case was characteristic of post-Reconstruction interpretation of the Constitution, the Thirteenth, Fourteenth, and Fifteenth Amendments, and statutes passed upon their authority. This was an era in which the Supreme Court supported federal police power to regulate lotteries and oleomargarine, yet constricted the use of federal police power in incidences of racial violence. Perhaps the best expression of this judicial leaning was the Supreme Court decision in *Hodges v. United States* (1906). In this case, eight blacks in Arkansas contracted to work for a lumber manufacturer. Three armed white men forced them to leave their jobs for no other reason than their color. The blacks argued that they had been deprived of the protection of the Civil Rights Act of 1866, which asserts in part that blacks have the same right to make and enforce contracts as whites. They reasoned that since the inability to make contracts was a badge of slavery, the Thirteenth Amendment had been violated. The blacks further contended that the white defendants had violated that part of the Civil Rights Act of 1866 which made it a federal crime to deprive persons of federally protected rights. Violation of the act was punishable by a fine of one thousand dollars or imprisonment for one year, or both. Finally, the plaintiffs claimed that the defendants were guilty of a conspiracy to deny federal rights under the Act of 31 May 1870, which was punishable by a five thousand dollar fine or imprisonment for not more than ten years.[8]

Justice David J. Brewer, who wrote the majority opinion in the case, rejected these arguments on the grounds that the Thirteenth Amendment only prohibits forcing someone to work. Brewer felt that if Congress had determined to make blacks aliens, or wards of the nation, after the Civil War, they would be subject to federal protection. However, Brewer stated that whether "this was or was not the wiser way to deal with the problem is not a matter for the courts to consider." According to Brewer, the right to work was not a privilege of national citizenship or a federally created or protected right; the plaintiffs in such cases must look to the states for their protection. Brewer did not think that it was relevant that the plaintiffs were in federal court because the state had refused to give them protection.[9]

Interestingly enough, Justice John Marshall Harlan, the great dissenter in *Plessy v. Ferguson* and the *Civil Rights* cases joined with Justice William Day in asserting that it *was* the purpose of the Thirteenth Amendment to remove all incidents or badges of slavery. Being forced not to hold a job because of color was a badge of slavery. Harlan thought that the majority opinion in the *Civil Rights* cases had asserted that Congress had authority under the second section of the Thirteenth Amendment to remove all incidents of slavery. This was precisely what the court had done under the Civil Rights Act of 1866. Nonetheless, the overruling of the *Hodges* decision did not come until 1968 when the Supreme Court, in *Jones v. Alfred Mayer Co.,* declared the Civil Rights Act of 1866 to be valid legislation under the Thirteenth Amendment. The majority opinion written by Justice Potter Stewart stated that the Civil Rights Act of 1866 was designed to prohibit all racial discrimination with respect to the rights therein enumerated. The blacks in the *Hodges* case, however, received no relief, and for almost fifty years, the case became the rod and staff of those who denied that the federal government had the authority to intervene in race relations.[10]

The year of the *Hodges* decision, 1906, was punctuated with racial violence. In August, black soldiers of the Twenty-fifth infantry had been stationed in Brownsville, Texas for three weeks. Even before they arrived, the troops had heard rumors that they would not be sent out on maneuvers with the Texas National Guard because those units had said they would use real cartridges against black troops in war games. Word also circulated that the townspeople had sent letters to their congressmen objecting to the stationing of black troops in their area. When the soldiers arrived, the bars in town refused to serve them or, in some cases, the blacks would be asked to step off in a corner to surreptitiously buy drinks. The townspeople continually complained to the officers about the "uppity" black troops. Black soldiers were accused of not giving-way on the sidewalk to whites, of being drunk and disorderly, and of refusing to move on when told to do so. A white woman had also reported that a black soldier threw her on the ground and ran away. White people in the town were infuriated over this incident, and all army passes were cancelled.[11] On the night before the disorder broke out, a search and interrogation was conducted in the barracks for a black soldier who had reportedly assaulted a white woman in her home. One of the soldiers maintained that whites had prompted the woman to make this charge in order to get a soldier lynched and to downgrade black soldiers generally. The blacks bitterly resented being searched and insisted on their innocence.[12]

About midnight on 13 August, nine to fifteen armed black soldiers reportedly stole into the town and began shooting, resulting in the death of a bartender who had treated them shabbily and the wounding of a policeman. Later, they allegedly returned to the base, cleaned their guns, and went about their business. In an investigation conducted by the inspector general, threats and intimidations failed to produce informers. The soldiers again insisted on their innocence. The inspector general, relying upon the testimony of white citizens, recommended that the whole unit be given dishonorable discharges. Consequently, President Roosevelt dismissed the entire batallion of approximately 160 men and disqualified them from further military or government employment. Roosevelt was attacked by black groups who cited cases in which blacks were killed in racial assaults without prison sentences being given. They criticized the president for punishing both the innocent and the guilty and for exacting such harsh punishment. Through the efforts of Senator Joseph Foraker of Ohio and other interested members of Congress, a court of inquiry was eventually established, and the soldiers cleared of the charges were reinstated without loss of pay or privileges. No effort was made to reconcile the townspeople and the blacks, either before or after the incident; black troops were simply transferred to Nevada.[13]

In the same month, in the small town of Seaford, Delaware, a disturbance occurred when the news spread that a "strange Negro" had attacked a white boy. White citizens began parading the streets, assaulting any "strange Negro" they encountered. Blacks retaliated by beating whites. In response, the whites formed a squad of "police" and began jailing blacks, which succeeded only in alarming the outraged blacks. Although the town had only five hundred residents, at least two hundred blacks, reportedly from Maryland and Virginia, came to aid their brothers. Whites from out of town also rallied to the cause. When the destruction finally ended, the white community had driven out or jailed most of the blacks.[14]

The Atlanta Race Riot of 1906 was the bloodiest confrontation between the races in the period between 1900 and World War I. That summer, Atlanta was host to a state political campaign. The hotly debated issue of black disfranchisement, dramatized by the newspapers and the contending factions of the Democratic party, exacerbated the race hatred. Charges of black offenses against white women were box-scored in a newspaper for six months before the riot. Tension mounted, and apprehension gripped the city. On the afternoon of the riot, the headlines reported four alleged assaults against white women. Actually, one woman saw a black man outside her house and screamed. The other three assaults were never verified.

Tension, apprehension, and bigotry gave way to maniacal rage, and the purge began. That night, 22 September, whites indiscriminately began attacking blacks, killing and maiming many of them. Rioters broke into hardware stores and armed themselves, demolished black businesses, and even robbed stores kept by white men. When the mayor, the police force, and the fire department failed to control the rioters, the governor called out the militia, but, as usual, the major damage was already done.

Members of a black citizens' group hastily wrote Roosevelt, explaining the causes of the disorder and requesting prompt federal assistance to prevent further violence. Roosevelt had already demonstrated his reluctance to use federal forces even during the open warfare between the Industrial Workers of the World (IWW), the Western Federation of Miners, and the mine owners in Cripple Creek, Colorado in 1903–4. He sent no federal troops to Atlanta. Roosevelt's position was traditional—unless a formal request was made from the state indicating its inability to control a situation, no federal troops would be utilized in civil disorders. These requirements were not met in Atlanta.[15]

Although Sunday was quiet in Atlanta, rioting broke out again Monday night. For unknown reasons, a squad of police marched into the black suburb of Brownsville. By this time, the blacks were organized and had established methods of self-defense. The police arrests of black citizens for being armed threw light on an apparent contradiction: some white citizens aiding the police were armed and were apparently not deputized. When the whites, with their black prisoners in custody, approached one group of blacks and began firing to disperse them, the blacks returned their fire. One officer was killed, one was wounded, and several blacks were killed and injured. As the police started back to town with their prisoners, two of the blacks were killed by one or more unknown assailants.

Some twenty-four whites were arrested, found guilty in the rioting of Saturday night, and sentenced to short terms on the chain gang. Sixty blacks who were arrested for the shooting of the police officer were later released for lack of evidence. A grand jury was convened; the jury condemned the newspapers for creating the atmosphere which instigated the Saturday night riots. A committee of white citizens investigating the riot concluded that two whites and ten blacks had been killed and some twenty persons wounded. Those who suffered most, the committee revealed, were the law-abiding citizens.

The Atlanta riot left many questions unanswered. There was no explanation for the failure of the militia to prevent the violence on 24 September. Although federal troops were not formally called in, it was known that the commander of the Seventh Infantry at Camp Chickamauga had come to Atlanta to ask the commander of the state troops if he needed help. He had been told none was necessary. On the other hand, military authorities reportedly aided the police and white citizens in disarming blacks to prevent further violence. Lewis Douglass, son of the black abolitionist Frederick Douglass, expressed this view in the *New York Age:* ". . . [blacks] must die to be saved and in dying must take as many along with them as is possible to do with the aid of firearms and other weapons." However, blacks found it difficult to rebel, to make revolution, or even to mount successful self-defense when military authorities disarmed them, leaving them vulnerable to white intimidation and repression.[16]

The 1906 Christmas holidays were also filled with racial disorders. In the predominately black town of Wahalak, Mississippi, mayhem erupted when a black killed a white constable and a conductor of the Gulf, Mobile, and Ohio Railroad. The state militia, fortified with a Gatling gun and heavy armament, was sent from Meridian to protect the whites in the town and to keep order. Reports were circulating that bands of armed blacks and whites were killing each other; twelve persons were known dead. Governor James Vardaman and several staff members, accompanied by twenty-five soldiers, went to Wahalak to examine the situation because the disorder was spreading to surrounding towns. They were reassured when they discovered that the remaining trouble-makers were "tough white elements" who were still killing blacks to avenge the initial murders.[17]

The jailhouse riot in August 1908 in Springfield, Illinois is a landmark in black history. This perfidy in the birthplace of Lincoln, who was regarded by neo-abolitionists and blacks as the Great Emancipator, led to the formation of the NAACP and the beginning of a new phase of political protest in the black liberation movement. This riot was instigated, as was the Atlanta riot, by reports that blacks had assaulted white women. Before the riot occurred, Joe James, a black man, was in jail awaiting trial; he was accused of fatally stabbing a white man who had allegedly discovered James in his daughter's bedroom. On the way to jail, James had been snatched from the police and severely beaten, but was recovered and placed under protective custody. On 14 August, George Richardson was arrested for allegedly raping a white woman and was put in jail with James. When the word spread of another crime against white womanhood, a white mob gathered outside the jail. The ingenious sheriff arranged to have fire engines race down the street to distract the crowd while spiriting his prisoners to the state prison for safety. When the crowd, now an insurgent mob, demanded the prisoners, the sheriff let them inspect the jail. Finding the prisoners gone, the mob began to search for an object on which to vent its anger.

While the mob was milling aimlessly around the streets, a rumor was circulated that a local restaurant owner had driven the car in which the prisoners were carried to safety. The throng, with a purpose at last, demolished the man's restaurant and overturned his car. The outnumbered police and militia did not interfere. When the mob began burning the car and restaurant, the police fired a few warning shots, but to no avail. The mayor appeared and asked the mob to disperse, but when the mob pushed him aside, he took refuge in a cigar store. With added momentum, the mob turned its vengeance on the black populace. Black porters were beaten at railroad depots, blacks were dragged from streetcars, and the black quarter was sacked, looted, and demolished. Precedents were established when whites flew white handkerchiefs to indicate the ownership of their properties in order to protect them and when mobs refused to let the firemen put out the fires. Many people were killed; four white spectators were unintentionally killed by stray bullets. Blacks were killed indiscriminately. An elderly cobbler, who had been married to a white woman for thirty years was strung up and his throat was cut. The local militia did not, or could not, control the riot, and once again, the state troops arrived after the main surge of violence had passed. By daylight Saturday, the rioters had grown tired and gone home. The eighteen hundred troops who had entered the city busied themselves by clearing the wreckage and patrolling the devastation.

A grand jury investigating the riot was mainly thwarted because too few people were willing to testify against their associates, and most were implicated in some way themselves. The grand jury indicated three of the most vociferous leaders of the mob; one leader was a woman who had inflamed the crowd to mob violence in the name of the defense of white womanhood and who expressed pride in her own complicity in a number of the homicides. She was the only rioter found guilty, but escaped punishment by poisoning herself on the way to jail. Ironically, the woman whose alleged rape precipitated the riot confessed afterward that a white man whose identity she refused to give had attacked her.[18]

The Taft administration failed to break tradition on the issues critical to the black man. Taft followed the Republican tradition of appointing some blacks to "Negro jobs" and minor offices as patronage for their support as delegates to Republican nominating conventions; he appointed William H. Lewis, a prominent black Bostonian, as one of the assistants to Attorney General George W. Wickersham. In one case, he naively approved the appointment of a one-armed black as a deputy marshal in Houston at a salary higher than that of the marshal. When the deputy was fired because of the difference in salary, he complained to the attorney general, but the attorney general agreed with the marshal that the firing could be justified, without offending black patronage seekers, on the grounds that a one-armed man could not make arrests.[19]

The Taft administration faced its most severe test on the racial issue with an incident that occurred in Palestine, Texas. In August 1910, approximately twenty black plantation workers had been murdered because they had protested against their wages of one dollar a day, and the payment in script which they had to spend at the company store. Wickersham was made aware of the event through a letter written to Taft by Cecil Lyon, the chairman of the Texas state republican committee. Lyon enclosed a letter from a local white man, John Siddon, who asked that his name be kept secret and who asserted that he knew the guilty parties. Siddon said, and Lyon agreed, that since the state of Texas would never undertake the prosecution of anyone for these crimes, a federal investigation was the only hope for ending such incidents. Wickersham replied to Lyon that the matter would receive careful attention. There is no evidence that it did.[20] In addition, a group of black ministers wrote Taft, complaining about the incident and demanding that the government make it clear that blacks were not to be executed without a trial, indictment, and conviction. A staff attorney replied that there was no federal crime involved. However, if the ministers knew of some federal violation, they would submit the facts and an investigation would certainly be made.[21]

When W. H. Ellis, an attorney and concerned citizen, sent a telegram to Taft, he struck at the heart of the issue of constitutional power as it related to the Palestine affair. Ellis thought that if Grover Cleveland could find justification to send troops to Illinois to stop rioting, then Taft should be able to find a means to send troops to Texas to stop the "massacre" of black people, if for no other reason than for the sake of humanity. Taft did not reply; if he had, the answer probably would have reflected all those conventions which had determined federal policy for twenty-five years. Since the national government relied on *Hodges v. United States,* murder was not a matter of federal concern.[22]

As the Republican era drew to a close, is was clear that Roosevelt, who had made progressivism nationally respectable, and

Taft, the trust-buster, had failed to develop a program for resolving America's racial problem. They, like the Progressives, must have felt that impure food and drugs, the trusts, corruption in government, and the plight of the immigrants were more important issues. In the meantime, troops and white citizens had rather successfully kept blacks in their place. Perhaps the disorder and violence was not yet profound or continuous enough to grasp the attention of the government or the general public.

NOTES

1. Kirk H. Porter, comp., *National Party Platforms* (New York, 1924), p. 232, 263, 305; Rayford Logan, *The Betrayal of the Negro* (New York, 1965), pp. 346–7; Leslie Fishel and Benjamin Quarles, *The Negro American: A Documentary History* (Glenview, Ill., 1967), pp. 359–62.

2. Seth M. Scheiner, "President Theodore Roosevelt and the Negro, 1901–8," *Journal of Negro History* 47 (July 1962), pp. 169–82; William Howard Taft, *Political Issues and Outlooks* (New York, 1909), pp. 231, 237, 350. *Annual Report of the Secretary of War for 1900,* p. 134.

3. Logan, *The Betrayal,* p. 348; NAACP, *Thirty Years of Lynching, 1889–1918. (See* Sections 241, 242, 332, and 333 of the *United States Code* in Appendix.) *Congressional Record,* 57th cong., 2nd sess. (1902–3), pp. 2511–5, 2559, 2558–64; Francis Butler Simpkins, *Pitchfork Ben Tillman* (Baton Rouge, 1944), pp. 394–401.

4. *New York Times,* 8–12 March 1904, p. 1; Ray Stannard Baker, *Following the Color Line, American Negro Citizenship in the Progressive Era* (New York, 1964, orig. pub. 1904) pp. 204–9.

5. *New York Times,* 17 August 1904, p. 1; 18, 19, and 27 August, p. 2. Fred Gordon to Theodore Roosevelt, Department of Justice, R.G. 60, National Archives, Letters Received, 19 August 1904, Letters Sent, 26 August 1904, file no. 40036. *See also* U.S. Commission on Civil Rights, *Freedom to the Free, A Century of Emancipation, 1863–1963* (Washington, 1963) pp. 75–6.

6. *See* entire file no. 40036, Department of Justice, R.G. 60, Statesboro, Georgia, 1904.

7. Department of Justice, file no. 40036, R.G. 60; Baker, *Following the Color Line*, pp. 187–201.

8. *Hodges v. United States*, 203 *U.S.*, 66, 70, 71 (1906) (*see* Sections 240 and 242 of the *U.S. Code* in Appendix).

9. Ibid., p. 70.

10. Ibid., pp. 73–5; *Plessy v. Ferguson*, 163 *U.S.* 537 (1896), separate but equal facilities on passenger trains are constitutionally permissible; *Civil Rights Cases* 109 *U.S.* 3 (1883), the Fourteenth Amendment does not permit Congress to outlaw individual acts of racial discrimination, but only state discriminatory action. *Jones v. Alfred Mayer Co.*, 392 *U.S.* 409 (1968).

11. Department of Justice, file no. 88139, R.G. 60, 1906.

12. *New York Times*, 15 August 1906, p. 1; Department of Justice, file no. 88139, R.G. 60.

13. *New York Times*, 16 August 1906, p. 3; 18 August, p. 1; 20 August, p. 1; 21 August, p. 2; Department of Justice, file no. 88139, R.G. 60.

14. *New York Times*, 19 August 1906, p. 1; 22 August, p. 11.

15. Charles S. Crowe, "Racial Massacre in Atlanta, September 22, 1906," *The Journal of Negro History* 54 (April 1969) sheds little new light on the subject; however, Crowe's paper (copy in my possession), "Race Riots in the Progressive Period," delivered at the Association for the Study of Negro Life and History in October 1969 was much more informative. Letter from J. E. Sistrunk to President Roosevelt, Department of Justice, file no. 67459, R.F. 60.

16. Baker, *Following the Color Line*, chap. 1; *New York Times*, 24 September 1906, pp. 1, 2; 25 September, p. 1; 26 September, p. 1, 5; 28 September, p. 1; *see* Aptheker, *Documentary History*, p. 868, for the speech of Lewis Douglass. Crowe believes that if blacks had engaged in serious retaliation, the federal troops would have aided the militia in repressing them: *see* fn. 15.

17. *New York Times*, 25 December 1906, p. 1; 26 December, p. 1; 27 December, p. 3; 28 December, p. 3.

18. The following account of the Springfield riot is based on James L. Crouthamel, "The Springfield Race Riot of 1908," *The Journal of Negro History* 45 (1906), pp. 168–81; *New York Times*, 15, 16, 17, August, p. 1; 18 August, p. 5; 19 August, p. 2; 20 August, p. 14; Mary White Ovington, "The Founding of the NAACP," *The Journal of Negro History* 9 (1924), pp. 107–116; Herbert Aptheker, *Documentary*

History of the Negro People in the United States (New York, 1951), pp. 915–28.

19. Department of Justice, file no. 9282–02, R.G. 60, 1909.

20. Department of Justice, file no. 152961–1, R.G. 60, 1910; file no. 152961–2, 1910.

21. Department of Justice, file no. 152961, R.G. 60, 1910; file no. 152961–3, 1910.

22. Department of Justice, file no. 152961–1, R.G. 60, 1910.

11 / Moving Off Dead Center

The administrations of Woodrow Wilson were remarkably fruitful in passing reform legislation; the tariff revision, financial renovation, and the "Magna Carta of Labor," the Clayton Antitrust Act, were proud accomplishments of the "New Freedom." But there was no "New Freedom" or reform related to race relations. Many blacks supported Woodrow Wilson in the campaign of 1912, only to find him less interested in their plight than the Republicans had been. Even in federal jobs and office buildings in Washington where black employees had once worked freely with whites, segregation was reestablished. Lynching, pogroms, jailhouse riots, and mob violence continued unabated; racial murder remained a seemingly unpunishable state crime.[1]

Aside from the continuing lynchings of individual blacks, the largest racial disorder in the Wilson era was a riot in East St. Louis in the spring and summer of 1917. The sizeable immigration of blacks into the city resulted in an oversupply of labor; apprehensive whites felt that job competition ought to be eliminated. Pressures mounted, and after a labor dispute in May, groups of disgruntled whites roamed the streets attacking blacks in an attempt to coerce them into leaving the city. The National Guard, which had officially been established in the Dick Act of 1903, was called out by the governor, all saloons were closed, and the violence subsided. Many alarmed blacks left the city.[2] The tenuous peace was shattered when a group of blacks, anticipating further hostilities, fired upon a car which approached them in their neighborhood, believing the car to be full of armed whites. However, the car turned out to be a police car; five policemen were shot, and one was killed. Afterwards, the car was parked in front of the police station where crowds gathered to look at this symbol of black perfidy. The purge began; nine whites and thirty-nine blacks were killed.

The racial violence in East St. Louis generated protest across the country. Even Theodore Roosevelt spoke out in support of an investigation of the riot and murders and of the city government's apparent inability to prevent them. Black spokesmen believed federal aid should have been introduced to end the violence, as it had been in the Colorado mining disputes of 1892, 1894, 1899, and 1914, in the railroad strikes of 1877, and in the Pullman dispute. Even businessmen asserted that for the sake of preventing the destruction of plants essential to the war effort, federal force should have been utilized in the absence of state protection.[3]

Despite pressure from the NAACP, concerned citizens and local businessmen, Wilson refused to intercede. The protests continued, eventually centering upon a request for a federal grand jury investigation to ascertain the causes of the riot and to suggest ways to prevent similar incidents. Lawyers in the Justice Department correctly put forth interpretations of the Civil Rights Act of 1866, which provided a basis for federal punishment of racial violence. However, Wilson and Attorney General Thomas Gregory refused the rationale for intervention provided by their staff attorneys. The governor had not requested federal aid and, in their view, no federal statute had been violated.[4]

In the House, Leonidus Dyer of St. Louis, Missouri introduced a resolution which requested a committee investigation based on the power of Congress to regulate interstate commerce. Lawrence Sherman of Illinois introduced a similar resolution in the Senate. A committee was set up in August, hearings were held, but access to Justice Department files were denied because Gregory felt that release of the materials would not be in the public interest. No action grew out of the committee report, despite its condemnation of community mores, politicians, labor organizations, and others who had created the environment that precipitated the riot in St. Louis.[5]

Even those blacks who were in the military service were not immune to the infection of violence which spread throughout the country during the summer of 1917. In August, a rebellion involving black soldiers occurred in Houston, Texas. Several companies of the Twenty-fourth Infantry, consisting of about six hundred men, were assigned as guards during the construction of a training base for Illinois National Guard troops. Houston was found to be just as inhospitable to blacks as Brownsville had been in 1906. Jim Crowism and racial insults were common. As the atmosphere became increasingly charged, the commander of the infantry organized an ersatz black military police unit, which was ordered to keep the black soldiers in order, although no arms were issued the unit. Newspaper advertisements placed by local prohibitionists who wanted saloon closing endorsed in the coming election reminded the populace of Brownsville that the presence of black soldiers was an additional reason for prohibiting liquor sales. Conditions were ripe for disorder.[6]

The exact circumstances of the ensuing events are difficult to establish. Reportedly, two Houston police officers arrested a black woman for being drunk and disorderly. A black MP from the base asked the officers to release the woman to his custody. The police refused his request, and when the soldier insisted that they comply, the police struck him and then jailed him along with the woman. Later, another encounter between the same police officers and another black MP heightened the tension. Upon inquiring about the charges made against his fellow officer, the MP was told by one of the police officers that he did not answer questions posed by a black man. When the MP insisted that he needed the information to file a report, the police officer answered him with a pistol butt and an escort to jail. When the MP tried to escape, the police officer shot at him to subdue him. The rumor quickly spread among the black soldiers that other blacks were being brutalized by the police. The vacuum created by the military's apathy was quickly filled. Preparations were made, and arms and ammunition were stolen. That night, approximately one hundred black soldiers marched into town, bent on punishing the police, especially those stationed around the black quarter. On the way to town, the soldiers encountered a group of white policemen and shot two of them. Houston policemen, members of the Texas National Guard, and the Illinois guardsmen who were in town when the trouble started pursued and arrested the black soldiers, wounding five in the process. Six hundred federal troops from Fort Sam Houston were assigned to aid in keeping order. When Assistant Attorney General William Fitts, completely missing the point of the disturbance, simplistically suggested that the opening of grog shops and their availability to the men might have caused the riot, the soldiers involved denied drinking.[7]

Evidence indicates that the army's desire for making an example of the insurrectionaries led the prosecution far afield. To aid in developing their case, the prosecution opened sixty letters addressed to the black soldiers, in an effort to find evidence of a plot, which would have incurred even heavier sentences than the ones given; no such evidence was found. The military believed that insurrections such as this did not occur as an immediate response to provocation, but as a result of a plan or design to create disorder. The black soldiers involved were court martialed; thirteen were hanged for murder, forty-four were sentenced to life imprisonment for mutiny, and five were acquitted. The Court of Claims was ordered by a Joint Resolution, passed by both houses of Congress in June 1919, to make an investigation and award damages to civilians killed or wounded by the soldiers. Justice was served.[8]

Racial violence on the home front and the war abroad contended for headlines. Amid the lynchings and jailhouse riots in 1918, one event captured the sympathy of the public. In Estill Springs, Tennessee, a black accused of killing two white men was burned at the stake after a confession was forced from him by red hot irons. The NAACP sent its usual letters of protest to the president and the attorney general, but there was a significantly increased volume of mail from private citizens. A lady who was on a cruise to Europe wrote the president that she was offended by having to explain these barbarities to foreigners.[9]

The most interesting letters from a social and constitutional point of view were those written by Nick Chiles, the editor of a black newspaper, *The Topeka Plaindealer*. Chiles first wrote to the president, who then sent his letter on to the attorney general as was customary. Assistant Attorney General William Fitts sent Chiles the standard *Hodges* response that murder was a state matter. Chiles scathingly replied that he had not asked for legal advice, but rather he had asked the president to make the suppression of lynching and mob violence a war measure. Chiles retorted that perhaps blacks did not know much, but at least they "know enough to know that the President could demand that the Governors of the several states see to it that their citizens desist from such outrages, as such acts interfere in the prosecution of the war between these countries and the allies against Germany." Chiles continued: "If a local miner's union in Kansas can strike and the Federal officers can be sent to this union to find out the difficulty and trouble and adjust the same, for the reason that it will stop the mining of coal and interfere with the prosecution of the war, the same thing could be done to put a stop to the lynching and burning of colored men who could be used to dig the coal or use guns in the defense of the country." According to Chiles, the *Hodges* decision was not applicable under war conditions. With governmental control of food supply, railroads, and fuel, states' rights were virtually nonexistent in some areas. Despite Chiles' understanding of the flexibility of constitutional law, his plea had no effect. The department filed his last letter without reply.[10]

In 1919, racial violence escalated. The general strike engineered by the IWW in Seattle in February, the organizing activity of William Z. Foster and steel workers for a large-scale strike which finally occurred in September, and the increasing militancy of coal workers frightened conservatives who blamed the tensions on a Bolshevist plot. Conservatives were as frightened of black rebellion as they were of strikes and, despite the fact that blacks were used as strikebreakers, sought a Bolshevist link between the two.[11] Federal aid was readily introduced to quell the violence accompanying these disputes, justified in part because the national guard had not yet been demobilized and returned to state control.

In Charleston, South Carolina, when white sailors went on a rampage after an embroilment between a black and two sailors, two blacks were killed and seventeen wounded; seven sailors and one white policeman were wounded. The sailors attacked stores owned by blacks and looted shooting galleries for rifles and ammunition. Blacks and sailors battled each other with clubs and guns. The marines arrived, subdued the sailors, and took them back to the base. Fifty soldiers were sent from North Charleston with orders to arrest only military personnel. The army report on the incident carefully pointed out that their intervention was not official and that any blacks who were killed were killed by the navy. Six sailors were convicted at a court martial of conduct prejudicial to good order and discipline, and manslaughter and given short prison sentences. A coroner's jury in the city, where the population was sixty percent black, exonerated the blacks who insisted they fired in self-defense.[12]

Racial violence occurred in Longview, Texas that year as a result of white response to increasing black sophistication in business transactions. Black efforts to improve their circumstances were met with hostility and suspicion, and finally, open aggression. In order to obtain better prices for their cotton, black businessmen sent it directly to Galveston, thus avoiding local middlemen. A cooperative had also been established where blacks could buy goods more cheaply. In addition, many blacks read the *Chicago Defender,* a newspaper whose militant tone was a source of aggravation to the white community. On 4 July, the paper published an article intimating that a black man who had been lynched for raping a white woman was innocent, because the pair were lovers. Whites, suspecting that one of the local black businessmen had written the article, beat him with iron rods and gun butts and ordered him to leave town. A white mob bent on black suppression then marched into the black section and was fired upon; four whites were wounded. Mustering help from other whites, the mob returned to burn houses and shops. The police arrested a number of blacks for rioting; two hundred and fifty national guardsmen called in by the governor arrested a few blacks and whites. The arrested rioters were ultimately released, although the black ringleaders were ordered to leave town.[13]

Just as military intelligence kept labor organizations and black groups under surveillance throughout the country, it kept a careful eye on developments among the black population in Washington, as the epidemic of riots spread into the Capitol. On 5 September 1917, the First Battalion of the District of Columbia, the Negro National Guard, and a battalion of white infantry with two companies of artillery guarded the White House and two squadrons of cavalry were on reserve at Fort Myer to aid the infantries in patrolling Potomac Park.[14] *The Washington Post,* like other newspapers, played-up alleged racial incidents to bolster scare headlines. In July 1919, a story concerning a naval employee's wife who was jostled by two blacks who tried to steal her umbrella led two hundred sailors and marines to attempt the lynching of the two black suspects. Discovering that the blacks had been released by the police, the sailors and marines, joined by white civilians, marched into black neighborhoods, beating any black men and women they encountered. Police and MPs called to disperse the mob held two sailors and eight blacks for investigation. A NAACP request to Secretary of the Navy Josephus Daniels that orders for a cessation of violence be issued to naval personnel elicited no response.

The violence was intensified when a black held in custody on a minor charge was beaten by a crowd of whites. The police recovered the prisoner, but failed to arrest any of his aggressors. Soldiers and sailors then began dragging black citizens from streetcars and beating them. At midnight, the servicemen returned to their barracks, while civilians continued the violence. The Monday morning *Post* called servicemen to assemble at

9:00 P.M. to "clean up the town." A mob of blacks, now thoroughly alarmed, boarded a streetcar, and beat the motorman and conductor, while another group fired on sailors at the naval hospital, and others marched toward the Navy Yard. That night, whites and blacks both raided the other's neighborhoods in automobiles, which resulted in shoot-outs whenever the opposing sides met. Seven hundred Washington police and four hundred servicemen tried to keep order.

On Tuesday, President Wilson, Secretary of War Newton D. Baker, and Secretary of the Navy Daniels ordered additional troops into the city. That night, approximately twelve thousand federal troops were in the city. The NAACP and other organizations had encouraged people to stay at home. Following a rainy night, with only three casualties, one black and two whites, the riot ended. As in many other incidents, military troops did not arrive until after the violence had subsided.[15]

In the congressional debates on the possibility of an investigation of the riot, one southern senator thought that although everyone knew blacks were inferior to whites, whites should set an example by not participating in the riots. Representative Melvin McLaughlin of Nebraska objected to a suggestion made by a congressman from Alabama that the Germans were behind the riot, as there was no evidence of truth in this statement. No investigation was made.[16] However, the police chief naively suggested that hiring more policemen with higher wages would solve the problem. Even military intelligence admitted to the existence of a problem when their undercover man, William H. Loving, who was described as "the best type of white man's Negro," criticized the government for repression and discrimination against blacks. Nonetheless, no positive action to improve race relations in Washington was taken.[17]

A bloodier disorder than the one in Washington broke out in Chicago in July when a young black boy on a raft drifted into the "white" area at a bathing beach; he was reportedly stoned and drowned by the insulted whites. When a white policeman, refusing to arrest the alleged murderers, arrested a black on some minor offense, a mob of enraged blacks attacked the policeman. As news of the incident spread, mobs clashed all over Chicago.

The disorders continued for seven days, resulting in the death of fifteen whites and twenty-three blacks.[18]

The biracial Chicago Commission on Race Relation, established by the governor to investigate the riot, reported that the large-scale migration of blacks into the city at the beginning of the war, the efforts of blacks to buy housing outside of traditionally black areas, the hostility between black and white workers, and the tendency of the police to use force when arresting blacks precipitated the riot. Despite the intensity of the riot, no regular army troops were called in; however, on 30 July, the third day of rioting, six thousand national guardsmen were called to duty. In the grand jury investigation which had indicted fifty blacks and seventeen whites, the NAACP aided in the defense of the blacks and, at one point, considered placing the responsibility for black violence on those who had created the volatile conditions. However, that position was rejected as being too extreme. Most of the persons arrested, black and white, were acquitted.[19]

Aside from the report prepared by the Chicago Commission on Race Relations, whose conclusions, though valuable to the historian, were left to gather dust, one result of the riot was an increased effort to keep blacks disarmed. Gun retailers refused to sell weapons to blacks. Military intelligence kept Pullman porters under surveillance since it was reported that they were bringing guns and ammunition into Chicago to arm the black population. The American public and those governmental officials unacquainted with nineteenth-century disturbances and earlier twentieth-century riots in Atlanta, Brownsville, and Houston, the events in Chicago and Washington forced one conclusion—blacks would not simply accept attacks against them without retaliation.[20]

Attempts to lynch black prisoners continued to cause jailhouse riots in 1919. In Knoxville, Tennessee in August, Maurice Mays, charged with the murder of a white woman, was surreptitiously moved to Chattanooga because a mob had gathered outside the jail. Not believing Mays was gone, the mob ransacked the jail, releasing white prisoners. Having been ordered to move away from the jail by a company of national guardsmen, the mob moved on without purpose or direction, looting stores and stealing weapons. When the rumor circulated that whites were being robbed in black areas, they moved into black neighborhoods and were met with gunfire. Twelve hundred national guardsmen, called in to control the riot, advanced against the blacks. The troopers then fanned out to disarm the blacks; two blacks were shot and two bayoneted in the process. The only two fatalities were national guardsmen who were accidently shot by other guardsmen. The sheriff arrested fifty whites and called a grand jury, despite receiving threats for acting contrary to the interests of the white community; most of the whites were acquitted. The National Guard, in this instance, successfully aided the mob.[21]

Another classic lynching riot occurred that year in Omaha, Nebraska. Again, there had been a plethora of newspaper stories about assaults on white women. On 28 September, when a black named William Brown was jailed on the charge of assault, a mob quickly gathered. The mayor, interfering with the lynchers, narrowly escaped hanging. The mob burned the jail and abducted Brown, who was then shot and hanged. Before the lynching, the police had requested aid from the army commander at Fort Crook, but the request was denied, along with one submitted by the federal marshal, on the grounds that troops could be used only to enforce federal law or in response to a formal state request. Red tape in the governor's office had slowed preparation for the official request. Finally, after Brown was killed, the commander at Fort Crook, deciding he could no longer await instructions from Washington, ordered two hundred army troops to disperse the white crowds who had moved into black neighborhoods.

By dawn the following day, the town was quiet. Remaining on guard, the soldiers advised the black population to stay indoors. The machine guns set up by the troops and a heavy rain that evening dampened the enthusiasm of the potential violators. The next morning when General Leonard Wood, Commander of the Central Division of the Army, arrived in Omaha, he began arresting those implicated in the lynching for trial by civilian authorities. Public meetings were prohibited and gatherings of two or more were broken up. Fifty-nine men were arrested for complicity in the lynching. The army remained in the city until early November.

As indicated by the official army report on the incident, the governor's official request for aid went to the chief of staff and secretary of war in Washington where it was approved shortly after the eight hundred troops had already left for Omaha. The War Department did not insist that the governor address himself to the president, which is required by statute, since most National Guard troops were federalized during the war and many states failed to organize volunteer militias as a first line of defense.[22]

While federal troops were still patrolling in Omaha, the last major racial disorder of 1919 broke out in Elaine, Arkansas. Desiring higher prices for their cotton and lower prices for goods, the blacks in Phillips County organized a union and began holding meetings in a black church. Robert L. Hill, a black farmer, emerged as the leader of the union movement, which had followers in several black communities in Arkansas. When the disturbances erupted, the Phillips County group was holding a meeting in the church to decide if they should retain U. S. Bratton as a legal advisor. Bratton was a white lawyer who was known for his efforts to press federal prosecution of white plantation owners who held blacks in peonage in Arkansas.

The account of the events surrounding the violence is punctuated with contradictions. According to the whites, deputy sheriffs had been fixing a flat tire near the church when they were fired upon by the black guards who stood outside the church and then attacked by the union members who feared that the sheriffs had heard of their plans to massacre whites. The blacks said that the whites, fearing the economic organization of the blacks, had fired into the church without provocation and then burned the church to hide any evidence that might contradict the white version of the event.[23]

Colonel Isaac Jencks, commander of the army troops at Camp Pike, did not move in immediately upon receiving word that the secretary of war had approved the governor's request for aid but had awaited further orders. The War Department, perturbed by his hesitancy, issued expanded orders that governors could receive aid from division commanders without informing the adjutant general in Washington.[24] When Jenck's troops finally arrived in Elaine, they aided the white posses who had formed to scour the countryside in search of blacks. Of the several hundred arrested blacks, a few were released when a white person vouched for their reliability. In the next few days, Jencks, believing he had been ordered into Elaine to suppress a black rebellion, joined the local officials in questioning blacks, in hopes of obtaining confessions of the planned "insurrection." In a report submitted to the military intelligence office in Washington, the district officer indicated that approximately twenty blacks were killed for resisting arrest; in addition, a black guard ·at the mass meeting had killed a deputy who came to arrest a bootlegger. In his opinion, the incident was caused by the money-making schemes of a few blacks who informed ignorant blacks that whites were cheating them, and that the black masses should arm themselves. Another investigator reported that he could find no Bolshevist or IWW connection with the riot.[25]

The NAACP put up a long and expensive battle to overturn the convictions of blacks who were the alleged leaders of the Elaine insurrection. The effort met with some success in *Moore v. Dempsey* (1923), when the Supreme Court condemned the atmosphere at the trial on the grounds that the defendants lacked proper counsel and that the courtroom was filled with people who were forestalled from lynching the defendants only because guilty verdicts were assured. Another NAACP battle was designed to keep the governor of Kansas from extraditing Robert Hill, who was charged with impersonating a federal officer. In March 1920, after the federal government had dropped charges against Hill, partly because the only evidence submitted was that some of Hill's organizing literature had indicated that the black union had the support of the United States government, the governor of Kansas decided to refuse the request for extradition from the governor of Arkansas.[26]

A spate of letters encouraging intervention on behalf of the Elaine blacks inundated the Justice Department. William Pickens, President of Morgan State College, wrote on 26 November 1919 that blacks would not riot without good cause and that it was peculiar that with all the blacks killed in Arkansas, only blacks were convicted.[27] In Congress, the House listened with great interest as Thaddeus Caraway of Arkansas interrupted Thomas Heflin of Alabama, who was speaking on the evils of anarchy, to give the white version of the Elaine events. Caraway hoped that President Wilson would ignore the NAACP pleas for intervention on behalf of the black insurrectionaries because to Caraway, the NAACP was an "association for the promotion of revolution and inciting to riot." [28]

The national government remained greatly concerned about black rebellion and possible ties with radical organizations. On 1 August 1919, J. Edgar Hoover, who was appointed Director of the General Investigating Division of the Justice Department, began compiling a report on black radicals. Secretary of War Baker, in a speech reported in the *New York Times* on 16 October 1919, linked race riots with labor disturbances as forces of social revolution and made it clear that the government would suppress every attempted revolt. The War Department prepared an Emergency Plan White, which specified instructions on riot control duty to guarantee effective suppression of revolts.[29]

Military intelligence maintained its surveillance of black organizational activity to determine the extent of black radicalism. On 13 October 1919, when it was reported that the Urban League, a "radical" black organization, would be holding a convention in Detroit at the same time Big Bill Haywood of the IWW was scheduled to speak, attention was focused on Detroit. On 29 October, a Chicago operative reported that two brothers, Chan and Charlie Jackson, had left 17 October from Philadelphia for New Orleans with instructions from Big Bill to start trouble among blacks. A description would be sent so they could be watched. Incidents such as this one were commonly reported by military intelligence as evidence of black ties with radical groups.[30]

J. Edgar Hoover's report on radicals was issued in mid-November 1919. Attorney General A. Mitchell Palmer, who submitted the report to the Senate Committee on the Judiciary, gave his opinion based on the findings of the report; he asserted that white radicals who tried to use blacks were sometimes successful. He added that major radicalism on the part of blacks was evident in their threats to retaliate for lynchings and in their demands for social equality; they were defiantly making assertions for equality and, in some cases, superiority. The NAACP responded by stating that blacks were not doing anything disloyal by pressing black demands.[31] Another response to the report came in a letter to the attorney general from Neval Thomas, a teacher at Dunbar High School in Washington, who expressed the view that black self-assertion had nothing to do with Bolshevism. In another letter on 29 December 1919, Thomas told Palmer that the government should pay no attention to "the servile Negro patronage hunter who would tell you that we are contented, and the discontented few," as those persons had no following in the black community. He pointed out that blacks had been drafted disapproportionately to their number "to fight for a freedom they have never known, and we their blood kin, regardless of consequences are going to get the freedom [for] which we were told to die." [32]

While Hoover diligently pursued his investigation of possible black ties with radical organizations, racial violence continued. In Wilson's administration, in Lexington, Kentucky in February 1920, a white mob, intent on lynching a black man who had been convicted of raping a ten-year-old white girl, were denied entrance to the jail by state troopers. Subsequent threats were made by whites that vengeance would be taken on the authorities and that the tobacco warehouses of those who interfered would be burned. A riot ensued in which state troopers killed four whites and wounded eighteen. The governor asked for federal aid from General Leonard Wood, the division commander at Camp Zachary Taylor, who sent 953 officers and 46 enlisted men to aid in controlling the disturbance. At this time, military intelligence was reassured by the officers involved that there were no outside agitators or foreigners present, that the rioters thought the black man should have been lynched, and that white civilians had informed them that even the blacks thought he should be lynched. The officers added that although twenty percent of the federal troops were foreignborn, they all seemed trustworthy. Despite the violence, the prisoner escaped injury and was sent to the state penitentiary.[33]

Despite the severe attacks on the NAACP, it continued its protest against the continuing violence. James Weldon Johnson, Executive Secretary of the NAACP, irately pointed out to President Wilson that black voter organizations were being brutalized in Florida and that federal troops should be used to oversee the elections instead of the unsympathetic state troops. Assistant Attorney General Robert P. Stewart responded that the government could do nothing since all the Reconstruction statutes on voting rights had been repealed. However, although the NAACP was seldom successful in achieving its goals, the American public could often pressure the national government into acting on their demands.[34] The increasing public pressure forced Secretary of War Baker to clarify the constitutional basis for supplying federal troops in domestic disorders. In a memo to the chief of staff on 2 December 1920, he stated that troops should be supplied only when the state had exhausted all its resources and was still unable to deal with the disorder. He might have asserted that when the National Guard was federalized during the war, the states could be assumed to have exhausted all their resources. Instead, he admitted that the constitutional rule had been relaxed during the war because the guard had been drafted into federal service. He thought that as enough time had elapsed for demobilization, governors or legislatures should now apply directly to the president as required by the Constitution and the statutes.

The law was now clarified; but the Wilson administration went no further. Even though the Wilson administration had witnessed the most severe racial disorders since Reconstruction, no really positive response was given. The only legislative attempt to curb racial disorders was made by Dyer of Missouri who introduced an antilynching bill to Congress. Dyer proposed that the failure to protect a citizen from lynching be made a denial of equal protection under the Fourteenth Amendment and that the act should include a provision that the county in which the violation occurred pay damages to the family of the victim. Dyer's committee took testimony on lynching and the major riots of 1919 to support the necessity for this legislation. Opponents of the bill responded that antilynching legislation was an NAACP tactic to keep black violators from being punished. Dyer's bill passed in the House but was filibustered to death in the Senate. It was apparent that the resolution of the problem of racial violence would again be passed to the next administration.

NOTES

1. Kathleen Wohlgemuth, "Woodrow Wilson and Federal Segregation," *The Journal of Negro History* 44 (April 1959), pp. 158–173; Arthur Link, *Woodrow Wilson and the Progressive Era 1910–17* (New York, 1954), pp. 64–6.

2. Elliott M. Rudwick, *Race Riot at East St. Louis, July 2, 1917* (Carbondale, Ill., 1964), pp. 39–40, *New York Times,* 29 May 1970, p. 3; 30 May, p. 6; 31 May, p. 1.

3. Department of Justice, Glasser File Box 14, R.G. 60, East St. Louis, 3 July 1917.

4. Department of Justice, Glasser File Box 14, East St. Louis, July 1917; Rudwick, *Race Riot,* p. 137.

5. Department of Justice, Glasser File Box 14, East St. Louis, October 1917; Letters Received, file no. 186835–55, R.G. 60, December 1917.

6. Edgar Schoulder, "The Houston Race Riot, 1917," *The Journal of Negro History* 29 (July 1944), pp. 300–38, is based on a report in the *Houston Daily Post* during the riot.

7. Department of Justice, file no. 196821, R.G. 60, National Archives; *New York Times,* 24 August 1917, p. 7; 25 August, p. 1; 26 August, p. 3; 27 August, p. 7.

8. Department of Justice, file no. 196821–x, R.G. 60; *Sen. J. Res.* 51, 10 June 1919.

9. Department of Justice, file no. 190267–1 through 4, R.G. 60; *see also* 158260, February 1918.

10. Department of Justice, file no. 190267–5, R.G. 60, February 1918.

11. Foster Rhea Dulles, *Labor in America, A History* (New York, 1949), pp. 231–40; Robert Kerlin, *The Voice of the Negro, 1919* (New York, 1920), pp. 68–70; Allen A. Holland, Jr., "The Negro and the IWW,"

(unpublished seminar paper, 1942), Michigan Historical Collections, University of Michigan, Ann Arbor, Michigan.

12. Arthur Waskow, *From Race Riot to Sit-In–1919 and the 1960's* (New York, 1966), pp. 13–6, is a useful study, although based primarily on NAACP files; he does not include the riots between 1919 and 1960. Department of Justice, Glasser File Box 14, R.G. 60, Charleston, S.C., 10, 11 May 1919.

13. *New York Times,* 12 July 1919, p. 20; 14 July, p. 2. Peonage (debt slavery) was endemic in the South despite the federal law of 1867 outlawing it. It was one means used by some southerners to continue their exploitation of black labor. Justice Department efforts to enforce the law were feeble at best; *see* Pete Daniel, "Peonage in the New South" (unpublished doctoral dissertation, University of Maryland, 1970).

14. Department of Justice, Memo for Chief of Staff, Glasser File Box 14, Washington, D.C. and Virginia, September 1917.

15. Department of Justice, Memo for Chief of Staff, Glasser File Box 14, Washington, D.C., September 1917; War Department, A.G.O. 370, p. 6; Department of Justice Glasser File Box 14, Washington, D.C., Executive Branch, Military Intelligence, "Negro Agitation"; *New York Times,* 21–24 July 1919, p. 1, Waskow, *Race Riot,* chap. 3.

16. *Congressional Record,* 66th cong., 1st. sess. (1919), pp. 3367, 3646, 8979.

17. Department of Justice, Glasser File Box 14, Office of Chief of Staff, Executive Branch, Military Intelligence, August 1919.

18. Chicago Commission on Race Relations, *The Negro in Chicago* (Chicago, 1922), pp. 4–5; *New York Times,* 28 July–1 August 1919, p. 1; 3 August, p. 9; 4 August, p. 6; 5 August, p. 1.

19. *New York Times,* dates cited in fn. 18; Waskow, *Race Riot,* chap. 4.

20. Waskow, *Race Riot,* p. 57 and notes there cited; Department of Justice, Glasser File Box 5, Chicago Riot, 1919.

21. *New York Times,* 31 August 1919, 1 September, p. 1; Waskow, *Race Riot,* pp. 105–10.

22. Report of Lt. Col. Jacob West, commanding troops in Omaha, to War Department, Department of Justice, Glasser File Box 14, October 1919; *see also* telegram from General Leonard Wood to the Adjutant General, October 1919.

23. *New York Times,* 3 October 1919, p. 6; 4 October, p. 7; 5 October, p. 10; Waskow, *Race Riot,* p. 125.

24. Memo for Adjutant General, War Department, File A.G.O. 370, p. 6, 29 September 1919, Box 15, Use of troops, Memo from Major General Jery to the Adjutant General, October 1919.

25. Passailogue to Ass't. Chief of Staff G–2, 3rd div., Eugene Bates Intelligence Officer, Camp Pike to Acting Intelligence Office Army, Department of Justice, Glasser File Box 14, Elaine Riots, 1919.

26. Waskow, *Race Riot,* chap. 8, discusses the difficulties involved.

27. Department of Justice, file no. 158260–1–12, R.G. 60, 1919.

28. *Congressional Record,* 66th cong., 1st sess. (1919), p. 8818.

29. Department of Justice, Glasser File Box 10, War Plan White, 27 May 1920.

30. Department of Justice, Code Military Staff in Chicago to Chief of Staff, Executive Division, Military Intelligence, Glasser File Box 14, Chicago, 29 October 1919.

31. *Sen. Doc.* 153, 66th cong., 1st sess. (1919), ser. no. 7607, p. 162.

32. Department of Justice, file no. 158260–119, R.G. 60, 1919.

33. Department of Justice, Office of Chief of Staff, Executive Division, Military Intelligence, Glasser File Box 14, Lexington, Ky., 19 February 1920; Department of Justice, file no. 158260–1–20, R.G. 60, 1920.

34. Department of Justice, Baker to Chief of Staff, Glasser File Box 15, 2 December 1920; Russell F. Weigley, *History of the United States Army* (New York, 1967), p. 396; *Congressional Record,* 67th cong. 1st sess. (1921), p. 81; Waskow, *Race Riot,* p. 206–7.

12 | The Illusion of a New Era

The optimism of the beginning of the century was not abandoned; the illusive myths of progress and reform and the American Dream provided a nucleus of aspirations to which the deprived could cling. The War to End All Wars was over and a new isolationism emerged, buoyed by "good times" and public indifference, characterized by toleration of the excesses of prohibition and the deification of Big Business. Treatment of blacks altered slightly with the great depression of the thirties and the economic boom of the war-time forties. Still, there was no national antilynching law, and though the number of persons lynched was decreasing, blacks were still repressed and racial disturbances continued. But, the widening world audience of the new media of radio and film brought an immediacy to racial situations that heretofore had been lacking. The trouble was now on Main Street.

The situation of the blacks became increasingly difficult to ignore because blacks themselves were more vocal in the pursuit of their rights. The dispersion of the blacks and the improvement of the status of many members of the black community provided a leadership which challenged the white community in ways that were less susceptible to direct coercion. Whether the white governmental officials liked it or not, legislation designed primarily to improve the welfare of white citizens had the incidental effect of improving the status of some blacks. Yet, the lynchings and the surveillance of blacks in an effort to prevent the development of rebellion continued. Racial disturbances recurred, reaching a height in the Detroit riot in 1943, which was suppressed by federal troops.

When the segregationist Wilson administration ended in 1920, many blacks welcomed the election of Warren G. Harding; a Republican administration could be no worse, and it was hoped that the party would fulfill the promises of Reconstruction and enforce a solution to the racial problem. The party platform of 1920 resolutely denounced lynching and supported the Dyer Bill, still pending in Congress. Harding's acceptance speech on 22 July 1920 was very sympathetic to the black cause, reaffirming that blacks deserved full citizenship rights. Optimism increased as a result of Harding's speech to a special session of Congress on 12 April 1921, in which Harding asked Congress to pass legislation against lynching, although he did not specifically mention the Dyer Bill. After making these overtures, Harding pressed Congress no further and made no additional public moves to support the Dyer Bill. Attorney General Henry Daughtery was asked to prepare a memorandum for the Congress expressing the opinion that the Dyer Bill was constitutional. In response to the memorandum, an attorney in the Justice Department indicated that the Dyer Bill was in clear violation of the Constitution and that the attorney general "advertises his asininity in holding to the contrary." [1]

Although militant interracial leadership, as represented by the NAACP, was disenchanted with Harding, Marcus Garvey of the Universal Negro Improvement Association (UNIA) thought Harding, in his lukewarm response to racial problems, was headed in the right direction. Since Garveyites rejected social integration as unworkable and impossible and proposed a separate homeland for blacks, they could tolerate anti-integrationist politicians and even the Ku Klux Klan. The integrationists feared his ability to mobilize the masses and ridiculed his lack of sophistication. Garvey's conviction for stock fraud and subsequent deportation in 1927 removed his disquieting influence from their midst. Black leaders who declined to utilize Garvey's ability to organize the masses, or aid him in his programs, continued to optimistically assert integrationist ideals.[2]

Despite the increasing success of the NAACP in bringing more black rights cases to the attention of the government, racial violence continued. In Tulsa, Oklahoma in June 1921, blacks were killed or ordered to leave town in large numbers for protesting against peonage. In Little Rock, Arkansas, when threats were made to lynch an accused rapist, the governor, reflecting an increased objection to lynching in the state, requested federal troops from Fort Pike to help protect the prisoner. Citing constitutional and statutory grounds, the War Department refused to send aid until the state had exhausted its resources. Senator Joseph Robinson asked the department to honor the governor's request, but received the same reply. State officials wanted to protect the defendant against lynching; even though they knew that national guardsmen drawn from local people could not be trusted to disperse a mob of fellow citizens, their request for aid was denied.[3]

The Justice Department continued to release its *Hodges*-type responses to requests for federal intervention in outrages involving the civil rights of blacks. C. B. Allison, a concerned citizen, wanted to know if the federal government felt there was cause for action when a citizen was forced to leave a state by violence and intimidation. John Shillady of the NAACP wanted to know if federal troops could be used to protect citizens when lynchings were advertised in advance and the state refused to take action to protect the due process of law. Black farmers in Laconia, Arkansas were unhappy because they were being forced to work cotton crops without pay and were told that if they sought legal relief, they would be killed. In response, the Justice Department stated that these legal problems were all matters under state jurisdiction.[4]

As the election of 1924 approached, disorders resulting from black voters' attempts to register increased. In September, blacks in Oklahoma complained that they could not find the registrars, since they were appointed at the last minute and moved about without advance notice. After looking at the numerous complaints of intimidation and at the devices used to inhibit black voting, Assistant Attorney General Paul Holland prepared a memorandum for Attorney General Harlan Stone, on 24 October 1924, in which he expressed the view that if the suggested plan to have marshals protect the black voters were instigated, whites would be driven from the polls. In his opinion, the problems reflected the old prejudices of the South toward blacks; if the administration attempted to protect blacks, it would incur the enmity of white people. He suggested that the administration should indicate its intention to exercise its constitutional responsibilities and take no other action, a position ambiguous enough to deter the enmity of anyone.[5]

Blacks, as groups or individually, continued the barrage of written complaints during the Calvin Coolidge administration. In a letter to the administration, Charlie Thompson, a house painter in Florida, wrote that blacks were hired to work for pay, but when they finished, all they received was the point of a Winchester to hurry them away. He expressed the belief that the national government had duped blacks during Reconstruction, and although Garfield had offered some hope, he was dead, and promises of justice had been made ever since with no results. He wanted the government to provide protection and compensation for blacks in the South and to aid migration out of the South. The only response Thompson received was a letter from a staff attorney acknowledging his comments.[6]

Even when the information on civil rights violations reaching the NAACP was not always entirely correct, the organization became increasingly successful in obtaining explanations from the government. In September 1926, Executive Secretary James W. Johnson exploded in a letter to the president when he read in the newspapers that, after a hurricane in Miami, blacks were rounded up and ordered to clean up the debris and that marines had shot some black who refused to cooperate. The Justice Department investigated and reported to Johnson that the order was, in fact, directed to blacks and whites, and that no one was forced to work, although many blacks had willingly responded. The marine commander reported that the marines had only helped to clean up the wreckage; they had not shot anyone.[7]

When the Coolidge administration offered no solutions to the race question, black groups continued to make every possible argument to obtain federal intervention when violence occurred. On 11 April 1930, A. Phillip Randolph of the Brotherhood of Sleeping Car Porters and Maids wrote Attorney General William Mitchell that a porter named J. H. Wilkins was found hanging a short distance from the track in Locust, Georgia after the train had been forced to stop between Atlanta and Macon. The state government would not investigate, and Randolph thought that since Wilkins was an employee in interstate commerce, the government had jurisdiction. Although the Justice Department responded that working in interstate commerce did not invoke federal jurisdiction, Randolph felt that if the department had been sufficiently interested, it could have found a constitutional basis for interference. On the basis of the Supreme Court decision in *Mondou v. New York, New Haven & Hartford R.R. Co.* (1912), which upheld a federal employees' liability statute covering employees in interstate commerce, and a myriad of other cases on the commerce power of Congress, Randolph's opinion was correct.[8]

The search for a means to invoke federal jurisdiction and to rouse state officials continued during the eight depression years of Franklin Roosevelt's prewar administration. The immediate responses to complaints made by Justice Department officials in the new administration seemed cold-blooded and callous. In July 1933, when Corinne Banks wrote to inform the Justice Department of the murder of her brother in Mississippi in the hope that they would investigate, she was told by Patrick Mallory, an assistant attorney general, that "it . . . is believed that if you enlist the aid of your friends among the white people in that vicinity and appeal to the proper state authorities, your cause will receive the consideration it deserves." Mallory's reply was naive at best.[9]

Numerous violations of constitutional rights went unpunished during the thirties. In August 1933 in Tuscaloosa, Alabama, three teenage blacks, Dan Pippen, Elmore Clark, and A. T. Hardin were accused of murdering an eighteen-year-old white girl. Lawyers from the International Labor Defense (ILD) organization, the legal aid arm of the Communist party, wanted to defend the three blacks, but were ordered out of town. The state militia guarded the courthouse while the trial was in progress on 1 August, but after the trial, it was decided to move the prisoners from Tuscaloosa to Birmingham for safekeeping. The sheriff, two deputies, and a private detective reported that while driving to Birmingham, a group of armed men abducted the prisoners. The four guards and the sheriff were unharmed. The details of the incident were never clear. Later, two of the youths were found dead; one who was left for dead was found in a shanty and returned to jail. His story of the incident was never made known, as he was too frightened to testify. However, questioning the fact that the sheriff and four guards, who were supposed to defend the prisoners, had escaped the confrontation unscathed, the ILD and the NAACP presented a brief to the Justice Department, declaring that the sheriff should be arraigned to explain the episode. The brief asserted that the sheriff was a government official who had denied persons equal protection and due process of the law under the Fourteenth Amendment, thereby negating the state action policy. The Justice Department decided not to prosecute since it was deemed impossible to prove that the sheriff had willfully deprived the victims of their constitutional rights.[10]

Perhaps the most well-known court decision favorable to blacks during this period is the Scottsboro case. Nine black youths were indicted for the rape of two white girls, both of whom were reportedly prostitutes. The National Guard was called out to protect the defendants from lynching during their trials. After long court battles, charges against five of the nine youths were dropped; four were convicted, three of these were later paroled, and one escaped but later died in a Michigan penitentiary. In the final resolution of the cases, the Supreme Court affirmed the constitutional right to counsel in state criminal cases and the right of blacks to serve on juries.[11]

One of several sensational lynchings occurred when attempts to invoke federal jurisdiction were thwarted. In October 1934, when Claude Neal, an accused rapist of a Florida girl, was kidnapped in Alabama by white citizens and brought back to Florida, blacks gathered to protect him from lynching but were driven off by national guardsmen. Federal action was requested when his lynching was forecast in the newspapers. There was no federal response.[12]

The NAACP continued to press for an antilynching law. Three times, in 1922, 1937, and 1940, an antilynching bill was passed in the House, but failed to get by the Senate. The Justice Department files of the twenties and thirties bulge with letters from blacks and whites on the subject. Most of those who wrote in favor of an antilynching law did not expect federal troops to be called every time a lynching was threatened; rather, they hoped that the successful prosecution of a few cases in which troops controlled the mobs would serve as an example to lynchers.[13] The same answer was given each time a reply was made: murder is not a federal crime. For over fifty years, the lawyers in the Justice Department failed to find a connection between the Constitution and issues of civil rights.

Despite the failure to intervene when lynchings were threatened, a new attitude was evident in Franklin Roosevelt's prewar administrations. The president spoke out clearly against lynching and appealed for antilynching legislation, but to protect other legislation, he compromised with southern Democrats. Antilynching legislation invariably died in the Senate. In 1941, he responded to A. Phillip Randolph's threat of a march on Washington by issuing an executive order forbidding discrimination in government employment and defense industries.[14] Roosevelt's Attorney General Frank Murphy set up the Civil Rights Section in the Criminal Division of the Justice Department so that civil rights matters might receive greater attention.

For some unknown reason, racial riots during the Depression were almost nonexistent. Crime also reached a national low.

Aside from a riot in Harlem in March 1935 in which no troops were used, significant racial disorders did not erupt again until World War II. In May 1943, when the upgrading of blacks to welding jobs caused a rash of beatings at the Alabama Dry Docking and Ship Building Company in Mobile, management ended the disturbances by separating workers on the job and limiting the openings for black welders. In June in Beaumont, Texas, a pogrom in black neighborhoods resulted from a white woman's complaint that she had been raped; two blacks were killed and seventy-three wounded. The Texas Rangers arrived after the damage was done. After an all-white fact-finding committee announced that efforts would be made to compensate innocent black victims, the city manager and other officials met to determine in advance if blacks were planning reprisals.[15]

In June 1943, "Zoot Suit" riots erupted in scattered cities across the country. In Los Angeles, Chicano and black youths wore suits with wide lapels, broad shoulders, fitted waists, and full pants that were tight at the ankles called *zoot suits*. Exaggerated key chains were a standard part of the outfit. The press harped on the irresponsible criminality of the "zoot suiters." Soldiers and sailors, claiming that military personnel had been attacked by zoot-suiters, roamed through Mexican–American and black neighborhoods beating, kicking, and tearing the clothes of the "guilty." The police did little except to make way for the rioters. Although most of the emmity was directed toward Mexican–Americans, many blacks were attacked.[16]

The most extensive disturbance of the World War II period exploded in Detroit, a city with a long history of racial troubles; for example, in March 1863, a pogrom through black neighborhoods developed as a response to the claim that a black man had raped a white woman. Federal troops were used to disperse a crowd that tried to storm the jail. Five companies of militia marched from nearby Ypsilanti to subdue the mob. In 1925, a mob tried to force Ossian Sweet, a black physician, out of a house he had bought in a white neighborhood. Police watched the mob gather and only acted when Sweet, along with his relatives and friends, fired at the approaching whites. When eleven blacks, including Sweet, were charged with murder, the NAACP hired

Clarence Darrow to defend them. Because of Darrow's eloquence and the impartiality of Judge Frank Murphy, the blacks were acquitted by an all-white jury.[17]

In the twenties and thirties, racial tension in Detroit was provoked by the Ku Klux Klan and the Black Legion, a white group which tried to prevent blacks from obtaining employment. The use of black strikebreakers during the sit-down strikes and the increased migration of blacks into the city in the midst of a severe housing shortage during the thirties and forties further inflamed the atmosphere. In February 1942, rioting broke out when whites gathered to prevent blacks from moving into the Sojourner Truth Federal Housing Project, because they felt the project should be occupied by white people. Over two weeks later, when whites realized that the federal government would not give the project to them, the blacks were finally able to occupy the building.[18]

The first massive Detroit riot began on Sunday, 20 June 1943, when a series of affrays occurred between whites and blacks. The incidents increased in frequency and severity, as whites began attacking blacks who happened to be outside their own neighborhoods, especially on Woodward Avenue, the main thoroughfare of the city. In the black neighborhoods, blacks destroyed and looted stores owned by whites and attacked whites whenever they encountered them. The police were apparently more lenient with white violators than black ones, as depicted in one photograph which shows a white man beating a black who is being held by two policemen. Thirty-four persons were killed in the violence, twenty-five blacks and nine whites. Fifteen of the blacks, and none of the whites, were killed by policemen. Of the nineteen hundred persons arrested, three-fourths were black.[19]

By 1:00 A.M. Monday, it was clear to military policemen that the riot was of major proportions. The commander of the military police passed this information on to Colonel August M. Krech, who was the highest military official in Detroit. Krech alerted a military police battalion and met with Mayor Edward Jeffries and Police Commissioner John Witherspoon in order to review the procedure for obtaining federal troops. They decided that Jeffries had to ask the governor for assistance, who would request aid from General Henry S. Aurand, commanding the Sixth Service at Chicago, who would then order Krech to use the troops in the area. The whole process would take about forty-five minutes.

No request was made for troops immediately, because Mayor Jeffries thought the riot was over. However, at 9:00 A.M. on Monday, when the rioting intensified, Jeffries called Governor Harry F. Kelly, who called General Aurand's office at the Sixth Service Command. The officials in Detroit thought federal troops would arrive immediately; however, General Aurand's staff in Chicago interpreted Kelly's call as a *possible* request. While they waited to hear from him again, Aurand began reading a textbook on aid to civilian authorities, put troops on stand-by orders, and sent Brigadier General William Guthner to Detroit to take command when, and if, a formal request was made.

Meanwhile, Jeffries and black leaders met with no success when they tried to subdue the rioters. The army staff in Washington received a call from Aurand, who wanted to know if he could use infantry troops in addition to the military police. The staff, recognizing that the riot was similar to those outlined in Emergency Plan White, the official army manual for riot control duty, did not bother to inform the president, but decided that military police could be used to protect stores related to the Defense Department or the war effort. Aurand ordered troops to guard an outlet where weapons were kept, while the army staff hesitated in ordering a large number of troops into Detroit.

On his way to Detroit, General Guthner read the army regulations and concluded that he could not use troops until martial law was declared by the president and informed Aurand of the regulation upon his arrival in Detroit. Governor Kelly, who was in Detroit by that time, did not want martial law declared because he did not wish the American public to think the situation was as uncontrollable as it was. As the Michigan National Guard had been federalized for the war effort, the remaining volunteer state troops were asked to mobilize. However, only thirty-two state troopers were in touch with the governor's office two hours later, and they did not have transportation to the area. Kelly went on the radio and declared a state of emergency in the three counties surrounding Detroit. When Aurand was informed of the developing problems, he called the army staff in Washington, who finally talked to the Secretary of War Henry Stimson about the situation. In accordance with the form in Emergency Plan White, a presidential proclamation extending federal aid was drafted. Aurand authorized Guthner to send military police battalions into action, and they rapidly dispersed the rioters with gas grenades and rifle butts. After the riot was somewhat subdued, Aurand called Washington again and was told that Governor Kelly had to request troops from the president. Kelly telephoned Roosevelt at Hyde Park, whereupon Roosevelt signed the presidential proclamation immediately. More military police and an infantry division was called into action, and the riot was quickly ended the next day.

The usual investigations and expressions of shock followed the riot. The Dies Committee, predecessor of the House Un-American Activities Committee, wanted to pursue claims that Japanese had inflamed blacks into rioting. With Thurgood Marshall as chief interrogator, the NAACP took affidavits and cited examples of police brutality. A citizen's committee composed of the district attorney general, the police commissioner, and the local prosecutor concluded that despite black complaints of prejudicial treatment in their arrest and the disportionate number of blacks convicted, the judiciary, police, and prosecutor had been fair. They concluded that the riot was caused by blacks.

The bungling efforts by city, state, and national authorities to invoke federal assistance in the Detroit situation typify the negligence of authorities in acquainting themselves with the appropriate means for invoking federal aid. The army Emergency Plan White was still available and had been revised from time to time since 1919. Army regulations in force in 1943 outlined the proper constitutional and statutory procedure for obtaining troops, but cited an exception: if public property of the United States was endangered, or an equivalent emergency made it necessary to act immediately, the army commander could take action, reporting the situation immediately to the adjutant general for the information of the president. This was the kind of action initiated in slave revolts, without any express authorization for it, and was in the spirit of the 1919 orders issued by Newton Baker, which were revoked in 1920, but later reissued. In this case, the authorities had plenty of time to inform the president, but apparently were not familiar with the regulations, Emergency Plan White, or Section 333 of the *United State Code* (see Appendix).

After the riot, President Roosevelt wrote to Secretary of War Stimson, stating that he understood from the attorney general that there was confusion on how to obtain federal troops. He ordered that a memorandum explaining the proper procedure be prepared and circulated to service commands. Secretary of War Robert Lovett replied that a memorandum had already been prepared and sent to service commands and governors and that Emergency Plan White and the army regulations were already at every command post before the riot. It was believed that at least in the future, officials could obtain federal troops immediately in order to prevent loss of life and property.

While the riot raged, the House of Representatives listened to Clare Hoffman of Michigan explain that while he commended the president for sending troops, Frank Murphy, labor leaders, and the president himself were responsible for the disorders, along with Secretary of Labor Frances Perkins who had aggravated conditions by supporting sit-down strikes. Hoffman added that the seizure and retention of private property during labor disputes had set the stage for the riot, and that the only remedy was a return to law and order with justice. William Lambertson of Kansas agreed with Hoffman. However, John E. Rankin of Mississippi stated that those congressmen who supported the anti-poll tax amendment were responsible; since riots were caused by "uppity" blacks and race-mixing, the sooner everyone accepted segregation, the sooner it would be more peaceful for all races.[20]

There was, however, some immediate benefit from the lessons learned in the Detroit riot. Mayor Fiorello La Guardia of New York City sent two high-ranking officers to Detroit to see how the riot was handled. When, on 1 August, a policeman shot a black soldier who interefered with the arrest of a black woman, New York was prepared for the resulting rumors and disorder. Thousands of blacks swarmed into the streets, attacking policemen, pulling fire alarms, smashing windows, and looting stores. The mayor immediately cut off all traffic to the area, walked the streets with black leaders, kept all policemen on duty, and made a radio speech explaining the incident. Six truckloads of military police were sent by the army to clear out all military personnel so they would not be involved. By the next day, everything was under control. Even though five blacks were killed and four hundred blacks and forty policemen injured, the riot did not become a clash between white and black citizens as had the one in Detroit; no white gangs formed and the area was isolated from white neighborhoods. Even though white persons walked through the ghetto unarmed, they were not touched. During the riots, shops that were owned by blacks or had "colored" scrawled in the windows were spared destruction. Policemen who were, to blacks, symbols of white authority, white-owned ghetto property, and white businesses which refused to employ blacks were the major targets.[21]

A number of other riots and clashes between black and white soldiers and citizens during World War II were caused by Jim Crowism or attempts to put "uppity" blacks in their places, but they were suppressed by local or military police; no further invocation of federal aid was necessary. The American Civil Liberties Union (ACLU) published a pamphlet on riot prevention which suggested that rumor control centers be set up in tension-ridden communities. In addition, the pamphlet discouraged police brutality and described how to obtain federal troops quickly. Its conclusions were left to gather dust with all the commission reports and suggestions accumulated over the past thirty years.[22]

However, there was evidence of a new attitude on the part of the national administration in the wake of the wartime riots. Attorney General Francis Biddle made several public speeches in 1943 and 1944 which underscored the administrative concern about the problems of race and racial violence. On 11 November 1943, he told a meeting of the Jewish Theological Seminary in New York City that the recent disorders were not fostered by Axis propaganda. His greatest concern was the "corroding effect" racial violence had upon the friends of America and the American people. Biddle asserted that under existing law, the federal government could take no action in such cases. However, he rejected the idea of a conscious governmental effort to mold public opinion on the subject, believing instead, that community action on the local level could create a climate in which states could prosecute violators and remove the causes of racial disorders.[23]

Also in November, Biddle informed a group of black lawyers, meeting at the National Bar Association, that he feared a recurrence of race rioting "at any moment" and that he was "profoundly disturbed by ever-growing racial tension." The attorney general blamed the following five factors for racial unrest: war tension, bad housing, reduced police protection through a manpower shortage, the poor treatment of black servicemen, and the "contradiction between our profession of faith in democracy and our acts." Charles H. Houston, a black member of the District of Columbia Bar, suggested that the Justice Department ought to more actively intervene whenever a citizen's civil rights were unprotected locally. The fruits of a constitutional revolution in federalism, in which the Supreme Court approved the expanded use of federal authority to control the economy after the court-packing fight of 1937, had not yet been used by the Justice Department in the area of race relations. But the administration was willing to speak out publicly on the issue and, in doing so, helped to mold public opinion. Part of this willingness was perhaps in recognition of the unpleasant analogy between American racism and the Nazi attitude toward the Jews.[24]

A more enlightened attitude toward extending federal protection in racial incidents in the absence of state action, was, in fact, emerging. The new departure was in part due to the constitutional evolution in federalism achieved during the New Deal. The national government stepped into the vacuum created by state inability and took responsibility for welfare measures, economic planning, and commercial regulations in an unprecedented manner. Although the exigencies of prosecuting a war against the Nazis partly necessitated this new policy, hope was revived that perhaps the government could find some effective means of dealing with black oppression and racial violence.

NOTES

1. Richard Sherman, "The Harding Administration and the Negro, An Opportunity Lost," *The Journal of Negro History* (1964), Department of Justice, Letters Received, file no. 158260–18–5, R.G. 60, 1921.

2. Edmund David Cronon, *Black Moses, The Story of Marcus Garvey and the Universal Negro Improvement Association* (Madison, 1962), pp. 74, 110, 194–5; NAACP, *Crisis* (July 1921), pp. 115–6.

3. Department of Justice, Glasser File Box 14, Elaine, Ark., March 1921. For a rare case in which a white man was convicted of murdering a black person in a state court, *see* Pete Daniel, "Peonage in the New South" (unpublished doctoral dissertation, University of Maryland, 1970), chap. 10. John Williams and his black foreman killed more than eleven peons, some for attempting to escape from Williams' Georgia plantation, others after an FBI investigation into peonage on the plantation because Williams feared they might testify against him.

4. Department of Justice, file no. 158260–95, 158260–135, 158260–1–29, R.G. 60, 1923.

5. Department of Justice, file no. 72–59–1–21, R.G. 60, 1924.

6. Department of Justice, file no. 50–18–6–1, R.G. 60, 1925.

7. Department of Justice, file no. 50–18–7–13, R.G. 60, 1926.

8. Department of Justice, file no. 158260 R.G. 60—Lynching, April 1930.

9. Department of Justice, file no. 158260, R.G. 60, July 1933.

10. Department of Justice, file no. 158260, R.G. 60, 1933. Lynching, Memo from Assistant Attorney General Kennan to Parrish.

11. Dan T. Carter, *Scottsboro, A Tragedy of the American South* (Baton Rouge, 1969), pp. 123, 174. Carter's book is a comprehensive study which discusses the clash between the NAACP and the ILD over who would defend the youths; the ILD won; Carter also describes communist efforts to organize black sharecroppers which led to white terrorism and rumors of a black uprising in Camp Hill and Tallapoosa County, Alabama in 1931 and 1932.

12. Department of Justice, file no. 158260, R.G. 60, October 1934.

13. Department of Justice, file no. 158260, R.G. 60, and its subdivision

contain an abundance of letters and other material on the subject of lynchings.

14. U.S. Attorney General, *Annual Report,* 1939; *Congressional Record,* 74th cong., 1st sess. (1935), pp. 5750, 6292, 6350–73, 6520–47; Exec. order 8802, 6 *Fed. Reg.* 3109 (1941), Exec. order 9346, 8 *Fed. Reg.* 7183 (1943); Robert K. Carr, *Federal Protection of Civil Rights, Quest for a Sword* (Ithaca, N.Y., 1947).

15. *Report of the Commission on Conditions in Harlem,* E. Franklin Frazier *et al.,* eds. (New York, 1935); Foster Rhea Dulles, *Labor in America, A History* (New York, 1949), pp. 301–6; *New York Times,* 17 June 1942, p. 1; 18 June 1943, pp. 8, 27.

16. Charles R. Lawrence, Jr., "Race Riots in the United States, 1942–1946," *Negro Year Book* (Tuskeegee, Ala., 1947), pp. 236–7.

17. David E. Lilienthal, "Has the Negro the Right to Self-Defense," *Nation* 121 (1925) pp. 724–5; Langston Hughes, *Fight for Freedom, the Story of the NAACP* (New York, 1962), p. 43; *A Thrilling Narrative from the Lips of the Sufferers of the Late Detroit Riots, March 6, 1863* (Detroit, 1863), Burton Historical Collections, Detroit.

18. Walter White, "What Caused the Detroit Riots," Frank Murphy's Papers, Box 109, Michigan Historical Collections, Detroit.

19. This account is largely based on Alfred McClung Lee and Norman D. Humphrey, *Race Riot* (New York, 1943); Robert Shogan and Tom Craig, the *Detroit Race Riot—A study in Violence* (New York, 1943); *see The Detroit News, Free Press,* and *New York Times* for the dates indicated and Harvard Sitkoff, "The Detroit Race Riot 1943," paper read at the Association for the Study of Negro Life and History, October 1969 (copy in my possession); War Department, Adjutant General's Office; R.G. 319/209, 207 Office of the Provost Marshal General.

20. *Congressional Record,* 78th cong., 1st sess. (1943), pp. 3180–1, 6344, 6554, A3463, 6303, 6371.

21. *New York Times,* 2, 3 August 1943, p. 1; Walter White, "Behind the Harlem Riot," *New Republic,* 10 August 1943; Shogan and Craig, *Detroit Riot,* pp. 91–4. Lawrence, "Race Riots in the United States, 1942–6," *Negro Year Book,* p. 245; according to official police reports in the LaGuardia papers, six men were killed and 172 were injured.

22. *New York Times,* 27 February 1946, p. 44; 1 March, p. 2; Lawrence, "Race Riots in the United States, 1942–6," pp. 246–56. *New York Times,* 11 June 1943, p. 122—the riot of black soldiers at Camp Stewart, Georgia; Winifred Rashenbush, *How to Prevent A Race Riot in Your Home Town* (New York, ACLU, 1943).

23. *New York Times,* 12 November 1943, p. 9.

24. Ibid., 28 November 1943, p. 34. For the decline of dual sovereignty and the affirmation of federal responsibility in critical areas of national economic concern during the New Deal, *see* any textbook; for example, Kelly and Harbison, *The American Constitution, Its Origins and Development,* pp. 791–5.

13 / Toward Federal Protection

The end of World War II heralded the advent of the Atomic Age, the Cold War, and a revived Red Scare of McCarthyism. As the economic and military influence of the United States enlarged greatly, Americans took on a new and unaccustomed role of responsibility in international affairs. Americans were not particularly comfortable in this new role, nor were they accustomed to the constant international spotlight on their internal problems. It rapidly became evident that the economic prosperity of the war years, as well as new post-war responsibilities, engendered significant social changes. The administrations of Harry Truman and Dwight D. Eisenhower saw the beginnings of an era of reform in race relations. Mounting pressure from black individuals and civil rights groups, as well as increased white sympathy, and the enfranchisement of large numbers of blacks in northern urban areas whose votes aided Truman's victory in 1948, gave impetus to reform. The Cold War, the struggle for economic and social development in the nonwhite nations, the pressure from organizations such as the NAACP who now possessed adequate financial, technical, and legal resources were factors which made this new reform politically expedient. A new departure in enforcing old laws and enacting new ones evolved. The constitutional revolution in federalism ushered in by the New Deal provided the national government with a framework in which to utilize federal military power in enforcing and realizing these new policies.

Initial steps in reform were slow to come. In the Supreme Court case of *Screws v. United States* (1945), the shadow cast by the *Hodges* doctrine was lengthened. The court refused to affirm the murder conviction of a sheriff in Baker County, Georgia who had brutally and fatally beaten a black man, Robert Hall, who was accused of stealing a tire. It had been impossible to secure a murder conviction in a state court; the Civil Rights Section of the Justice Department, taking an enlightened view of the statutes, had decided to attempt a federal conviction despite the *Hodges* tradition. The statute under which the sheriff was indicted required proof that the deceased had been *willfully* deprived of his right to trial in a court, not merely evidence that he had been beaten to death. Four justices concluded that, at the trial, the instruction on the statute given to the jury had not been clear. However, the justices were not only unsure whether the jury had understood this technical distinction but also whether the sheriff had the specific intent to willfully deprive the black man of his constitutional rights. Justice Wiley B. Rutledge thought the conviction should be affirmed, but in order to have a majority, he concurred with William O. Douglas, Harlan F. Stone, Hugo L. Black, and Stanley F. Reed in their findings. Justice Frank Murphy dissented separately and voted to affirm the conviction. He asserted that the sheriff knew he lacked the authority, and was, in fact, forbidden from beating his prisoner to death. Owen J. Roberts, Felix Frankfurter, and Robert H. Jackson dissented because the effect of the majority opinion was to assert federal jurisdiction in such cases, and they reasoned that in enacting the statute, Congress had no intention of interfering with areas of state responsibility; the sheriff, if he was guilty of a crime, was guilty of the state crime—murder. In view of the legacy of the past, the last three dissenters were saying, in effect, that the sheriff should not be punished.[1]

On 5 December 1946, President Truman created The President's Committee on Civil Rights, which was charged to investigate and determine where and how governmental authority could be strengthened to safeguard the civil rights of the people. To redress inequalities, the committee proposed expansion of the Civil Rights Section in the Justice Department, establishment of a permanent Commission on Civil Rights, and a federal anti-lynching act. A Fair Employment Practices Commission (FEPC) law and new legislation covering voting rights and criminal procedures were also suggested. In a special message to Congress on 2 February 1948, Truman urged the passage of these recommendations. Although Truman's program met strong resistance in Congress, many of the recommendations were effected in the next twelve years. Executive orders, court decisions, and legislation desegregated the armed forces and created fuller opportunity for middle-class and educated blacks in education and other areas of American life.[2]

Although lynchings and jailhouse riots had diminished, three sensational episodes raised the question of federal intervention during Truman's presidency. On 25 February 1946 in Columbia, Tennessee, a black woman and her son were jailed. The son had reportedly knocked a white man, who had slapped his mother, through a plate glass window. A white mob gathered at the jail with the intent to "punish" the two prisoners. Four city policemen were shot when they entered the tense black district. The five hundred state troopers and guardsmen who were ordered into the area arrested at least one hundred blacks. Thurgood Marshall, then special counsel for the NAACP, alleged that the troopers had roped off the black section and fired indiscriminately at black residents. Two of the blacks arrested were reportedly machine-gunned to death by state troopers at the jail. Walter White, Executive Secretary of the NAACP, as well as spokesmen for other black and white organizations, sent letters and telegrams to Attorney General Tom C. Clark and Truman, pointing to the denial of due process of the law and demanding federal intervention to protect blacks in Columbia. Blacks were particularly incensed to discover that Clark had delegated responsibility for an investigation to a local district attorney who was a white resident of Columbia. Apparently, there was no federal intervention.[3]

An even more sensational racial incident in the summer of 1946 was cause for great public and administrative concern. Two black men and their wives were passengers in a car driven by a white farmer who had provided bond for one of the blacks who had been jailed for allegedly stabbing his white employer during a dispute. Near Monroe, Georgia, twenty masked white men surrounded the car, forced the four blacks out, and proceeded to pump approximately sixty shots into their victims, leaving the bodies alongside the road. Black and liberal white individuals and organizations, appalled by this horrifying incident, were skeptical of a prosecution by Georgia state officials, and they wrote President Truman and Attorney General Clark, demanding federal intervention in the case.[4]

President Truman ordered Clark to take every action to apprehend and convict the murderers. Clark began an FBI investigation but turned the results over to state officials, concluding there was no basis for federal prosecution. Fifty black women from the National Association of Colored Women (NACW) began picketing outside the White House. James Carey, Secretary-Treasurer of the Congress of Industrial Organizations (CIO) sent the president and the attorney general messages urging action to supplement the efforts of "admittedly impotent" local officials. Rewards totaling $12,500 were reportedly offered by various groups.[5]

By October 1946, no criminal proceeding had begun. Attorney General Clark, at a meeting of the *New York Herald Tribune's* "Fifteenth Annual Forum on Current Problems," said that he would ask that the facts gathered by the FBI be presented to a federal grand jury, possibly permitting conviction for a civil rights violation, since no state indictments for murder had been initiated. Oliver Harrington of the NAACP demanded to know why a federal government capable of tracking down every single spy in World War II was curiously unable to determine who was responsible or involved in the incidences of racial violence in Tennessee and in Georgia. He admonished the government for its lack of convictions in lynching cases over the years and maintained that "the government should spend less time finding legal reasons for not acting and more time acting in behalf of human justice." However, Clark asserted that the government's record for prosecuting civil rights cases was improving; during his sixteen-month tenure, there had been three hundred investigations, twenty-three prosecutions, six convictions, eight acquittals, and nine persons were awaiting trial.[6]

In June 1949, after two years of sporadic racial violence, including the North Carolina lynching of a black prisoner who had allegedly raped a white woman and the acquittal of twenty-eight defendants who had admitted lynching a black man in Greenville, South Carolina, Attorney General Clark urged Congress to pass an antilynching act. Before the House judiciary committee, whose chairman Emanuel Celler had drafted a new antilynching bill, Clark said it was imperative that the federal government have the authority to prosecute lynchers, even when no action was requested by the state. According to the court decisions in the *Hodges* and *Screws* cases, federal prosecution was illegal even for a civil rights violation unless some state action was involved in the violation.[7]

When Clark was elevated to the Supreme Court, the new attorney general, J. Howard McGrath, still faced complaints of lynching and racial violence. In Miami, Florida in December 1951, Harry T. Moore, State Coordinator for the NAACP, was killed when his house was bombed. The bombing was reportedly in retaliation for Moore's efforts to force the prosecution of a sheriff who allegedly shot two handcuffed blacks in his custody. The black men had been granted a trial by the Supreme Court after being convicted of rape by an all-white jury. Walter White, Executive Secretary of the NAACP, the Federal Council of Churches of Christ, and numerous veterans' and social organizations wrote McGrath demanding a federal investigation. But no investigation was made.[8]

Although instances such as the one in Miami continued, racial violence during the next few years was largely associated with attempts to desegregate schools and public accommodations. The Supreme Court decision in *Brown v. Board of Education,* which declared that segregated schools violated the Fourteenth Amendment, brought blatant hostility. At first, the NAACP was forced to attack individual school systems on a case-by-case basis. One antagonistic response to these activities came on 12 March 1956 when a group of southern senators and congressmen presented a "Southern Manifesto," largely the work of Senator Sam Ervin, Jr. of North Carolina, which asserted their intention to use every legal tactic to resist desegregation.[9]

President Eisenhower, who had no reputation as a great liberal on the race question, but who was a former army officer with a firm belief in the importance of obeying orders, received reports of numerous civil rights violations in 1955 and 1956. The FBI reported that the Communist party was trying to curry favor with the NAACP by its assertion that federal troops should have been sent to avenge the murder of Emmett Till, who had been murdered for whistling at a white woman in Mississippi in August 1955. The Montgomery, Alabama bus boycott, led by Martin Luther King, Jr. in December 1955, resulted in bombings and violence. White Citizen's Councils and the Ku Klux Klan were using threats and intimidation to prevent blacks from achieving desegregation and equal voting rights. In response to these racial problems, the administration proposed the Civil Rights Act of 1957, which established the Civil Rights Commission, made the Civil Rights Section a division in the Justice Department, and gave the government limited injunctive powers in voting rights disputes.[10]

While the Civil Rights Act was under consideration, the administration's attention was turned toward the school crisis in Little Rock, Arkansas. Although federal troops had been used under Section 332 of the *United States Code* (see Appendix) on numerous occasions to enforce such federal purposes as the Fugitive Slave Act and injunctions in labor disputes, the incident at Little Rock was the first occasion in American history when federal troops were used to enforce a federal court order favorable to blacks. But the troops were used in Little Rock, not because the black cause was just, but apparently because Eisenhower could not let a court order go unenforced. In 1956, when Autherine Lucy's presence at the University of Alabama set off rioting which forced her removal, the university's request to Attorney General Herbert Brownell for aid received no response. She had been admitted to the school without state interference, even though she was later expelled for criticizing the board of trustees, so ostensibly, the court order had been followed.[11]

But, in Little Rock, circumstances were different. The Little Rock school board, complying with the Supreme Court's direction, had announced a plan for gradual desegregation, beginning with their senior high school in the fall of 1957. As desegregation day approached, opponents filed a petition in the Arkansas State Chancery Court to prevent the plan from taking effect. On 29 August, Governor Orval Faubus appeared before that court to express his concern over the possibility of violence if the court refused to order a stay. The chancery court issued a restraining order forbidding desegregation in September. The federal district court, upon the request of the school board, ordered noninterference with desegregation. An obvious clash of federal and state authority existed.[12]

On desegregation day, Governor Faubus ordered the Arkansas National Guard to prevent the nine black children from entering the school. The school board responded to Faubus' show of force by asking the black children not to appear. However, the children did appear on 3 September and were turned away. Faubus had defied the federal court. The school board, stymied in these cross-purposes, went before the federal court and asked for exemption from contempt proceedings for not executing the court order. Judge Ronald Davies ordered desegregation to proceed.

In the next few days, while Faubus continued his defiance, the school board asked Judge Davies to set aside his order. He refused. The United States entered the case as a Friend of the Court and set 20 September as a date for a hearing on whether to issue an injunction against Faubus. Brooks Hays, congressman from Little Rock, who later lost his seat for his role in the controversy, offered to act as intermediary between Eisenhower and Faubus. A meeting was arranged between the two at Newport,

Rhode Island on 14 September. At the conclusion of that meeting, Faubus had agreed that upon returning to Arkansas, he would keep the National Guard on duty and admit the black children, but he did not comply. On 20 September, without the presence of Faubus or his lawyers, the federal court prohibited him from further interference. Faubus had again thumbed his nose at the judiciary by refusing to appear.[13]

That night, Faubus announced that although he would remove the guard, he was going to appeal the court order and hoped black parents would keep their children away from the school in the meantime. In effect, this action would have postponed desegregation indefinitely. By Monday, 23 September, three weeks of federal irresolution had passed. The National Guard had been removed, and a white mob had gathered at the school to enforce vigilante justice. Eight black children were brought into the school through a side door; when the mob discovered their presence, they attacked the police. The mayor ordered the black children removed in the interest of their safety. At last, the issue seemed clear enough to the president. Attorney General Brownell indicated that since the governor had abdicated his mandatory duty under Article VI of the Constitution to remove obstruction to federal law, the president could use troops to enforce the court orders. Eisenhower issued a proclamation asserting that the events were willful obstruction of the laws of Arkansas and the United States and constituted a denial of equal protection under the Fourteenth Amendment. He commanded all law violators to cease and desist.[14]

When the mob gathered again the next morning, the mayor frantically wired that troops were needed. Eisenhower immediately ordered five hundred paratroopers from nearby Fort Campbell, Kentucky to Little Rock. Another five hundred troops arrived later in the day. Meanwhile, Eisenhower issued an executive order authorizing the use of force and federalizing the Arkansas National Guard. By the next morning, the mob was dispersed with few injuries. The nine blacks entered school and stayed the whole day. The crisis subsided. On 14 October, Eisenhower approved withdrawing half the federal troops and defederalizing four-fifths of the guard. On 23 October, the students entered the school without military escort; on 22 November, the last paratroopers left the city to the protection of the National Guardsmen who remained on duty until the end of the school year.[15]

While Eisenhower acted too slowly to suit some civil rights supporters who failed to understand why he waited three weeks and too quickly for opponents who thought he should not have acted at all, his broad view of presidential authority under the Constitution and statutes had offered him other alternatives. Even in the face of the *Brown* decision and the federal court orders in the case, he could have asserted that the mob violence outside the high school did not require a federal response. Had he chosen this course, Eisenhower would have found support in a mass of precedents; however, public opinion at home and abroad would not have accepted that interpretation. In a nation greatly concerned about its world image, a new view of old statutes was required. Unlike the Autherine Lucy case, the school board had been willing to comply, until the governor interfered. In any event, the Supreme Court affirmed Eisenhower's position in *Cooper v. Aaron* in 1958, when they declared that the constitutional rights of children could not be nullified by state officials or by evasive schemes for segregation. However, Arkansas did not give up the fight for segregation. The legislature closed all high schools in September 1958 only to have them declared reopened by a federal court order in June 1959. Two blacks entered school that fall after police and firemen dispersed a mob of 250 whites.[16]

In Congress, the Little Rock crisis generated an expected controversy between detractors and supporters of civil rights with little enlightening constitutional debate. In the House, John Bell Williams of Mississippi wanted to know why troops were not sent to Brooklyn when newspapers reported incidents of racial strife in the schools. He thought the Little Rock crisis substantiated arguments for opposing federal aid to public schools, as the government would then have additional authority over the schools. Elijah Forrester of Georgia thought that the soldiers sent to Little Rock should have been implemented to root out communism around the world. In the Senate, Jacob J.

Javits of New York and Richard L. Neuberger of Oregon strongly defended the president's position, while Joseph C. O'Mahoney of Wyoming denounced Thomas H. Kuchel of California for inserting a speech on the subject given by Assistant Attorney General Warren Olney III into the *Congressional Record.* Olney had asserted that James O. Eastland of Mississippi and John L. McClellan of Arkansas, who vitriolically attacked the president, were on the committee which reenacted Sections 332 and 334 of the *United States Code,* which constituted the legal basis for the president's action (see Appendix). O'Mahoney pointed out that statutes which are only revised and codified are not reenacted in the same time. However, Eastland and Mc-Clellan, although appointed to the committee, took no part in the revision, which left them free to criticize the president.[17]

The school desegregation crisis persisted after Little Rock, as southern states kept searching for ways to maintain *de jure* segregation. When the Louisiana legislature attempted interposition in defiance of a federal court order in November 1960, President Eisenhower retreated to the historical position by asserting that marshals should first be used to enforce court orders. Large numbers of marshals poured into New Orleans and interposition collapsed. The Supreme Court in *United States v. Louisiana* in 1960 reaffirmed the federal position on interposition and discounted the legal significance of massive resistance as a tactic.

The concern of the national government in regard to lynchings and mob violence was expressed by its response to the lynching of Mack C. Parker, a black man accused of raping a white woman. In April 1959, Parker was taken from the unguarded jail in Poplarville, Mississippi. President Eisenhower, hoping to facilitate a quick apprehension of the violators, pledged FBI assistance in solving the case. After seven days of searching, the FBI found Parker's body in the Pearl River.[18] Seven months later, Attorney General William P. Rogers told a press conference that the handling of the Mississippi case was "a travesty on justice." The FBI had spent eighty thousand dollars investigating the Parker case and had given their report to Mississippi officials to be used in a state murder prosecution. However, the state grand jury adjourned without indictments; none of the FBI witnesses or evidence had been used. Rogers said he believed in states' rights, but state irresponsibility should be reconciled by the federal government. The Justice Department attempted to obtain indictments from a federal grand jury in Mississippi on the basis that Parker's civil rights had been violated. From a local jury of one black and twenty white residents, twelve affirmative votes could not be obtained for an indictment. Roy Wilkins, Executive Secretary of the NAACP, suggested that Rogers make the FBI report public; his request was not honored.[19]

Despite the failure of prosecution in such incidents as the Parker case and the continued lynchings and racial violence, reform had begun. The Truman and Eisenhower administrations had responded to increasing public pressure and to the exigencies of maintaining moral leadership in the world with innovations in the area of race relations. Military power had been used to enforce court orders favorable to black people. School desegregation, which began rather feebly, was upheld by the federal government. It was even suggested that federal intervention and protection might be proper in the prevention of the indiscriminate murder of black people and in the prosecution of their executors. There was hope that constitutional authority could be used to equitably adjust black-white relations.

NOTES

1. *Screws v. United States,* 325 U.S. 91 (1945): *see* memo of Justice Robert Jackson on this case in Frank Murphy's Papers, Box 133, Michigan Historical Collections, in which he states that the Justice Department had received eight to fourteen thousand complaints of violations of civil rights a year since 1939, but relied heavily on state officials to punish violators. No more than seventy-six cases a year were even investigated.

2. Exec. order 9808, 11 *Fed. Reg.* 14153 (1947); *Congressional Record,* 80th cong., 2nd sess. (1948), p. 929. U.S. Commission on Civil Rights, *Freedom to the Free* (Washington, 1963), pp. 122–55.

3. *New York Times,* 2 March 1946, p. 26.

4. Ibid., 27 July 1946, p. 1; 29 July, p. 36.

5. Ibid., 31 July 1946, p. 1, 48.

6. Ibid., 29 October 1946, p. 1.

7. Ibid., 24 May 1947, pp. 1, 32; 17 June 1949, p. 6.

8. Ibid., 27 December 1951, p. 1; 29 December, p. 1.

9. *Congressional Record,* 89th cong., 1st sess. (1965), pp. 4460–1, 4515–6; *Brown v. Board of Education,* 347 *U.S.* 483 (1954).

10. Dwight D. Eisenhower, *Waging the Peace 1956–61* (Garden City, N.J., 1965); 71 *Stat* 634, 42 *U.S. Code* 1975c (1958); *New York Times,* 12 January 1957, p. 38.

11. Anthony Lewis, *Portrait of a Decade: The Second American Revolution* (New York, 1965), pp. 91–2.

12. Eisenhower, *Waging the Peace,* pp. 163–5; Virgil T. Blossom, *It Has Happened Here* (New York, 1959), pp. 62–3.

13. *United States v. Faubus,* civ. no. 3113, E.D., Ark., 20 September 1957, 2 *Race Rel. Law Reptr.* 958 (1957).

14. *Opinions of the Attorney General* 41 (1957), p. 67, Proclamation 3204, 23 September 1957.

15. Exec. order 10730, 22 *Fed. Reg.* 7628 (1957); Eisenhower, *Waging the Peace.* Troops could be used without a governor's request because federal law was being violated; *see* Section 332 of *U.S. Code* in Appendix.

16. Eisenhower, *Waging the Peace,* pp. 162–75; Civil Rights Commission, *Freedom to the Free,* pp. 154–5; *Cooper v. Aaron,* 385 *U.S.* 1 (1958).

17. *Congressional Record,* 85th cong., 2nd sess. (1958), pp. 763, 1388, 3825, 5090, 18872, 19975.

18. Ibid., 26 April 1959, p. 1; 29 April, pp. 1, 23.

19. Ibid., 18 November 1959, pp. 1, 25; 15 January 1960, pp. 1, 16.

14 / The States Act Despite Themselves

Federal intervention and enforcement in cases of black-white violence and discrimination, already underway when John Kennedy was elected president, continued into the 1960s. The way had been partially paved for the national administration to provide protection for black people when state governments abdicated their responsibilities. The public concern expressed by governmental officials in the Roosevelt, Truman, and Eisenhower administrations had established precedents for executive action. The antidiscrimination decisions of the Supreme Court in *Brown v. Board of Education* and its progeny, the increasing influence of liberal ideas in the white community, and the exigencies of moral leadership in international affairs provided a firm foundation for vigorous federal response to racial disorder.

On 1 February 1960, when four black freshmen from A & T College at Greensboro, North Carolina sat down at a segregated lunch counter and refused to move, the Sit-In era began. Countless young blacks were caught up in a proliferating movement on college campuses across the South. White college students joined the movement, out of which the Student Non-violent Coordinating Committee (SNCC) evolved. Southern police responded to sit-ins and civil rights marches with fire hoses, tear gas, beatings, and arrests. When white liberals, as well as Martin Luther King's Southern Christian Leadership Conference (SCLC) and the Congress of Racial Equality (CORE), joined and supported the movement, the conscience of the nation was stirred. There was no immediate federal response, since sit-ins and the response they engendered were regarded as completely within the purview of the state. When the cases of sit-inners who were arrested for violation of state trespass and disorderly conduct statutes were appealed to the Supreme Court, the court did not resolve the issue of whether the use of state law enforcement officers to protect the property of those who practiced racial discrimination violated the Fourteenth Amendment. In some of the cases, the court decided in favor of the sit-inners on technical grounds of statutory interpretation and remanded others for reexamination by lower courts. The court chose not to face head-on the problem of a state trespass statute which conflicted with constitutional prohibitions against racial discrimination.[1]

In 1961, the New Abolitionists focused their attention on segregation in interstate transportation. Although outlawed by the Supreme Court as being in conflict with the Interstate Commerce Act of 1887, segregation existed as a matter of common practice throughout the South. No administration had directed the Interstate Commerce Commission to order discontinuance of this practice in conformity with the court decisions. In 1947, CORE Director James Farmer took a freedom ride to see if the court decisions were being obeyed; he found they were not.[2] On 28 April 1961, Farmer wrote President Kennedy that freedom rides would be attempted again and asked for federal protection. Although none was given, the rides proceeded. When a bus was burned at Anniston, Alabama and some of the riders were attacked, Attorney General Robert Kennedy asked the state to give the riders protection. Governor John Patterson agreed at first and then changed his mind. As the rides continued across

Alabama, the Kennedys tried to reach the governor, but were not able to do so. On 20 May, Patterson announced publicly that he would not protect outside agitators. As the riders approached Montgomery, the FBI warned the Montgomery police in advance that riots might occur when the bus arrived. The police replied that local authorities could keep the peace. When the bus arrived, the freedom riders, as well as sympathetic blacks and whites who had no connection with the protest, were attacked. Robert Kennedy tried to reach the governor again; when he was unable to do so, he sent marshals to Alabama and obtained a federal court injunction against the Ku Klux Klan and others who interfered with the riders. Kennedy's action was based on the constitutional obligation of the national government to enforce the right to travel in interstate commerce if the state failed to do so.

Having taken the first step, the administration sent Deputy Attorney General Byron White to Montgomery and assigned more marshals to him. When Martin Luther King came to address a black meeting at a church, a mob of white youths which had gathered outside was dispersed by marshals and local policemen. Federal intervention now forced state officials to take some action if they wanted to insist on their ability to keep order. Governor Patterson proclaimed martial law, called out the National Guard, denounced federal intervention, and blamed the disturbance on the federal marshals. The American Nazi Party of George Lincoln Rockwell announced they were going to protest against the riders by sending a "hate bus" from Washington to New Orleans. When the Nazis arrived in Montgomery, marshals escorted them through town.

As some of the riders proceeded across the state into Mississippi, Alabama congressmen protested to the attorney general against federal intervention. Kennedy responded by stating that marshals would be removed when state officials kept order and conformed to federal law. Consequently, the riders were escorted to the state line where Mississippi patrol cars took over; Governor Ross Barnett of Mississippi did not want federal marshals to displace his authority. In Jackson, twenty-seven riders, including James Farmer, were arrested for using white facilities. The Justice Department asked the federal district court for an injunction to keep state officials from interfering with interstate travel and also requested black leaders to enforce a cooling-off period. They refused and the rides continued.

In response to a request from Attorney General Kennedy, the Interstate Commerce Commission issued an order forbidding discrimination in interstate travel on 22 September 1961. Although the freedom rides were costly in terms of injuries and legal and travel expenses, the national government had enforced the law. The correct interpretation of federal law—that the national government could intervene in all cases in which a class of persons were subjected to widespread private violence which the state refused to suppress—although used in this instance, was not firmly established as a matter of continuing policy. It could still be argued that governmental interference was based only on court decisions. The Kennedys showed the same careful concern for the delicate balance between national and local authority in a federal state as Eisenhower had in Little Rock. The government intervened only when repeated efforts to persuade state officials to keep order failed.[3]

The desegregation of education became front-page news again during the Kennedy administration. James Meredith, a black Mississippian, decided he would like to attend the University of Mississippi, the all-white state university in Oxford. Meredith attempted to register at the university in January 1961, but was turned away. He and the NAACP went to federal court where they lost at the district level, but won in the court of appeals. When the Fifth Circuit Court ordered Meredith's admission, Governor Barnett asserted his intention to defy the court.[4]

When Barnett first announced his position, Attorney General Kennedy pointed out the foolishness of such a course and indicated the willingness of the administration to use marshals to enforce the court order. The state's position clearly defied federal law. On 20 September, when Meredith appeared with marshals to register, Barnett told him that his application for admission had been rejected. On 23 September, after repeated efforts to convince Barnett to desist, the Justice Department went into court to have the university officials cited for contempt for failure to comply with the original order to register Meredith. At the hearing, university officials agreed to register Meredith without further delay. Meanwhile, Barnett went into state court and obtained an injunction forbidding university officials to enroll Meredith and issued an executive order directing state police to arrest anyone who tried to arrest or fine a state official in connection with the case.[5]

On 25 September, by prearrangement with university officials, Meredith and his marshals appeared in Jackson, Mississippi, where the trustees normally met, to proceed with his registration. Barnett arrived with a group of state troopers and legislators, blocked the doorway, and read a proclamation denying Meredith admission in order to uphold the peace and dignity of the state. By this time, the patience of the administration and the Fifth Circuit Court was exhausted; the court directed the Justice Department to begin contempt proceedings against Barnett and issued a temporary restraining order prohibiting the governor and all others from interfering with its orders.[6]

The next day, when Meredith and his marshals appeared again at the "Ole Miss" campus, state police shoved the marshals back and Lieutenant Governor Paul Johnson denied Meredith admission on the same grounds that Barnett had the previous day. The Justice Department ordered additional contingents of marshals to the campus and continued negotiations with Barnett.[7] On 27 September, Barnett and Attorney General Kennedy agreed that Meredith and the marshals would confront Barnett and unarmed state policemen at the gate, the marshals would draw their guns, and Barnett would then give way to this show of force. By agreeing to the staged confrontation, Barnett would save face while permitting Meredith to register. However, this little drama was never performed. State police on duty knew nothing of Barnett's negotiations, and a crowd of civilians had gathered to watch the proceedings. Barnett frantically called Attorney General Kennedy saying he had changed his mind because he feared bloodshed might occur. The marshals and Meredith were ordered back to Memphis.[8]

Additional marshals, as well as a support detachment of one hundred army engineers, were ordered into Oxford. On 28 September, the court stated that if the governor ignored the order, he would be jailed and fined ten thousand dollars a day until he complied. Meanwhile, the attorney general again stated that Meredith would be enrolled and called attention to federal law which makes it a crime to interfere with the exercise of constitutional rights. Responding to the threat of national intervention, southern spokesmen referred to the old *posse comitatus* act of 1878, which prohibited the unrestricted use of troops to enforce federal laws. However, the Justice Department correctly pointed out that the act in question applied in all cases, except those in which the Constitution or an act of Congress permitted the use of troops. Article II of the Constitution, which relegates the responsibility for the faithful execution of the laws to the president, as well as the specific powers in federal statutes, was sufficient legal authority for intervention.[9]

While the army engineer troops were on their way to Oxford to set up a tent city and provide food and lodging for the marshals on duty there, Robert Kennedy conferred with Major General Creighton Abrams about the possible use of federal troops, as pressure for federal action was mounting. Meredith's lawyers, Constance Baker Motley and Jack Greenberg of the NAACP staff, complained about the delay in enforcing the court order; various other black organizations accused the court of being too lenient with Barnett. Citing Mississippi's historical opposition to interposition, Robert Kennedy appealed to Barnett to cease his attempt at nullification.[10]

By Saturday, 29 September, the Kennedy administration felt that since all possible alternatives had been exhausted, it was time to use federal force. That afternoon, as they worked on a proclamation, Barnett called with a new plan: while he and his troopers waited at the university, Meredith would go to Jackson and be registered; the governor would then complain of federal trickery and the episode would be closed. At 7:00 P.M., the president and Barnett agreed on this subterfuge. Three hours later, Barnett called the attorney general to change the plans and proposed that the marshals and Meredith appear at the university where he would be registered. The administration, rapidly losing confidence in Barnett's promises, agreed with this plan, but ordered army troops to a position nearer the university. The president signed an executive order federalizing the Mississippi National Guard, both for possible service and to prevent Barnett from using them. A cease-and-desist proclamation required by federal law was prepared and signed at the same time. The basis for action cited in the proclamation and order were specific federal enforcement statutes, the necessity for enforcing the court order, and the refusal of Barnett to assure maintenance of law and order.[11] Early Sunday morning, Secretary of the Army Cyrus Vance telegraphed Barnett that the Mississippi National Guard had been ordered into federal service and informed him of the contents of the proclamation and executive order. Fourteen hundred men, one-half taken from the 503rd Military Police Battalion at Fort Bragg and the remainder from the 716th Military Police Battalion at Fort Dix, were already ordered to the area. Meanwhile, white people were gathering from other parts of the state and the South to defend segregation at "Ole Miss." [12]

When Meredith was brought on campus Sunday evening, he was taken to a dormitory where he was guarded by marshals and state police. Meanwhile, other federal officials on campus were working out registration procedures. An angry crowd gathered, confronted the police who showed little interest in dispersing them, and began taunting the marshals. By the time President Kennedy went on nationwide television to explain the necessity of federal intervention and ask for peace and order, the marshals on the campus were under heavy attack. They had to use tear gas to drive off the rioters. The students on the campus jeered at the president's plea for calm. Claiming their masks were ineffective against the gas employed by the marshals, the state troopers withdrew from the campus. Paul Guihard, a French reporter, was shot and killed. As the number of marshals injured by shotgun pellets and rocks increased, sixty local national guardsmen were ordered to aid the marshals, but since they had been told by their squadron commander not to bring guns or ammunition, they were largely ineffective. Attempts made by three students and a campus priest to end the riot failed. President Kennedy ordered the army and other National Guard units to move into the campus, but it took them at least two hours to arrive. Meanwhile, Governor Barnett, after his earlier statements indicating his acquiescence, went on the air to declare he would never surrender.[13] However, later that night President Kennedy finally persuaded Barnett to order state troopers to man the roadblocks outside the campus to prevent further incursions of potential rioters. By 3:00 A.M., regular army troops arrived in force, some five hours after they had been ordered to leave Memphis eighty-seven miles away. By morning, twenty-five hundred soldiers were on the campus, and the riot ended. Fifty persons had been injured and a newspaperman and a white bystander killed. After almost two weeks of negotiations between Barnett and the Kennedy administration and several false starts which culminated in violence, Meredith was finally registered without incident.[14]

While the Meredith crisis was in process, liberals and conservatives in Congress sparred over the legality of federal intervention in Oxford. In the Senate, Javits described the whole episode as unpleasant, but thought everyone should support the president in the exercise of his duty to uphold the law. Eastland of Mississippi inserted a long article in the *Congressional Record* as a definitive statement of the southern constitutional position on the subject; the article outlines one lawyer's opinion that the president cannot use troops to enforce court decisions. Since the laws which he must enforce consist only of statutes, the president, therefore, must rely upon the state for enforcement of court orders, and if the state fails to enforce court orders, the president must have Congress pass a specific law making the court decision law. Then, and only then, would he be justified in interceding.[15]

This argument is easily controverted. The Supreme Court decided in *Erie v. Tompkins* (1938) that the expression *laws* included court decisions as well as statutes. However, in this discussion, it does not make much difference which argument is controlling. If the laws the president must enforce were only statutes, the question of why Congress had not passed laws to outlaw discrimination would arise, instead of why the executive did not enforce the laws already in existence. At the same time, if the president could not use troops to enforce court decisions, then the national government would simply have to mobilize enough marshals or let the decisions go unenforced.

John C. Stennis of Mississippi, reinforcing his colleague's argument, said that the power to initiate antidiscriminatory actions was not given to the attorney general by the Civil Rights Act of 1957 and that Robert Kennedy was, in fact, initiating Justice Department action in the Meredith case. Javits, responding to the two Mississippians, admitted that ordinarily in Congress, comments could be made about affairs in one's home state without rejointer from others present. However, he was sponsoring a resolution with Kenneth B. Keating of New York and Paul H. Douglas of Illinois in support of the president's actions. He knew the resolution would be filibustered to death, but thought it should be in the *Congressional Record*. When the resolution was introduced, Eastland intimated it had been prepared by the NAACP. To this, Keating replied that the NAACP had no part in its preparation, but he was happy that they were interested. Douglas, in a long speech in defense of Javit's resolution, asserted that he knew southerners were simply prisoners of their institutions, suggesting that once Meredith was in the university, they might discover that he was not so bad. Allen J. Ellender of Louisiana made it known that Meredith had been accepted at other schools, but since he merely wanted to attend a white institution, his motives were suspect. Wayne Morse of Oregon and Hubert Humphrey of Minnesota were concerned that this incident might feed the flames of communist propaganda and mar America's world image.[16]

Once troops were on campus, Morse made a flowing speech commending the president for federalizing the guard before sending in regular troops, action he thought Eisenhower should have taken in the Little Rock crisis. Herman C. Talmadge of Georgia and Sam J. Ervin of North Carolina felt that although the government had the power to use troops, it was inexpedient to do so. Eastland wished the president would show a similar interest in decontaminating Cuba.[17] During the discussion, Senator John M. Butler of Maryland made one of the strangest proposals ever articulated in Congress; he demanded that an act be passed which would restrict the jurisdiction of the Supreme Court to giving advisory opinions in cases "the consequence of which will have a serious impact upon the people of a sovereign state, or when the domestic tranquility is liable to be disrupted and our foreign relations embarrassed." Morse correctly replied that such an act would be unconstitutional, and that the state sovereignty issue had been settled in the Civil War.[18]

In the House, Mississippians and Alabamians castigated the administration while northern liberals defended it. Thomas G. Abernethy said the Mississippi and Alabama congressional delegates had asked the Justice Department to wait until Monday when the students would have been prepared for Meredith, but the request was denied. Abernathy made no statement about the abortive negotiations with Barnett. Jamie L. Whitten pleaded that his "poor little Mississippi" had only two hundred state troopers and intimated that it was a shame to ruin a great university for one black. A suggestion was made by George W. Andrews that Martin Luther King was the mastermind behind the Meredith incident. Robert Nix of Pennsylvania was not saddened by the plight of "poor" Mississippi, but by the fact that the partial payment on a grievous debt was so long overdue. William F. Ryan of New York agreed with Nix and commended the president for his action.[19]

In April 1963, the administration's difficulties with racial violence escalated when the SCLC began a campaign for jobs and freedom in Birmingham, Alabama. Southern police responded with frenetic repression. When Martin Luther King called for a march on Good Friday, Eugene Bull Connor procured an injunction forbidding the demonstration. Along with his use of dogs and cattle prods to disband the marchers, Connor arrested King, Ralph Abernathy, and other leaders who were released after serving fifteen days in jail. As the demonstrations continued, fire hoses and dogs were increasingly relied upon for crowd control. On 4 May, a now well-known picture of a police dog lunging at a demonstrator was flashed around the world. President Kennedy, speaking before a group of Americans for Democratic Action (ADA), said that in this situation, the Constitution left him powerless; there were no court orders or statutes to enforce. However, Kennedy sent Assistant Attorney General Burke Marshall to Birmingham to mediate a settlement. Meanwhile, the president, Secretary of Defense Robert McNamara and Treasury Secretary C. Douglas Dillon tried to persuade business leaders to mediate with black leaders on solutions to the crisis. On 10 May, an agreement was reached—promotion and hiring would be on a nondiscriminatory basis; black demonstrators would be released on bail or their own recognizance, and a biracial civil rights commission would be established.[20]

Governor George Wallace of Alabama, expressing his dissatisfaction with this agreement, announced that he would never be a party to a compromise on the principle of segregation. On Saturday, 11 May, whites responded to his incantations by bombing hotels and houses in black neighborhoods, including the home of King's brother and a motel owned by a black, A. D. Gaston, where the negotiations for the agreement had taken place. Blacks retaliated by attacking policemen and whites who were in their neighborhoods. The rioting continued until dawn. Wallace finally deployed state troopers who used shotguns and indiscriminate beatings to suppress the blacks.[21] Disheartened by the precipitous breakdown of the negotiated civil rights settlement and the resulting violence, President Kennedy consulted with his advisors all day Sunday. In the evening, he went on nationwide television to announce that he had alerted army units on bases in the area and had taken preliminary steps to federalize the National Guard. Challenging the president, Governor Wallace stated that as no state request for aid had been made, there was no authority for federal interference. The Justice Department pointed to Section 333 of the *United States Code,* which empowered the national government to intervene when states refused to protect citizens from private violence (see Appendix). The President could use his constitutional powers to move troops about at his discretion. The *Hodges* doctrine, with its limited interpretation of federal power, was well on its way to extinction.[22]

On 13 May, Birmingham was quiet; threatened with intervention, local police decided they could keep order. President Kennedy assured Wallace that federal troops would be used only if the state abdicated its responsibilities. Wallace responded by blaming blacks for the trouble. The administration believed events in Birmingham were shameful, but the level of violence had not been sufficient to warrant federal intervention until the rioting on Saturday night. When a new administration took control of Birmingham's city government on 23 May, Albert Boutwell, who replaced Connor, expressed his approval of the desegregation agreement. As a result of the crisis in Birmingham, the administration prepared a new, broadly drawn civil rights bill which was sent to Congress on 19 June and expanded the use for Section 333 of the *United States Code*.[23]

Events in Birmingham precipitated a high level of constitutional, as well as emotional, argument in Congress. In the Senate, Keating announced that when the marches began, he had asked Deputy Attorney General Nicholas Katzenbach whether new legislation was needed to enable the administration to deal with attacks on marchers, but had received no reply. Keating wondered if the Justice Department could seek an injunction against those harassing the marchers. Harrison A. Williams, Jr. of New Jersey supported the president for putting troops on a standby basis outside Birmingham, but felt that their use indicated failure to peacefully resolve the racial problem. Javits of New York opposed the president's initial statements that he lacked constitutional authority to intervene; a state's action or inaction denying the First Amendment guarantee of the right of petition constituted a clear basis for federal action. Stennis of Missisippi maintained that the absence of a validating court order or a statute prevented federal interference. Apparently, he had repudiated the argument that court orders could not be enforced with troops, which he had supported during the Meredith incident. He asserted that the mere threat of using troops to support demonstrators was the same as using troops. Morse responded by advancing Section 241 of the *United States Code,* which prohibits conspiracies that prevent the free exercise of federally secured rights, as a basis for federal action (see Appendix).[24]

In the House, Armistead Selden of Alabama suggested that if the president had the authority to send troops to Birmingham, he had authority to send them to Fisk University in Nashville, where students were creating a disturbance. His colleague asserted that state officials were keeping order and that Martin Luther King was violating laws with the approval of the president. Joe D.

Waggoner of Louisiana chimed in with the observation that the whole situation was a stratagem to raise funds for the NAACP.[25] Despite the congressional criticism, the president's decision to station troops strategically to enforce the peace was effective.

Wallace stubbornly defied federal law again in June 1963, when a federal court ordered the admission of two blacks, James Hood and Vivian Malone, to the University of Alabama. President Kennedy informed Wallace that if he stayed home when the students arrived for registration, there would be no disorder. Wallace insisted on dramatically staging a stand in the schoolhouse door, but retreated when Kennedy sent units of the National Guard to the campus to clear the way for the black students. President Kennedy issued a proclamation and executive order, citing Sections 332 through 334 of the *United States Code* as the basis for his action (see Appendix). Although intervention in racial crises was becoming a routine matter, the president responded to Robert Kennedy's insistence that any such action ought to be explained to the public.[26] On 12 June 1963, twelve hours after Medgar Evers, an NAACP leader in Jackson, Mississippi had been shot and killed by a white assassin at his home, President Kennedy spoke on nationwide television, explaining not only his intervention in Alabama, but giving a stirring address on the problems of blacks in America and the necessity for the passage of his new civil rights bill. But the controversial bill was not welcomed in Congress.[27]

However, the bombing of a black church in Birmingham on 15 September 1963, resulting in the death of four little girls, and the assassination of President Kennedy in November, along with President Johnson's vigorous support of Kennedy's bill, compelled Congress to pass the broadest civil rights act since Reconstruction. The new act, passed on 2 July 1964, contains provisions for enforcement of black access to jobs, public accommodations, education, and voting without discrimination. One significant section specifically empowered the attorney general to bring suit against suspected violators in the name of the United States, upon the written complaint of persons that they were being denied access to public facilities or the right to equal protection of the laws on the basis of race.[28]

With fresh impetus provided by the passage of the civil rights bill, the civil rights movement gained momentum. In the summer of 1964, whites and blacks joined in SNCC's Freedom Summer, which was a concentrated effort to register black voters in the South. More than twelve hundred students, the vanguard of the movement, arrived in Mississippi early in June to get the drive underway. They were greeted with open hostility. The local police frequently arrested students for exceeding the speed limit or other minor infractions of the law. On 22 June, one black and two white workers, James Chaney, Michael Schwerner, and Andrew Goodman, were reported missing while traveling from Meridian to Philadelphia, Mississippi to investigate a church burning. Initial reports indicated that Philadelphia county authorities had stopped the workers for speeding at 5:30 P.M. According to Sheriff Lawrence Rainey, they were released about 10:30 P.M. when Chaney paid a twenty dollar fine. The sheriff was unconcerned about their whereabouts.[29] When the group failed to appear, President Johnson, expressing concern about their fate, sent Allen Dulles and a few FBI agents to organize a search. One administration official indicated that the government was in a quandary over the course of action: although they felt that sending troops all over the South was too provocative and reminiscent of Reconstruction, they did want to take some action to protect student workers. Civil rights groups, as well as Mrs. Medgar Evers, pleaded for federal support.[30]

Although Sheriff Rainey expressed complete confidence in the safety of the three workers, FBI agents found Chaney's fire-gutted car in a swamp outside Philadelphia on 23 June. At this point, the incident was faintly reminiscent of the Huntsville case in which the sheriff claimed that two carloads of persons had spirited his prisoners away when he, in fact, had conspired in the murder. Some weeks later, the bullet-riddled bodies of Goodman, Schwerner, and Chaney were found buried in an earthen dam.[31]

The disposition of these cases was different from the abortive attempts to punish the sheriff in the Huntsville case in 1933 and to obtain an indictment of the murderers in the Mack Parker lynching. When a Georgia state court acquitted two klansmen who were accused of murdering Lemuel Penn, a black educator, it became even more evident that it was useless to attempt the state prosecution of Deputy Sheriff Cecil Price and his six co-conspirators who were charged with the murder of the three workers. However, federal prosecutions were begun under Sections 241 and 242 of the *United States Code,* which made the deprivation of civil rights through conspiracy a criminal act (see Appendix). Hopes for success were narrowly limited by the disaffection shown by previous administrations for these statutes, except in the *Hodges* and *Screws* cases which the government prosecuted and lost. In the cases growing out of the Penn, Chaney, Schwerner, and Goodman murders, *U.S. v. Price* (1966) and *U.S. v. Guest* (1966), the lower courts decided against the government, but the Supreme Court reversed the decision and ordered new trials held in lower courts. In the new trials, all defendants were found guilty and their sentences of three to ten years were upheld by the Supreme Court in 1970.

Sections 241 and 242 were given new vitality in these two cases. The indictment in the *Price* case stated that the deputy sheriff and seventeen others had intercepted Chaney, Goodman, and Schwerner, assaulted and shot them, and then buried their bodies where they were found forty-four days later. The Supreme Court decided there was sufficient state involvement to justify conviction under Section 242 for willfully subjecting the three to a denial of the right to due process of the law which is outlined in the Fourteenth Amendment.

In the *Guest* case, Justice Potter Stewart, who wrote the majority opinion, asserted there was sufficient state involvement in the crime to invoke federal prosecution under Section 241. Hugo Black, Abe Fortas, and Tom Clark concurred, but wanted it understood that Congress had the power under Section 5 of the Fourteenth Amendment to punish conspiracies, with or without state action, when they interfered with the rights outlined in the amendment. William Brennan, Earl Warren, and William Douglas concurred with Stewart's finding in that they also felt that there was sufficient state involvement and that a conspiracy to interfere with the right of interstate travel violated Section 241. But they dissented from Stewart's assertion that Section 241 did not cover private action. They thought that Section 241 forbade private, as well as state, action, when that action deprived persons of the right to free interstate travel. Justice John Marshal Harlan dissented on the grounds that the right to interstate travel is not a federally protected right and that the federal government cannot punish private action; he concurred, however, in the view that there was sufficient state action in this case to sustain a reversal. The *Guest* decision is a landmark in the area of civil rights because there was now a clear chance for conviction under federal law if states refused to prosecute or convict. The penalties designated for this crime were much less severe than those for murder, but even the possibility of a short sentence might deter such brutality. Additionally, at least three judges thought that private racial violence could be punished under existing laws, and another three thought Congress could pass a law making such an action a federal crime.[32]

The congressional debates on the Chaney, Schwerner, and Goodman incident foreshadowed the court opinions in *Guest* and *Price*. Apparently, the murder of the lone black, Penn, was unworthy of note. In the Senate, Javits affirmed the right of interstate travel without interference and thought marshals should be used to protect civil rights workers, but Stennis of Mississippi intimated that such persons were nothing but trouble-makers. When a group of law professors expressed the view that there was a basis for protection and intervention under the Civil Rights Act of 1866, the 1957 and 1960 Voting Rights Acts, and Sections 332 through 334 of the *United States Code,* Javits had these comments inserted in the *Congressional Record* (see Appendix).[33] After President Johnson authorized FBI agents and sailors to join in the search for the bodies, Stennis complained that he and Eastland had not been informed of the president's decision to move into their state. Stennis had asked Hoover about the situation and when he was told that these men had simply constituted a searching party, Stennis suggested that the government could have used the Mississippi National Guard for the search.[34]

In the House, John Bell Williams of Mississippi said communists were demanding that the president send troops to Mississippi. The president, he incorrectly reported, had already assigned two hundred marines to aid in the search of persons who came to Mississippi looking for trouble. William Colmer of Mississippi agreed with Williams and expressed the view that the president ought to send troops to find missing persons in New York; however, Colmer failed to mention that missing persons in New York were not likely to have been riddled with bullets and buried surreptitiously by police officers.[35]

The murders of Chaney, Goodman, and Schwerner, along with the march from Selma, Alabama, and the killing of three additional civil rights workers were part of a chain of events which precipitated the enactment of the Voting Rights Act of 1965. In March 1965, Governor Wallace's police harassment of persons attempting to register and vote led to a protest march from Selma to Montgomery. When the marchers were beaten and gassed, out-of-state black and white supporters came to join the effort. In the case of *Williams v. Wallace,* federal Judge Frank Johnson decided that the march could continue as a reasonable exercise of the right of petition. At this point, Governor Wallace asked President Johnson for aid, claiming his force was inadequate to curtail the potential violence, action that was probably motivated by the fact that Wallace knew he could not prevent intervention and wanted the national government to bear the responsibility. The march continued. President Johnson sent seventy deputy marshals to cooperate with the Alabama National Guard and the military police in providing protection for the marchers. As grounds for his action, Johnson cited the necessity for enforcing the court decision and also the states' inability to provide for the safety of the marchers, which was an exercise of his authority under Sections 332 through 334.[36]

In the Senate, Javits deprecated the violence which occurred during the voter registration drives and hoped federal troops would be used to deter it. Walter F. Mondale of Minnesota and Joseph S. Clark of Pennsylvania asked that the Justice Department prepare the Voting Rights Act for immediate passage, for they felt that if the federal enforcement supported the registration and voting efforts, such marches would become obsolete. Despite the protestations of southern congressmen and senators that outside agitators were responsible for their civil rights prob-

lems, the sweeping Voting Rights Act of 1965, which suspended
literacy test in states where less than fifty percent of the adults
had voted in 1964 and which provided for federal supervision of
registrations and elections, was passed.[37] The terms of the act
were similar to those of the Lodge elections bill of 1890, which
was labeled unconstitutional by its opponents. However, this bill
was saved from the onslaught of southerners by the Supreme
Court decision in *South Carolina v. Katzenbach* (1966), in which
the act was determined to be a value exercise of constitutional
power under the Fifteenth Amendment.[38] The act, if enforced,
would be a godsend for southern blacks who might gain a share
of control in areas where they lived in substantial numbers.

By enacting the 1964 and 1965 Civil Rights Acts, the national
government indicated its willingness to provide a basis for the
achievement of full equality for blacks. The legislation resulted
in part from pressure generated by a civil rights movement that
had taken to the streets. While the three previous administrations had taken some interest in civil rights enforcement, the
Kennedy administration seriously intervened in cases of racial
violence under the authority provided in Sections 241, 242, and
333 of the *United States Code,* which had been in existence since
Reconstruction. Now states found it more difficult to hide behind
the facade of states' rights to abdicate their duties.

NOTES

1. *See Bell v. Maryland,* 378 *U.S.* 226 (1964); *Garner v. Louisiana,* 368
U.S. 157 (1961); *Peterson v. City of Greenville,* 373 *U.S.* 244 (1963);
Bouie v. City of Columbia, 378 *U.S.* 347 (1964); *Barr v. City of Columbia,* 378 *U.S.* 146 (1964); and Monrad G. Paulsen, "Sit-In Cases of 1964,
but Answers Came There None," *Supreme Court Rev.,* 1964, p. 137;
the whole issue was made moot by the enactment of Title II of the
Civil Rights Act of 1964, insofar as the facilities in question are covered
by the terms of that act.

2. *Crandall v. Nevada,* 6 Wallace 35 (1868); *Mitchell v. United States,*
313 *U.S.* 80 (1941); *Morgan v. Virginia,* 328 *U.S.* 373 (1946); *Boynton v.*

Virginia, 364 *U.S.* 454 (1960); Robert G. Dixon, "Civil Rights in Transportation and the ICC," *George Washington Law Review* 31, 1962, p. 198.

3. Arthur Waskow, *From Race Riot to Sit-In—1919 and the 1960's* (New York, 1960) pp. 231-2; *New York Times,* 21 May 1961, pp. 1, 78; Louis Loma, *The Negro Revolt* (New York, 1962), pp. 135-44. As Dixon points out in "Civil Rights in Transportation," this was a good example of how the executive branch can achieve a goal by taking the initiative in requesting specific action from an independent regulatory commission which possesses rule-making power.

4. Michael Dorman, *We Shall Overcome* (New York, 1964), pp. 15-6, 142-3; This eyewitness account by a reporter is most useful for the chronology of events. Burke Marshall, *Federalism and Civil Rights* (New York, 1964), discusses Justice Department attitudes.

5. Dorman, *We Shall Overcome,* pp. 25, 27, 30-2; *see* Section 332 of the *U.S. Code* in Appendix.

6. *New York Times,* 26 September 1962, pp. 1, 22; Dorman, *We Shall Overcome,* pp. 30-1.

7. *New York Times,* 27 September 1962, pp. 1, 28, 29.

8. Dorman, *We Shall Overcome,* pp. 34-6.

9. *New York Times,* 27 September 1962, pp. 1, 28, 29; *see also* sections of the *U.S. Code* in Appendix.

10. *New York Times,* 28 September 1962, p. 22.

11. *New York Times,* 30 September 1962, p. 1, 68; Arthur Schlesinger, Jr., *A Thousand Days, John F. Kennedy in the White House* (Boston, 1965), p. 946; Dorman, *We Shall Overcome,* pp. 53-5; *see also* sections of the *U.S. Code* in Appendix.

12. Dorman, *We Shall Overcome,* pp. 56, 58-9.

13. *New York Times,* 1 October 1962, p. 23; U.S., *Public Papers of the Presidents of the United States, John F. Kennedy, January 1–December 31, 1962* (Washington, 1963), pp. 726-8.

14. *New York Times,* 1 October 1962, pp. 1, 23; 2 October, pp. 1, 24.

15. *Congressional Record,* 87th cong., 2nd sess. (1962), pp. 19622, 19649; Alfred J. Schweppe, "Enforcement of Federal Court Decisions: A Recurrence to Fundamental Principles," *American Bar Association Journal* (February 1958).

16. *Congressional Record,* 87th cong., 2nd sess. (1962), pp. 19622, 19649, 19876, 20114, 20115, 20117–8, 20144.

17. *Congressional Record,* 87th cong., 2nd sess. (1962), pp. 20250, 20251, 20262–3, 20310, 21401, 22569.

18. Ibid., p. 20523.

19. Ibid., pp. 20346, 20347–8, 20437, 20649, 21329, 21552, 20523.

20. *New York Times,* 11 May 1963; Schlesinger, *Thousand Days,* p. 959; Dorman, *We Shall Overcome,* pp. 181, 192.

21. *New York Times,* 12 May 1963; Dorman, *We Shall Overcome,* pp. 194–7.

22. *New York Times,* 13 May 1963, pp. 1, 25; U.S., *Public Papers of the Presidents, John F. Kennedy, January 1–November 22, 1963,* pp. 397–8; *see* Section 333 of the *U.S. Code* in Appendix and *Constitution of the United States,* Article II. *See also State of Alabama by and Through Wallace v. United States,* 373 U.S. 545 (1963) in which the Supreme Court refused to permit Alabama to sue the national government for damages arising from the general adverse effects on the state created by the president's threatened use of troops in Birmingham.

23. *New York Times,* 14 May 1963, p. 1, 26.

24. *Congressional Record,* 88th cong., 1st sess. (1963), pp. 8322, 8291–3, 9115, 9293, 9140. *See* Section 241 of the *U.S. Code* in Appendix.

25. Ibid., pp. 8501, 8613.

26. Exec. order 11111, Proclamation 3542, 28 *Fed. Reg.* 5209, 5707 (1963); *New York Times,* 11 June 1963, pp. 1, 20; 12 June, pp. 1, 21; U.S., *Public Papers of the Presidents, John F. Kennedy, January 1–November 22, 1963,* pp. 406, 468, 477; *see* sections of *U.S. Code* in Appendix.

27. Schlesinger, *Thousand Days,* p. 966; Dorman, *We Shall Overcome,* pp. 251–2.

28. 78 *Stat* 241 (1964), Title 42, USC Sec. 2000A.

29. *New York Times,* 21 June 1964, p. 21; 22 June, p. 15; 23 June, p. 1; 23 June, p. 13.

30. *New York Times,* 24 June 1964, p. 21; 25 June, p. 18; U.S., *Public Papers of the Presidents, Lyndon B. Johnson, November 22, 1963–June 30, 1964,* p. 808.

31. *New York Times*, 24 June 1964, p. 1; *United States v. Price*, 383 *U.S.* 787 (1966), *United States v. Guest*, 383 *U.S.* 745 (1966).

32. *Price* and *Guest; see also* sections of *U.S. Code* in Appendix.

33. *Congressional Record*, 88th cong., 2nd sess. (1964), pp. 14813, 15645, 15851, A3626; *see* sections of *U.S. Code* in Appendix.

34. Ibid., pp. 15005–6, 15158.

35. Ibid., 15005–6; 30 *Fed. Reg.* 3739, 3743 (1965).

36. U.S., *Public Papers of the Presidents, Lyndon B. Johnson, January 1—May 31, 1965,* pp. 274–6, 296, 299. Governor Wallace tried a new twist: he asked for aid, claiming his peace keeping forces were insufficient. *Race Relations Law Reporter* (1965), pp. 218–34; *see also* sections of the *U.S. Code* in Appendix.

37. *Congressional Record*, 89th cong., 1st sess. (1965), pp. 4311, 4350, 4545, 4563, 5178.

38. 79 *Stat* 437, 42 *U.S.* 1973 (1965), *South Carolina v. Katzenbach*, 383 *U.S.* 301 (1966).

15 / Riots, Rebellion, and Repression

In the last half of the 1960s, the national government was faced with an expanded, but significantly transformed, black revolutionary movement; black and white "togetherness" was challenged by black activists who recognized violence as one tactic for achieving their goals and whose thinking was greatly influenced by cultural black nationalism. Black activists, with due respect to the contributions of older civil rights organizations such as the NAACP and the SCLC, began to think of economic and social revolution, of black power, and of forging alliances with white radicals and with the Third World of other people of color (nonwhite people in developing nations) as means for gaining their objectives. The black masses continued to lash out at "whitey" through his person and his ghetto property, while some militants devised plans and projects to move black people from reform to revolution. The president turned his attention to constitutional means of suppressing rioting black masses and supporting state and local law enforcement, while searching for programs to meet the needs or thwart the anger of the hostile people. Congress, even as it put the finishing touches on civil rights legislation, was perplexed by the new problems arising out of the violence perpetuated by blacks who seemed ungrateful for congressional beneficience.

The superficial issue that most often brought retaliatory violence from the black masses and retaliatory repression from the federal government in the 1960s was police brutality. Blacks had complained about police harassment for generations. In many of the incidents leading to preceding riots, police action was a precipitant. More recently, in 1959, Robert F. Williams, then director of the Monroe, North Carolina branch of the NAACP, asserted that blacks should respond violently when attacked by whites, since justice could not be expected in local court systems. His caustic expression of bitter disillusion reflected the verdicts of a local county court which handed an acquittal to two white men accused of brutally assaulting two black women and gave a jail sentence to a mentally retarded black man for having had an argument with a white woman. Williams asserted that blacks must understand that a liberation struggle had to be flexible; there was a place for violence as well as nonviolence. In August of 1961, during an outbreak of racial violence in Monroe, Williams was falsely accused of kidnapping a white couple. Fearing for his life, Williams fled the United States to seek asylum in Cuba and later in China. Williams returned to the United States in 1969 to fight the kidnapping charges and to rejoin the black revolutionary struggle.[1]

It was in 1959 too, that Malcolm X, the most articulate spokesman for Elijah Mohammed's Black Muslims, gained national attention for his analysis of the shallowness of earlier civil rights movements and their leadership and his program for black nationalism. Malcolm, until his assassination on 21 February 1965, frightened whites and bourgeois blacks as he aroused the disillusioned black masses by ridiculing integration and calling for the blacks to maintain their cultural identity as they worked for economic and political self-sufficiency in American life. While whites castigated Malcolm for preaching hatred, the black masses, weary of promises, knew he accurately described the "Man" and his injustice to blacks. Black revolutionaries and the masses, even when ignorant of the Muslim organization, believed that the rhetoric of organization and manliness made good sense.[2]

The new era of riots overlapped the nonviolent phase of the black liberation struggle. Even while the Civil Rights Act of 1964 was being passed, disturbances surfaced in Harlem and to a lesser degree in Rochester, New York, in Elizabeth and Jersey City, New Jersey, and in Philadelphia, Pennsylvania. The Harlem riot erupted when an off-duty policeman killed James Powell, a teenage boy who had allegedly attacked him. Blacks moved in protest, demanding establishment of a police review board to investigate cases of alleged brutality. On 18 July, the local CORE chapter organized a mass protest march to a police precinct in Harlem. The police tried to restrain the marchers and arrest the leaders. Instead of acquiescing as most blacks had done in the nonviolent marches in the South, the crowd attacked the police. By the next morning, one black had been killed by the police, twelve policemen and at least one hundred blacks had been injured, dozens of shops had been looted, and more charges of police brutality were made by James Farmer of CORE. Intermittent violence continued for the next few nights. President Johnson announced that the FBI would investigate the riots. In the investigation report, the FBI cited that it had found no evidence of systematic organization or planning, although it claimed that communist organizations had tried to exploit black unrest. The government still found it difficult to acknowledge the fact that blacks were moved to violence without external influence.[3]

Those blacks recognized as leaders by whites, such as Roy Wilkins, A. Phillip Randolph, Whitney Young, and Martin Luther King, embarked on the policy they would follow for the next few years: blacks would make their voices heard in the political process. Renunciating the riots, they insisted on a moratorium on sit-ins and other confrontation tactics in order to win the presidential election of Lyndon Johnson. However, black leaders, such as John Lewis of SNCC and James Farmer of CORE, dissented and articulated the seething black resentment against police brutality, rephrased by the whites as "law and order." [4]

Black leaders, counseling temperance, were unheeded by blacks in the ghettos. The Watts riot in Los Angeles in August 1965 exploded when a highway patrolman stopped an apparently intoxicated black man for speeding. A crowd of blacks gathered. The black people believed they were witnesses to an incident of police brutality. When one of additional patrolmen called to the scene struck a bystander with a billy club, the crowd began throwing things at the police. The next night, looting and burning of white-owned ghetto businesses began. As the conflagration grew, the chief of police asked for National Guard assistance. When the guard arrived, they and the police made heavy use of firearms. Four thousand persons were arrested, thirty-four were killed, and hundreds were injured. Property damage was estimated at thirty-five million dollars. Despite the enormous casualty figure, a major concern of governmental officials was that insurance cover property losses. Some blacks complained that they could not even retaliate against "whitey" by destroying his property without their efforts being neutralized.[5]

During the riot, Congress, having just appropriated some 950 million dollars in August 1964 for President Johnson's War on Poverty, was in a dither. During the nonviolent phase of the revolution, liberals and conservatives in Congress knew where they stood; now liberals were confused, while conservatives blamed liberals for the disturbance. While insisting that the movement toward equality should continue, Senator Javits of New York expressed horror at the "hoodlums" of Los Angeles. Richard Russell of Georgia intimated that civil rights leaders had pushed lawbreaking too far, setting the example for rioters. Walter Mondale of Minnesota denounced his colleagues who were blaming civil rights leaders for the riots. Then, Senator Robert C. Byrd of West Virginia proposed that planned parenthood be introduced to blacks so that they would not have so many children who would grow up and be unemployed. Michael Mansfield of Montana, defending the police against charges of brutality, insisted that mass defiance of law could not be justified by this charge. Strom Thurmond of South Carolina knew that communists and agitators were responsible for these racial problems.[6]

In the House, Selden of Alabama was pleased with the discomfort of his northern colleagues. He commented that even though the northerners had run to the South to investigate her racial problems and to advise southerners on solutions, he was not going to meddle in their communities. By now, he stated, the public must recognize that racial problems were nationwide, that the encouragement of law violation by demonstrators in Alabama had led to lawlessness in northern communities, and that the passage of civil rights bills would not eliminate racial friction. George Hansen of Idaho thought Martin Luther King and other leaders should put an end to the riots since their example had caused them. James Roosevelt of California felt that the House should investigate and make recommendations for riot prevention. At this time, Adam Clayton Powell of New York correctly enumerated the causes of the riots for his colleagues: blacks were angry and furious because the white power structure chose to work with "Uncle Toms." As a result, the "natives" were ready to take matters in their own hands. Civil rights legislation had absolutely no meaning to blacks in the North who were fed-up with police brutality, de facto segregation, unemployment and underemployment, inferior education, political tokenism, and Jim Crow justice. Powell predicted that Los Angeles was only the first of a long series of riots and episodes of lawlessness. Ignoring Powell's impassioned and accurate explanation, Richard H. Ichord of Missouri insisted that it was a simple matter of keeping the peace as exemplified in Selma. James D. Martin of Alabama was heartened by the fact that newspapers, by speaking out in favor of law and order, were finally assuming their responsibility for action when demonstrators were violating local segregation and trespass statutes.[7]

In the summer of 1966, there were approximately forty-three disorders, all initially precipitated by some minor incident between blacks and the police. Commentators stated that the country was in for a succession of long hot summers without realizing that racial disorders had characterized every American summer for years.[8] When rioting and violence erupted in 1966, liberals in Congress were understandably disturbed while conservatives felt vindicated. In the past two years, legislation was passed before the summer riots. But this year, when the riots came early, Javits feared that the Civil Rights Act of 1966 might not be passed. He was correct; the bill containing a fair housing section did not pass. Javits tried to explain the positive side of black power and to subvert the argument that blacks were not like other immigrant groups who simply had to work hard and who would someday become assimilated in the melting pot. In the first place, he said, there was no melting pot, and in the second place, blacks came in chains and had been subjected to accumulated oppression. Undismayed, conservatives, such as Byrd of West Virginia, called for strong repressive measures to end the riots.[9]

In the House, when northerners were, for the most part, silent, Abernathy of Mississippi rose to ask why those who were so vocal when racial troubles plagued the South had nothing to say now. Convinced, as were his fellow southerners, that outside agitators caused the riots, William C. Cramer of Florida introduced an amendment to the civil rights act presently under consideration which would provide for punishment of those who crossed state lines to cause riots. His bill would supplement the efforts of those state governments which were passing repressive legislation. The amendment passed the House on 9 August by a vote of 389–25. Interestingly enough, southerners who argued against federal intervention and for local control between 1962 and 1965 now wanted federal legislation, and northerners, such as Don Edwards of California and James Corman, who had supported federal intervention previously, opposed the bill on the grounds that law enforcement was a local matter. However, both groups were consistent; southerners wanted outside agitators suppressed, and northerners were opposed to the suppression of civil rights activists and civil liberties in an effort to end racial disturbances. In any case, the amendment was lost when the bill failed to pass.[10]

In the spring of 1967, disorders ignited by police attempts to make arrests on some minor charge began again. In April and May, disturbances broke out at several black colleges in the South where SNCC had been organizing youthful militants. In Tampa, Florida, riots in June occurred after policemen shot a black held on a robbery charge as he was attempting to escape. Police, with the aid of a hastily organized black youth patrol, restored order. In Cincinnati and in Atlanta, that same month, police encounters with blacks and accumulated grievances set off rioting. In Newark, New Jersey, the allegedly brutal arrest of John Smith, a black cab driver, for driving without a license and assaulting a police officer, set off retaliatory rioting in July. National guardsmen and police suppressed the violence which had spread to other New Jersey cities; in Plainfield, national guardsmen and police further antagonized the black community by making a warrantless house-to-house search for arms that had allegedly been stolen from a manufacturing plant.[11]

The most extensive racial disorder of 1967 grew out of a police raid on a "blind pig," an illegal after-hours drinking establishment, in Detroit on 22 July. A crowd gathered outside the after-hours club, vocally criticized the police for the way in which they made the arrests, charging they used excessive force. Window-breaking and looting spread. Early Sunday morning, Mayor Jerome Cavanaugh asked Governor George Romney for national guard support; Romney complied. When the violence increased, a request was made for federal troops and 4,700 paratroopers arrived in Detroit that evening. On Thursday, the rioting almost completely subsided and the paratroopers left on Saturday. National guardsmen remained in town until 1 August. Of the forty-three persons killed, thirty-three were blacks; 7,200 citizens were arrested, most of whom were black. One white national guardsman, one white fireman, and one black private guard lost their lives, all three being mistakenly killed by policemen and guardsmen. Claims of police brutality, wholesale violations of civil rights, illegal arrests, and unreasonable bail were commonplace. Seventeen of the persons killed were reportedly looters, two of whom were white. Some twenty million dollars damage was done, most of which was covered by insurance.[12]

Considerable discussion and controversy arose over the roles played by President Johnson and Governor Romney in introducing federal troops to suppress the disorder. Realizing that state troopers and the National Guard were virtually all-white units who might further aggravate the rioters, Mayor Cavanaugh reluctantly called the governor for aid. Romney, who began discussing the disorder with Attorney General Ramsey Clark about 3:00 A.M., was told that he should use the specific language required by statute in order to obtain federal aid; he was to assert that there was a state of "insurrection." Romney, fearing that insurance companies would not cover the property damage involved if that language was used, refused to use the term *insurrection*. In later conversations, Romney said that Clark told him there was a statute which permitted troop use in cases of domestic violence, so he could substitute that term in his request. At 10:00 A.M., Clark informed President Johnson that Romney thought he would definitely need troops and that the governor had been informed that he must send a written request. Romney charged that Clark first indicated that an oral request was sufficient, but changed his mind at 4:00 A.M. and stipulated that a written request was required. Although Romney said he had a telegram prepared by 8:00 A.M., he waited to send it until Clark agreed that he did not have to indicate the existence of an insurrection. At 11:00 A.M., President Johnson received the telegram in which Romney asserted that there was a reasonable doubt that looting and disorder could be suppressed without the use of federal troops.[13] At 11:20 A.M., Johnson ordered Secretary of Defense Robert McNamara to start sending troops to Detroit. He also decided to send Cyrus Vance as his personal emissary to study the situation. He then conferred with Clark and three Justice Department civil rights attorneys, Warren Christopher, Roger Wilkins, and John Doar, to draft a reply to Romney and a presidential proclamation and executive order. At 11:42 A.M., a reply was sent to Romney that troops would be landing at Selfridge Air Force Base. Shortly after 1:00 P.M., Vance and other federal officials flew to Detroit.[14]

When Vance arrived in Detroit that afternoon, he toured the riot areas with local officials and met with Cavanaugh, Romney, and a dozen black leaders. All of these men, except Representative John Conyers, agreed to send the troops into the riot areas at once. At 8:30 P.M., Vance reported to the president that the need was not critical enough to send the troops into the streets. Representative Charles Diggs called the White House, threatening to denounce the administration's behavior as being politically motivated in an effort to discredit Governor Romney, who was being considered a Republican presidential candidate, unless troops were used immediately. Shortly before midnight, federal troops moved into the city and the president went on nationwide television to explain the reasons for their use.[15]

Newspaper accounts and official reports from both sides correlate substantially. The administration, admitting they were reluctant to use federal troops, did not want to establish a precedent for sending regular troops all about the country whenever civil disorders occurred. Apart from the economics of the situation, it was not a tactic that would win favor at the polls. No troops had been used in Newark or Watts, and no request had been made for them. Romney, however, blamed the president for his own ignorance of the statutory and constitutional means for invoking the use of federal troops. Romney should have been familiar with the procedures. After the 1943 riots, instructions were reiterated and sample requests were sent to all states. The information on how to proceed was also available in any law library. Based on his own account as published in the newspapers and outlined in the statutes, Romney did not proceed in the proper manner.[16]

It is also evident that there was considerable confusion in the administration over the correct procedure. In his proclamation and executive order giving the basis for troop use, Johnson cited all of Chapter 15, Title 10 of the *United States Code* (see Appendix). However, a Justice Department memorandum, written to explain the federal grounds for the Detroit action, cited only Sections 331 and 333 of the same chapter. If the administration was relying upon Section 331, which is the only part of the statute that provides for action upon a state request, Johnson was correct in insisting upon the word *insurrection,* because that is the only situation in which the statute permits him discretionary authority to use troops. The statute is based upon Article IV, Section 4 of the Constitution, which provides that the United States shall, upon application, protect the states from domestic violence. It was decided by the Supreme Court in *Luther v. Borden* (1849), that Congress, by statute, must decide how Article IV, Section 4 shall be enforced. The presidential authority comes only from Section 331, which Congress enacted in response to the court decision. Since Romney refused to state there was an insurrection, technically troops should not have been sent. In addition, it is well accepted that as the president has discretionary authority under Section 331, he can make his own investigation before determining whether to send troops. Sending Vance under those circumstances, especially since riots earlier in the year had been suppressed without federal troops, seems quite proper.[17]

Since Romney never said there was an insurrection, perhaps the president was relying upon Sections 332 and 333 as authority for sending troops. Congress had passed these two sections to give the president authority to enforce federal law without a state request. If that was the case, he did not need a state request. Section 332 requires a rebellion against federal law before troops can be sent; however, no assertion was made that federal law was being opposed in Detroit. Section 333, which was used as a basis for action in Birmingham, Selma, and the investigatory stages of the Schwerner-Chaney-Goodman cases is the best statutory basis cited by the president. That section requires only that domestic violence hinder the execution of state or federal law so as to deprive persons of constitutional rights secured by law, along with evidence of state failure to provide protection. Again, no state request is necessary. It is very likely that neither Clark nor the president knew what constitutional authority they would use when the rioting was first reported; however, when Romney refused to aver that there was an insurrection, but insisted he needed help, and after politicians threatened to condemn the president's inaction as political ploy, the president probably decided in haste to cite all of Title 10.[18]

The president and the attorney general must have become aware that their refusal to send troops upon Romney's first request could only be based on the theory that they thought Section 331 covered riot situations. In a letter from Clark to the governors on 7 August 1967, the law on the subject is correctly explained. Clark cites only Article IV, Section 4 and Section 331, which requires a state request, and 334, which requires that the president issue a proclamation ordering citizens to cease and desist when troops are introduced upon state application. The sticking points in the Detroit riot situation seemed to be Romney's unwillingness to say that there was a state of insurrection *or* of domestic violence which he was unable to suppress and the administration's unwillingness to send troops, despite the seriousness of the riot, without Romney making these averments when both were relying upon statutes which seemed to require very specific language. In cases of state requests for troops before 1967, references had been made to either domestic violence or insurrection existing in the state. In cases in which a reference was made to domestic violence in the state applications, it was clear from the language that the reference was to Article IV, Section 4 and Section 331 by extension. In his wire to the president, Romney referred only to looting, arson and sniping, and the necessity for federal troops to assist local authorities in restoring order. If any blame must be given for the delay in acquiring federal assistance, it should probably fall on the governor.[19]

In Congress, the same jockeying for political capital, of which Johnson and Romney were accused, was evident. In the House, southerners, such as Waggoner of Louisiana, repeated the 1965 and 1966 charges that communists were initiating the riots. F. Edward Hebert, also from Louisiana, thought action should be taken to make the national guard more effective so that the use of federal troops would be unnecessary. Speaker of the House John McCormack of Massachusetts inserted Johnson's explanation of the sequence of events in the *Congressional Record*. Republican Gerald Ford of Michigan sparred with Wayne B. Hayes of Ohio and Democratic Whip Carl Albert of Oklahoma over the roles played by Romney and Johnson in the disturbances. Chet Hollifield of California and Hale Boggs of Louisiana supported the president. L. Mendel Rivers of South Carolina, the chairman of the Armed Services Committee, commended the military, but emphasized the responsibility of the guard to keep order. Abernathy of Mississippi could not resist needling the northerners again, and addressing them, he said that every time racial disturbances occurred in the South, you would all ". . . pack your shabby old valises and head down to revel in the activity. Ike and Kennedy sent the military at the drop of a hat. But President Johnson sort of held back until Detroit was on its knees." He stated that the national guard could have handled the situation, but Romney, "another Civil Rights expert, piddled around" before releasing the full force of the National Guard.[20]

In the Senate, Republican Robert P. Griffin of Michigan, supported the view that Johnson was attempting to make Romney appear incapable of handling affairs in his state, while Philip A. Hart, his Democratic colleague, opposed the allegation of such charges. Robert Byrd of West Virginia, consistent with his positions in disturbances in the South, said he was opposed to the use of federal troops except as a last resort. Asserting it was necessary for future historians and scholars to have material available from which to form an opinion about the dispute, Hart helpfully inserted a memorandum prepared by the attorney general, the proclamation and executive order signed by the president, the president's speech, and Romney's telegram into the *Congressional Record*.[21]

A number of strange circumstances and controversies grew out of the intense apprehension which followed the riot. One of these resulted in the death of three black youths at the Algiers Motel in Detroit on 26 July 1967. The police, responding to a report that there were snipers in the motel, discovered ten black males and two white females in the building annex. No guns were found. An hour later when the police left, the three youths were dead; they had been shot at close range. The other people, including the two women, had been beaten. There was no immediate acknowledgement or explanation of the incident. Later, one of the policemen, Ronald August, admitted shooting one of the youths, but claimed he had acted in self-defense. He was acquitted by an all-white jury in June 1969. Since a white judge ruled his confession inadmissible because it was made without proper constitutional warning, no trial is possible in the case of a second policeman, David Senak, who admitted shooting another one of the youths. Senak, August, and Robert Paille, a third white police officer, and Melvin Dismukes, a black private guard, were charged under the same statute used in the *Guest* and *Price* cases —conspiring to violate the civil rights of the three youths by murdering them. All four were acquitted by an all-white jury in February 1970.[22]

After the Detroit riot, the army organized a directorate for civil disturbance policy and operations and issued new riot control instructions to insure rapid response in an expected succession of long hot summers. If no major disorders had occurred in the next few years, those plans and preparations would probably have been forgotten. However, the assassination of Martin Luther King on 4 April 1968 set off a wave of rioting in black ghettos across the country, resulting in the use of federal troops in Chicago, Washington, and Baltimore. Troops were dispatched without problems. In response to state requests for aid to suppress domestic violence in Maryland and Illinois, the president issued proclamations and executive orders upon the authority granted him in Section 331. In the Washington riots, the president cited not only Sections 331 through 334 as authority, but also his position as commander-in-chief of the local national guard in respond to a request for aid from Mayor Walter Washington, Chief of Police John B. Layton, and Commissioner of Safety Patrick V. Murphy.[23]

Deaths and injuries in the King assassination riots were not as great as those in the summer disturbances of 1965, 1966, and 1967. However, in Chicago, 9 were killed and 500 injured; in Washington, 11 deaths occurred with 1113 injuries, mostly minor. There were 6 deaths and 900 injuries in Baltimore, and 6 more deaths in Kansas City. Racial violence was much more widespread after King's assassination, with disturbances occurring in 36 states and 138 cities. The decrease in casualties can perhaps be explained by the training given National Guard and the police after 1967 in which they were instructed to use tear gas and curfews rather than arms and ammunition, except in the most severe circumstances.[24]

The summer violence of 1968 continued into the fall and spring semesters on college campuses, and into the summer of 1969. The murder of three black college students by highway patrolmen in Orangeburg, South Carolina in February was reminiscent of many previous cases. The incident grew out of student efforts to integrate the local bowling alley. When no state charges were filed, Attorney General Ramsey Clark sought federal indictments of the nine highway patrolmen for civil rights violations.

A South Carolina grand jury refused to indict the patrolmen. The occurrence of violent confrontations on campuses and on the streets was no longer primarily confined to the summer months. By April of 1969, more racial violence and use of national guard and federal troops took place than in all of 1967. Militarism, too, was fast becoming a common occurrence; in Wilmington, Delaware, National Guard troops occupied the city from April 1967 to January 1969.[25]

For the first time in 1968, there was evidence of planned strategic acts of violence and conspiratorial warfare by blacks. In Cleveland in July, three policemen were ambushed and killed by black snipers. Black militant Fred Ahmed was later convicted of murder in the case. There were several attacks on policemen in Brooklyn late in the summer; in August, two policemen were wounded by shotgun fire; in early September, two policemen were hit by sniper fire as they waited for a traffic light; and in mid-September, a police communications truck was fire-bombed, slightly injuring the policemen. Also in mid-September in Harlem, two policemen, sitting in a parked patrol car, were shot and wounded, reportedly by two black men. Two attacks on policemen occurred in Illinois in September; in Kankakee, a policeman was wounded in an ambush in the black community; in Summit, black youths reportedly fired shotguns at two police cars, injuring two policemen. In the same month, eighteen black militants were arrested in St. Louis following a series of attacks on the police, including one incident in which shots were fired at a police station and at the home of a police lieutenant. Organized violence, involving Black Panther confrontations with police in Oakland, California and other cities developed into significant methods of racial confrontation in 1968.[26]

Some political science theorists and commentators assumed that as the black liberation struggle had changed its tactics to selected strategic violence, the era of the riot was at an end. Events in early 1969 seemed to support their opinion. In Detroit in March, black separatist members of the Republic of New Africa allegedly fired on policemen outside the New Bethel Church, wounding one officer and killing another. The police then stormed the church in search of the sniper and arrested 142 black adults and 5 children. Black Judge George Crockett, who began releasing the prisoners a few hours later since there was no evidence of their complicity, enraged the police department. However, these commentators seem to have forgotten that the level of consciousness of different groups of black people varies. Police brutality would still cause an outbreak of rioting and property destruction in the ghettos, while other members of the black community would react with guerilla warfare. This theory was borne out in the summer of 1969 by the Omaha, Nebraska rioting and looting precipitated by the killing of a young black girl by a white policeman investigating a robbery and incidents such as the one at New Bethel Church and the shooting of policemen in Kokomo, Indiana. There were approximately 683 race-related disorders in 1968 and 688 in 1969. The 1969 disturbances, unlike those of 1967 and 1968 occurred, for the most part, in smaller communities that had not experienced such disturbances before. Some black people still chose marching, picketing, or other nonviolent methods as evidenced in Resurrection City in June 1968, in the Charleston Employees' strike in the summer of 1969, and the Cairo, Illinois movement of 1969. All of these protests were coordinated by the SCLC, with Ralph Abernathy, Jesse Jackson, and others maintaining the tradition of Martin Luther King. The NAACP found a new cause in trying to insure that the Nixon administration would not bargain away recent civil rights legislation in a second Compromise of 1877.[27]

Congress was ever on the move to defend the public from manifestations of civil violence. During the disorders of 1968, Congress was faced with the resubmitted Cramer antiriot bill, which from the congressional debates on the subject might more accurately be titled the "Stokely Carmichael and H. Rap Brown Bill." Cramer and his supporters were convinced that agitators, such as Carmichael and Brown, who travelled from place to place around the country were responsible for the riots and that the national government must take action to end their ubiquitousness. The bill, based on the commerce power of Congress, provided that persons who traveled in or used facilities of interstate commerce with intent to incite a riot or to aid or abet a riot could be fined ten thousand dollars or imprisoned for five years, or both. Supporters, demanding assurance that the law would be enforced, added a section requiring the attorney general to prosecute speedily and to exhaust all possible appeals, or explain to Congress in writing why action was delayed. According to the bill, a riot is any public disturbance involving acts of violence by one or more persons as part of an assemblage of three or more persons.[28]

Page after page of the *Congressional Record* was filled with assertions by proponents of the bill that Rap Brown and Stokely Carmichael were the demons of the riot era. Opponents of the bill, such as John Conyers of Michigan and Don Edwards of California, pointed out that the bill was too simplistic to stop riots, but to no avail. Robert Nix of Pennsylvania was not convinced that the section of the bill which excluded punishment of mere oral or written expression of ideas not advocating violence would prevent infringements of First Amendment rights. Joseph Resnick of New York pertinently asked whether the legislation could be labeled as a Bill of Attainder, which is prohibited by Article I of the Constitution, since its framers had gone on record by stating that the bill was designed to "get" the two former SNCC chairmen, Carmichael and Brown.[29]

While passing this riot prevention measure, Congress, moved by King's assassination, enacted some civil rights legislation which had been left over from 1966. The Fair Housing Act reaffirmed the principle expressed in the Civil Rights Act of 1866 that the purchase of housing on a nondiscriminatory basis was a matter of national policy. Persons convicted of violating the act could be subjected to a ten thousand dollar fine or not more than ten years imprisonment, or both. Amendments to Sections 241 through 244, as well as the new Section 245 of the criminal code, were also enacted (see Appendix). The new legislation was designed to close loopholes which had been pointed out by the Justice Department and the Supreme Court in the *Price* and *Guest* cases of 1966.[30]

The new Section 245 made it a federal crime for any individual, whether acting under authority of law or not, to interfere with the right to vote or the right to participate in any activity administered by the United States government or under federal financial assistance. The act also made it a crime to interfere with anyone engaged in interstate commerce during a riot. The punishment for violators was a one thousand dollar fine or imprisonment for one year, or both; if bodily injury resulted, the fine was increased to ten thousand dollars or a prison sentence of not more than ten years, or both; and if death resulted, the punishment could be a term of years or life imprisonment. The penalties under Sections 241 through 244 were similarly increased. The impact of these changes was significant. Previously, the killers of Chaney, Goodman, and Schwerner, Mrs. Viola Liuzzo, and the three blacks in the Algiers Motel incident, if successfully convicted under federal law, could only be subjected to short prison sentences. Now, in cases involving civil rights, life imprisonment was a possible punishment for murder, even when a state refused prosecution. The section on injury to persons in interstate commerce during a riot was intended to provide a basis for prosecuting looters and rioters who attacked businessmen on the grounds that such business was federally protected and secured.[31]

The majority of the Senate committee that conceived the bill indicated that the measure was directed against brutal acts of violence done to blacks and whites, such as the Chaney-Goodman-Schwerner incident, and allowed the government to prosecute offenders without the necessity of proving a conspiracy when states failed to act. Its scope was based on the Fourteenth Amendment and the Commerce Clause of the Constitution. The minority on the Senate committee, consisting of Sam Ervin, George Smathers, Everett Dirksen, and Roman Hruska, ignoring the black protection theory of the Fourteenth Amendment, complained that the act was not in the American tradition, since it referred to acts done to people on account of race or color. Apparently oblivious to the violence perpetrated against blacks without state protection for 179 years, they asserted that there was no evidence that states had refused to provide protection for their citizens. Eastland of Mississippi and Thurmond of South Carolina filed a separate report in which they articulated the new tactics of the southern conservatives in the light of recent northern riots; they asserted that the bill would protect roving "fomentors of violence," such as Carmichael and Brown. Eastland offered an example: if Rap Brown, while making a speech, was yelled at and hit by a white man, the white man could be convicted of interfering with Brown's constitutional rights, while Brown would not be guilty of any violation. In Eastland's opinion, there was no reason for Brown not to be hit while making speeches.[32]

While the passage of the Fair Housing Act and Section 245 seemed to be a high-water mark at the end of the brief black protection-civil-rights era of the black liberation movement, at least one part of the legislation could be used to suppress black militancy. The Nixon administration considered using Section 245 to obtain injunctions against black and white radicals who used disruptive tactics to gain their objectives. Black students bent on making demands that universities offer them relevance and power in the academic community could find themselves proscribed by an act intended to protect them. White radicals, apparently incensed by the Vietnamese war and the military industrial complex, could find themselves in the same predicament. If the administration did act under Section 245, it would mean that the administration found suppressing students "in the public interest" as required by the terms of the bill.[33]

In the spring of 1969, Congress had its attention more and more drawn to the Students for a Democratic Society (SDS) and such groups as the Black Panthers and the Revolutionary Action Movement (Ram). The congressional attitude seemed to be that either there were no inequities that could generate radical liberation efforts, or that even if such inequities did exist, the oppressed could not possibly consider revolutionary action unless some group or individual encouraged them. The groups or individuals responsible must be communist-backed or actual communists. The Nixon Republicans, elected on a law and order platform in the midst of growing black militancy, with no debt to the white radicals and blacks who voted against them, took the same kind of repressive stance. The government responded to militancy in the traditional ways. The House Un-American Activities Committee (HUAC) continued its thorough investigation of subversive influences in riots, looting, and burnings begun after the riots in 1967. The committee heard a variety of testimony which was used to place the blame for the riots on communist influence: words of admiration for revolutionists such as Che Guevara; comments about the necessity for people to attain freedom by any means necessary; statements which expressed the refusal to discountenance violence; the enumeration of trips to communist countries; and comments by communists in support of riots.[34]

In 1968 and 1969, Senator John McClellan's permanent investigation subcommittee investigated the same organizations HUAC had probed but this time, the Black Panthers and the SDS drew more attention. McClellan stated that a year-long study by his investigators indicated that there was an anarchistic movement, operating under different labels, which was dedicated to the objective of overthrowing the government. Vice President Spiro Agnew aided the governmental effort by sending the committee a copy of coloring books reportedly circulated to black children, depicting white policemen and merchants as "pigs" and urging black children to "off" (kill) them. The Panthers had organized a "feed breakfast to the children" program across the country for ghetto children and, according to the committee, were preaching violence as part of the program. Panther Chairman Bobby Seale said the coloring book was unauthorized and that they had taken it out of circulation after only twenty-five copies were printed. Seale took this opportunity to state that Larry Powell, a star witness at the committee hearings who said he had been a Panther and who had charged the group with conducting robberies and having venal leadership, was a paid government agent who joined the group for the express purpose of finding a means to undermine its image with the people. While the committee determined what legislation was needed to suppress such groups, a Catholic priest in whose church some of the books had reportedly been circulated said he did not permit the distribution of the books, but in a society where "the only good Indian was a dead Indian" and "the only good nigger was a dead nigger," he was not alarmed when the victims of police brutality said "the only good pig was a dead pig." [35]

In late 1969 and 1970, attacks on policemen continued. These assaults were usually attributed to urban guerillas, including the Black Panthers, even when there was no evidence of their complicity. In 1969, eighty-six policemen were reported killed, a thirty-four percent increase over the casualties of 1968, and by mid-October 1970, sixty-seven were reported killed, sixteen of them murdered in allegedly unprovoked attacks. In each case, investigations were made and charges were brought against alleged attackers. Congress responded predictably to these events. Hearings were held by the Senate Internal Security Subcommittee chaired by Senator Eastland. Law enforcement officials testified to threats and attacks made on policemen, and the committee proposed the passage of a federal law, based on the Commerce Clause of the Constitution, which would make the murder of a policeman a federal crime.[36]

Many members of black revolutionary groups, particularly the Black Panthers, were killed or injured in confrontations with policemen in late 1969 and 1970. On 4 December 1969, two Panthers, Mark Clark and Fred Hampton, were killed in a police assault on the Chicago Panther Headquarters. A county coroner's jury ruled that the slayings were justifiable homicide in January 1970. A federal grand jury reported in May 1970 that the police fired eighty-three shots into the apartment while only one shot was fired toward the police. The grand jury, however, did not believe there was enough evidence to sustain the indictment of any of the police for violating the civil rights of the victims under the same statute used in the *Price* and *Guest* cases.[37] In addition, the Black Panthers' attorney, Charles Garry, claimed that twelve members of the organization had been killed unnecessarily by policemen between March 1968 and 21 December 1969. In each case cited by Garry the police indicated that the murders were justifiable.[38]

Aside from reported attacks on individual police officers, there was at least one black revolutionary action against the court system in the late summer of 1970. In August, Jonathan Jackson, a seventeen-year-old Black Panther carried weapons into the Marin County courthouse in San Rafael, California, tossed them to three black prisoners who were awaiting trial, and set off a kidnapping and shooting incident which led to the murder of Judge

Harold Haley, Jackson, and two of the prisoners. Two of the weapons were found to be registered in the name of Angela Davis, a twenty-five-year-old former philosophy professor at UCLA and an avowed Communist. The FBI started a nationwide manhunt for Miss Davis who was charged with kidnapping and homicide, even though she was not present when the incident took place. Under California law, if Miss Davis had given the guns to Jackson to be used in the slaying, she would be guilty of the actual crime.[39]

In addition to the tensions generated by the conflict between black revolutionaries and the police, serious confrontations between black and white servicemen became more evident in military bases around the world and in training camps in the United States. In July 1969, a brawl between black, Puerto Rican, and white marines resulted in the death of one white marine and the serious injury of another. Eleven black marines were charged with rioting. After this incident became publicized, the Defense Department began releasing information concerning the continuing disturbances and rioting between blacks and whites in Vietnam and on military bases in Europe. Out of this information grew widespread speculation over the ability of the military forces to successfully suppress racial disturbances when the military itself was torn by racial strife. Since the enforcement of the entire legal system of the United States ultimately depends on military suppression, the national government could be rendered powerless in widespread racial disturbances if the military should be found ineffective.[40]

Between 1965 and 1970, the "We Shall Overcome" principles of the Black Liberation movement were merged with, and in some cases, overwhelmed by an increased emphasis on violence as a tactic and strategy. Where the Kennedy administration had been forced by the movement to use federal military power to protect blacks within the framework of constitutional law, the Johnson and Nixon administrations found themselves using governmental power against blacks, who seemed to be law violators. Liberals in Congress who had fought for civil rights bills with great moral fervor were dismayed. While they supported the War on Poverty as one solution to ghetto ills, their programs lacked not only the breadth to adequately deal with the problem but the imagination to insure their success. Liberals were inundated by the law-and-order protagonists, led by the conservative southerners who were pleased to be able to say, "I told you so." Meanwhile, militant blacks, in unvarnished rhetoric, demanded economic and social revolution, making it clear that they did not believe America had the capacity to reform itself, as racism was fundamental in American life, in its foreign policies, and in its profit system. The response of the federal government, reflecting the administration's conservative position, seemed to be that police and military power would be used to suppress those who refused to submit to the system, a position which required no real alteration in constitutional theory; the techniques for instituting local and federal suppression of rebellion and disorder had always been in the Constitution and had always been effectively utilized when considered necessary.

Conservatives and black militants, as well as white radicals, seemed to have come full circle and all reached the same conclusions. Militants and radicals asserted that the Constitution was a property-minded instrument which failed to provide equality and justice for the masses; therefore, they wanted to change or subvert it. Conservatives agreed with them about the nature of the Constitution, but asserted that such change was undesirable and that militant efforts to "radicalize" the framework of government would be suppressed. The only voices not effectively being heard were those of the moderates and liberals who were left with the unpleasant and difficult task of proving that economic and social justice were constitutionally possible and that military suppression was undesirable and inexpedient. The future course of black revolution depends, in part, on the solutions they find.

NOTES

1. Robert F. Williams, *Negroes With Guns* (New York, 1962); Julian Mayfield, "Challenge to Negro Leadership," *Commentary* 31 (April 1961), pp. 297–305; NAACP, "The Robert F. Williams Case," *Crisis*

46 (June, July, August, September 1959), pp. 325–9; 409–10; Elliott Rudwick and August Meier, "Negro Retaliatory Violence in the Twentieth Century," *New Politics* 5 (Winter 1966), p. 42—the same article is reprinted in Rudwick and Meier, eds., *The Making of Black America, Essays in Negro Life and History,* 2 vols. (New York, 1969), pp. 407–17, and in Staff Report of the National Commission on the Causes and Prevention of Violence 3, *Violence in American Historical and Comparative Perspectives* (Washington, 1969), pp. 307–16; The North Carolina Supreme Court voided indictments against four blacks charged with Williams in the alleged kidnapping of 1961. Williams is fighting extradition from Michigan to North Carolina. *Detroit Free Press,* 2 November 1969, p. 3a, 21 November, p. 4.

2. C. Eric Lincoln, *Black Muslims in America* (Boston, 1961), Malcolm X, *The Autobiography of Malcolm X* (New York, 1964, paperback ed., 1966), pp. 237–44.

3. *New York Times,* 17, 27 July 1964, p. 7; 27 September 1964, p. 81; Arthur Waskow, *From Race Riot to Sit-in—1919 to the 1960's* (New York, 1960), pp. 255–60. *U.S. National Advisory Commission on Civil Disorders Report* (Washington, 1968), pp. 19–20 (hereafter cited as Kerner Report). U.S., *Public Papers of the Presidents, Lyndon B. Johnson, July 1—December 31, 1964,* p. 938.

4. *New York Times,* 30 September and 1 October 1964, p. 1.

5. *New York Times,* 13–15 August 1965, p. 1; Governor's Commission on the Los Angeles Riots, *Violence in the City: An End or a Beginning* (Los Angeles, 1965).

6. *Congressional Record,* 89th cong., 1st sess. (1965), pp. 20518, 20610, 20625, 20681, 21372, 22046, 20560–7, 20672, 20825.

7. *Congressional Record,* 89th cong., 1st sess. (1965), pp. 20488–9, 20490, 20793.

8. Ibid., pp. 20754–6.

9. Ibid., pp. 14765, 20825; 89th cong., 2nd sess. (1966), pp. 16764–6.

10. *Congressional Record,* 89th cong., 2nd sess. (1966), pp. 17652, 17654, 17659, 17669.

11. *Kerner Report,* pp. 21–47.

12. Ibid., pp. 47–61; *New York Times,* 24–9 July 1967, p. 1; 30 July, p. 52; 31 July, p. 17; 1 August, p. 17; 2 August, p. 16; *Detroit Free Press,* 24–30 July 1967, p. 1; at that time Hubert Locke, administrative assistant to Police Chief Girardin, said that troops were in fact needed immediately since there were never more than eleven hundred police-

men on the street during the riot. Interview on WJR Detroit, "Focus," 12 November 1969.

13. *Detroit Free Press,* 26 July 1967, p. 1; Allen Sultan and Richard Howard, in "The Efficient Use of Military Forces to Control Riots, Some Proposals for Congressional Action," *Journal of Urban Law* 45 (1968), p. 847, points out that standard insurance policies also included riots and civil commotions, a statement which could lead one to question the justification given by the governor for not calling for federal troops at an earlier time.

14. *Detroit Free Press,* 25 July 1967, p. 1.

15. *Detroit Free Press,* 26 July 1967, pp. 1a, 10a.

16. Ibid., 30 July 1967, pp. 1b, 4a; 25 July, p. 2a; *New York Times,* 26 July 1967, p. 38; 30 July, p. 1.

17. *Luther v. Borden,* 7 How. 1 (1849); Sultan and Howard, "Efficient Use of Forces," p. 861; 32 *Fed. Reg.* 10905, 10907 (1967). *See* sections of *U.S. Code* in Appendix and *Martin v. Mott,* 12 Wheat 19 (1827) for affirmation of president's power to decide when to use troops. A conversation with Ramsey Clark while he was chatting informally with a group of law students in Ann Arbor, Michigan on 18 September 1969 confirmed my analysis of the administration's behavior during the riot.

18. *Sen. Doc.* 209, 57th cong., 2nd sess. (1903), p. 256; U.S. Civil Rights Commission, *Law Enforcement: A Report on Equal Protection in the South* (Washington, 1965), pp. 150–4.

19. *Congressional Record,* 90th cong., 1st sess. (1967), pp. 21391–7; Ramsey Clark's Press Conference, pp. 21393–6; Romney's Telegram of 24 July 1967 to the President, p. 21396; Ruthanne Gartland and Richard Chikota, "When Will the Troops Come Marching In?": A Comment on the Historical Use of Federal Troops to Quell Domestic Violence, *Journal of Urban Law,* 45 (1968), p. 881, ignore Romney's refusal to allege that there was either domestic violence or an insurrection in pressing the argument that the president should have accepted an averment of domestic violence.

20. *Congressional Record,* 90th cong., 1st sess. (1967), daily edition, H9256–9.

21. Ibid., pp. S10854–9.

22. *Kerner Report,* p. 59; John Hersey, *The Algiers Motel Incident* (New York, 1968); *New York Times,* 15 June 1969; *Detroit Free Press,* 26 February 1970, p. 1.

23. Ben W. Gilbert, *Ten Blocks from the White House* (New York,

1968); Staff Report, National Commission on Causes and Prevention of Violence 2, *Violence in America: Historical and Comparative Perspectives*, p. 330; as example of army proposals, *see* Army FM 119–15; *Civil Disturbances and Disasters* (March 1968); *see* also *Detroit Free Press*, 9 July 1969, p. 6d on the unveiling of an enlarged fully manned operations center; *see also* sections of *U.S. Code* in Appendix.

24. Staff Report, National Commission on the Prevention and Causes of Violence 2, *The Politics of Protest, Violent Aspects of Protest and Confrontation*, p. 128, quoting from Lemberg Center for the Study of Violence, *Riot Data Review* 2 (Waltham, Mass., 1968), p. 60; Army FM 19–15 (1968).

25. Violence Commission, *Staff Report*, 2:128; 2:332. When three Negro college students were killed by state troopers during a South Carolina State College protest against segregation in a local Orangeburg bowling alley, state officials refused to bring charges. Attorney General Ramsey Clark attempted to obtain prosecution for a civil rights violation under Sections 241 and 242, but a grand jury refused to indict. Clark believed the policemen were literally getting away with murder. *New York Times*, 10 February 1968, p. 23; 9 November 1969, p. 25; Conversation with Ramsey Clark, see fn. 18 this chapter. *See also* Jack Nelson and Jack Bass, *The Orangeburg Massacre* (New York, 1970).

26. Violence Commission, *Staff Report*, 2:129; Lemberg Center, *Riot Data Review* 3 (Waltham, Mass., February 1969), pp. 1–38; *New York Times*, 24 July 1968, p. 1; 13 September, p. 1; 20 September, p. 37; 13 March 1969, p. 22; 29 May, p. 1; *St. Louis Post Dispatch*, 12 September 1968; Civil Violence Research Center, Case Western Reserve Univ., National Commission on Prevention and Causes of Violence, *Shoot-Out in Cleveland, Black Militants and the Police, July 23, 1968* (Washington, 1969).

27. *New York Times*, 15 June 1969, p. 40; 6 July, pp. 1, 30; *Detroit Free Press*, 1 July 1969, p. 1; 12 July, p. 10a; *Newsweek*, 7 July 1969, p. 19, *New York Times*, 6 September 1970, p. 1.

28. Title 18, *U.S. Code*, chap. 102, *Riots* (1968), *see* section of *U.S. Code* in Appendix. The Riot Control Act received its first court test in the trial of eight defendants for allegedly conspiring to incite the riots that erupted during the Democratic Convention in Chicago, 1968. Bobby Seale, National Chairman of the Black Panther Party, was indicted along with seven white radicals. Seale was gagged and shackled to his chair in the courtroom to prevent his outcries and protests over not having preferred counsel. Seale was finally adjudged guilty on sixteen counts of contempt and sentenced to four years imprisonment by the judge sitting without a jury. The seven whites, also indicted for violat-

ing Section 231 of the *U.S. Code* by teaching persons techniques of resisting and obstructing the police were found innocent of both charges but were convicted of contempt of court at the trial. Appeals are pending; *Detroit Free Press*, 30 October 1969, pp. 1a, 4a; 5 November 1969, p. 16; 20 November 1969, p. 20b; U.S., District of Illinois, Eastern Division, *United States v. David Dellinger, Rennard Davis, Thomas Hayden, Abbott Hoffman, Jerry Rubin, Lee Weiner, John Froines, Bobby Seale,* Indictment No. 69CR180 (1969).

29. *Congressional Record*, 90th cong., 1st sess. (1968), pp. 19347–19433.

30. Title 42, *U.S. Code* 3601 (1968), 82 *Stat* 81; *see* sections of *U.S. Code* in Appendix.

31. 18 *U.S. Code* 241–5 (1968); see sections of *U.S. Code* in Appendix.

32. 2 *U.S. Code, Congressional and Administrative News, 1837–1854* (1968), *Senate Report* 721 (1968).

33. 245 *U.S. Code* (1968), *see* sections of *U.S. Code* in Appendix. *New York Times,* 21 May 1969, pp. 1, 28.

34. *Hearings Before House Un-American Activities Committee,* 90th cong., 1st sess., *Subversive Influences in Rioting and Looting and Burning,* 6 pts. (1969).

35. *Detroit Free Press,* 27 June 1969, pp. 10, 13; *New York Times,* 15 June 1969, p. 57; *CBS Evening News,* 25 June 1969; *San Francisco Chronicle,* 25 June 1969, pp. 1, 10.

36. *New York Times,* 19 July 1970, p. 50; 6 September, p. 3e; 11 October, p. 4e; 20 September, p. 60; *Los Angeles Times,* 19 July 1970, p. 3; *Washington Post,* 1 September 1970, p. 3; 27 October, p. 2. These are examples of alleged attacks on police by revolutionaries. If one follows these reported attacks, he will find investigation and prosecution certain and conviction practically assured.

37. *Detroit Free Press,* 5 December 1969, p. 1a; 21 December, p. 1a; 16 May 1970, p. 1a.

38. *New York Times,* 21 December 1969, p. 47.

39. *Los Angeles Times,* 8, 13, 14, 17 August, 1970; *New York Times,* 13 October 1970, p. 1.

40. *New York Times,* 10 August 1969, pp. 1, 67; 31 December, p. 44; *Detroit Free Press,* 1 December 1969, p. 12b (from *New York Times*); *Los Angeles Times,* 3 October 1967, p. 7.

16 / Still

the "Disquieting" Presence

White oppression and black resistance has been a persistent part of the American scene since the colonial period. The response of the government in its effort to suppress racial disorder has reflected the tension between the lofty ideals expressed in the documents on which constitutional government is based and the tendency of the white majority to desire summary disposition of those they regard as unpopular, unlovely, hateful, or powerless. The predilection of the white majority to suppress efforts by black people to acquire real freedom and equality in America (as black *people,* not as single individuals who may achieve some recognition of the rights), even when white repression means resorting to illegal violence and brutality, has added to that tension. Black people have not been, of course, the only oppressed group in American society—the labor movement, Mexican-Americans, Indians, Mormons, and white radicals have experienced suppression. The black experience is unique because black people have been oppressed from the day they first set foot on English–American soil. The American government and people have persistently defended the repression of blacks in the name of law and order, without admitting that the Constitution was designed and has been interpreted to maintain the racial status quo. Racism, the promotion of white nationalism, is the primary reason why black people have served as the mudsills of American society. The need to respect constitutional government has been so twisted and perverted in the name of this objective that it is no wonder that its victims see beyond the fiction and regard law and order as a mere instrument for their repression.

Racial tensions and the rationalization for the justification of suppression originated in the theory and practice of law developed before the Civil War. The constitutional history of military power, as it relates to rebellion and black-white relations in the United States, indicates that the use of troops and the threat of force have always been of major importance. In the antebellum period, the willingness to use force against blacks, in large measure, effectively prevented widespread slave revolts. The United States used the regular army to return slaves to their masters, to execute a twenty-year war against blacks and Indians in Florida, and to keep the slaves in "awe" with the strategic stationing of troops. On the other hand, the government refused to oppose the suppression of the civil liberties of antislavery activists. Dominated by southerners and "doughfaces," the executive branch of the government ignored the mobbings and beatings of abolitionists, even when state officials were among the perpetrators. The national government chose to interpret its powers in such a way as to weaken and inhibit the development of the antislavery movement and later the Black Liberation movement. This inaction was another phase of legal racism.

At the beginning of the Civil War, the behavior of the Union government reinforces the view that the emancipation of slaves was not among the Union's war aims. Troops, in fact, protected and defended slaveholders, as they had done before the war. Although the Union was forced to issue the final Emancipation Proclamation, the fact that the proclamation was only a war measure made it still uncertain whether there was a national will to end the use of military power to suppress the newly-freed blacks.

Because military power was not used effectively to protect blacks and suppress white violators, even during Reconstruction, the status of black people remained in doubt. One indication of this continuing doubt was that the government was still unwilling to use force against white people for the injury or murder of blacks. However, after Reconstruction, the intentions of the government in cases of black-white confrontations and racial violence became somewhat clearer. From 1877 to 1957, federal troops or marshals were not used to prevent pre-advertised lynchings or other kinds of violence directed against black people when states refused them protection. The government's oft-asserted declaration that it lacked the power to intervene was based more on disinterest than on statutory or constitutional incapacity. Even though blacks were nominally free, the government was unsure about the extent of that status and uninterested in insuring blacks the opportunity to achieve the freedoms granted the American whites. On the other hand, the national government's pattern of inaction in cases of white violence against blacks indicated its certainty about the status of white people and its unwillingness to punish whites for murdering and assaulting blacks.

These conclusions were reinforced when, between 1957 and 1965, national power was used to enforce court orders and protect blacks from racial violence. It now became clear that the problem had not really been a constitutional one after all; the Constitution had merely been interpreted to support the disinclination of whites to regard blacks as persons. This interpretative behavior can be readily understood if one recognizes that white Americans, like people elsewhere, have historically demonstrated the human capacity to rationalize what is merely expedient into what is legally necessary.

The use of troops to suppress black riots and rebellions after 1964 was a return to the policy utilized before the Civil War. Federal force was used to defend white persons and property from blacks when state forces were inadequate or when states requested federal help. In such cases, black rioters and rebels were in the same position as slaves who attempted to revolt before 1965. They were outside the law, and federal military force has always been used to enforce the "law," whether it was the law of slavery, segregation, or disfranchisement.

The reflex action of the national government to black requests for federal action to aid in the improvement of their economic and social condition has always been token measures or assertions that no problem exists. If these tactics failed and black people persisted too vigorously, then force and suppression were used. If the slave experience is any indicator, a serious dislocation of American society might be necessary before the institutional response is changed. Also, if the failure of the economic promises of Reconstruction is relevant, satisfactory improvement in the conditions and status of blacks so as to remove the factors that give rise to riots and rebellion will be a long time in coming.

From 1789 through 1970, governmental action in response to the problem of black-white violence and black rebellion has been slow and uneven until some great cataclysm threatening white people has occurred. While white America and the government generally vacillated on the issue, black advances have been met with repression. And repression has proceeded in the guise of constitutionalism, despite the fact that the Constitution is much more flexible than those who hide behind its provisions will admit. Further, no concerted effort has been made to fully utilize its person-oriented and general welfare provisions to remove the economic and social causes of black rebellion.

Additionally, the government has demonstrated a lack of imagination in eradicating the racial prejudice which undergirds the constitutional suppression of black people. If blacks are to be a part of American society, the removal of racism should have the highest priority. Although racism may not be erased by legislation, educational techniques, even-handed justice, and black self-determination as positive government programs might prove effective. Since Americans are apparently enamored of the profit motive, perhaps a government policy for paying grants or giving tax credits to people and programs designed to end racial antagonism might be useful. Even if these ideas seem utopian, one superficial indicator of prejudice—continued racial violence—is amenable to solution. The enforcement of laws designed to make contact between whites and blacks less abrasive and a willingness on the part of the government to respond as quickly when blacks are the victims as when the persons or property of white people are at stake would be a good beginning.

This study also supports the view that the government allocates military power, as everything else, to defend those who are its friends and to injure those who are its enemies. Unfortunately, blacks in general and militants in particular have always been regarded as enemies. So long as the government possesses a virtual monopoly of military power, is unencumbered by widespread internal disorder, such as that which occurred during the Civil War, and remains able to cope with its enemies at home and abroad, white Americans apparently see no need to deal seriously with the factors which cause black rebellion. If real black revolution comes, it will result from this failure of the larger society to come quickly to an acceptable determination of the status of black people and to use the Constitution to effect needed social, economic, and political reform.

Bibliographical Note

All sources utilized are sufficiently described in the footnotes to enable scholars or students to consult them. However, brief mention of some of the most useful materials might be helpful.

MANUSCRIPTS AND PRIMARY DOCUMENTS

Of the manuscript collections consulted, letters received and sent in the Justice Department Record Group 60 were most informative both for governmental policy and for the grievances of black people. Correspondence on the subject of lynchings, mobbings, racial violence, and requests for federal aid was forwarded to the Justice Department by the president and other officials in the executive and congressional branches of the government. Also, many letters were sent to the Justice Department directly. War

Department records and files in the National Archives were most useful for the period of an actual riot or major disturbance. Typescript from manuscript records for most of the earlier disturbances are collected in the Glasser File of the Justice Department Records. Unfortunately, letters received and sent for the period after 1942 are closed to the scholar, and permission could not be obtained to examine them despite the Freedom of Information Act. (Letters from Richard G. Kleindienst, Deputy Attorney General, to M. F. Berry.)

Public documents such as the *Annals of Congress* (1789–1824), *The Register of Debates in Congress* (1824–37), *The Congressional Globe* (1833–73), and the *Congressional Record* (1873–) were relied upon for official congressional response to racial disorder, comment upon the president's power to intervene in domestic crises, and for the development of legislation on the subject. These same materials also contain many of the proclamations and orders issued by the president for the earlier period, which are most readily found in the *Federal Register* after 1936. House and Senate *Documents* and *Reports* on investigations contain a wealth of material on lynchings, mobbings, riots, and murder. These sources were particularly useful for the section on the Seminole War as a black freedom movement.

The opinions of the Supreme Court, published in *United States Reports,* of the courts of appeal, published in the *Federal Reporter,* and the federal district courts, published in the *Federal Supplement,* were used to ascertain when and how the judicial process was brought to bear on the perpetrators of racial violence. In a few cases, court opinions shed some light on the extent of the president's powers in cases of domestic disorder.

In the executive field, the *Messages and Papers of the Presidents* made important materials accessible through the administration of Woodrow Wilson. There is a gap in the series from Wilson to the administration of Franklin D. Roosevelt when commercial publishers began publication of *Public Papers and Addresses* of succeeding Presidents. For the period after 1936, most official executive materials on the topic under consideration were found in the *Federal Register.*

NEWSPAPERS AND PERIODICALS

Although one can find some information on official practices in the newspapers of particular communities at the time of a racial incident, such as the *Detroit Free Press* during the 1943 and 1967 riots, the issues of governmental practice and power are usually not given much attention. After the *New York Times* began publication in 1851, it increasingly became the best newspaper for the kind of information required for this study. It usually contained summaries of official statements and an analysis of policy, followed by interviews with governmental spokesmen.

GENERAL STUDIES AND SECONDARY ACCOUNTS

There is no one book or article on this subject. However, the facts of some disturbances can be found in monographs cited in the footnotes. I found Bennett Rich, *The Presidents and Civil Disorder* (1941) a useful constitutional analysis, although it contains only a footnote on the subject of racial domestic disorder. Frederick T. Wilson, "Federal Aid in Domestic Disturbances," *Senate Document* 209 (1903), contains significant information for the period before its publication. Robert K. Carr, in *Federal Protection: The Quest for a Sword* (1947), succinctly describes the unsuccessful attempt to use the federal criminal code to punish the perpetrators of racial violence after the Civil Rights Section was set up in the Justice Department in 1939. Richard Bardolph, ed., *The Civil Rights Record: Black Americans and the Law, 1849–1970* (New York, 1970) is a useful documentary collection. Allen D. Grimshaw, ed., *Racial Violence in the United States* (Chicago, 1969) contains some interesting sociological essays.

Arthur Waskow, *From Race Riot to Sit-In, 1919 and the 1960's* (1966), which is based almost completely on NAACP files, was useful for looking at the bloody confrontations of 1919 and the nonviolent movement before 1965 from the point of view of the NAACP. Individual riot studies, such as James L. Crouthamel, "The Springfield Race Riot of 1908," *The Journal of Negro History* 44 (1960), pp. 164–81; Edgar Schouler, "The Houston Race Riot, 1917," *The Journal of Negro History* 29 (1944); Elliot M. Rudwick, *Race Riot at East St. Louis, July 2, 1917* (1964); Alfred McClung Lee and Norman D. Humphrey, *Race Riot* (Detroit, 1943); Robert Shogan and Tom Craig, *The Detroit Race Riot: A Study in Violence* (1943); and Ben W. Gilbert, *Ten Blocks from the White House* (Washington, 1968), were relied upon heavily for the chronology of events during these disturbances. John D. Weaver, *The Brownsville Raid* (New York, 1970) and William M. Tuttle, Jr., *Race Riot: Chicago in the Red Summer of 1919* (New York, 1970) are recent treatments of these two disturbances.

Every major disorder brought forth official state or national commission studies. The most informative ones were the Chicago Commission on Race Relations Study of the 1919 riot and the Kerner Commission on the riots in the 1960s.

Appendix:
Excerpts from
the *United States Code*

TITLE 10, CHAPTER 15—INSURRECTION

§ 331—Federal Aid for State Governments

Whenever there is an insurrection in any State against its government, the President may, upon the request of its legislature or of its governor if the legislature cannot be convened, call into Federal service such of the militia of the other States, in the number requested by that State, and use such of the armed forces, as he considers necessary to suppress the insurrection. [*Earlier Laws*—Acts February 28, 1795, c. 36; 1, 1 Stat. 424; March 3, 1807, c. 39, 2 Stat. 413, RS. 5297]

§ 332—Use of Militia and Armed Forces to Enforce Federal Authority

Whenever the President considers that unlawful obstructions, combinations, or assemblages, or rebellion against the authority of the United States, make it impracticable to enforce the laws of the United

States in any State or Territory by the ordinary course of judicial proceedings, he may call into Federal service such of the militia of any State, and use such of the armed forces, as he considers necessary to enforce those laws or to suppress the rebellion. [*Earlier Laws*—Act July 29, 1861, c. 25; 1, 12 Stat. 281, RS. 5298]

§ 333—Interference with State and Federal Law

The President, by using the militia or the armed forces, or both, or by any other means, shall take such measures as he considers necessary to suppress, in a State, any insurrection, domestic violence, unlawful combination, or conspiracy, if it—

(1) so hinders the execution of the laws of that State, and of the United States within the State, that any part or class of its people is deprived of a right, privilege, immunity or protection named in the Constitution and secured by law, and the constituted authorities of that State are unable, fail, or refuse to protect that right, privilege, or immunity, or to give that protection; or

(2) opposes or obstructs the execution of the laws of the United States or impedes the course of justice under those laws.

In any situation covered by clause (1), the State shall be considered to have denied the equal protection of the laws secured by the Constitution. [*Earlier Laws*—Act April 20, 1871, c. 22; 3, 17 Stat. 14, RS. 5299]

§ 334—Proclamation to Disperse

Whenever the President considers it necessary to use the militia or the armed forces under this chapter, he shall, by proclamation, immediately order the insurgents to disperse and retire peaceably to their abodes within a limited time. [*Earlier Laws*—Act July 29, 1861, c. 25; 2, 12 Stat. 282, RS. 5300]

TITLE 18, CHAPTER 13—CIVIL RIGHTS

§ 241—Conspiracy Against Rights of Citizens

If two or more persons conspire to injure, oppress, threaten, or intimidate any citizen in the free exercise or enjoyment of any right or privilege secured to him by the Constitution or laws of the United States, or because of his having so exercised the same; or

If two or more persons go in disguise on the highway, or on the premises of another, with intent to prevent or hinder his free exercise or enjoyment of any right or privilege so secured—

They shall be fined not more than $10,000 or imprisoned not more than ten years, or both; and if death results, they shall be subject to imprisonment for any term of years or for life. June 25, 1948, c. 645, 62 Stat. 696; April 11, 1968, Pub. L. 90–284; Title I; 103(a), 82 Stat. 75.

§ 242—Deprivation of Rights Under Color of Law

Whoever, under color of any law, statute, ordinance, regulation or custom, willfully subjects any inhabitant of any State, Territory or District to the deprivation of any rights, privileges, or immunities secured or protected by the Constitution or laws of the United States, or to different punishments, pains, or penalties, on account of such inhabitant being an alien, or by reason of his color, or race than are prescribed for the punishment of citizens, shall be fined not more than $1,000 or imprisoned not more than one year, or both; and if death results shall be subject to imprisonment for any term of years or for life. June 25, 1948, c. 645, 62 Stat. 696; April 11, 1968, Pub. L. 90–284, Title I, 103(b), 82 Stat. 75.

§ 245—Federally Protected Activities

(a) (1) Nothing in this section shall be construed as indicating an intent on the part of Congress to prevent any State, any possession or Commonwealth of the United States, or the District of Columbia, from exercising jurisdiction over any offense over which it would have jurisdiction in the absence of this section, nor shall anything in this section be construed as depriving State and local law enforcement authorities of responsibility for prosecuting acts that may be violations of this section and that are violations of State and local law. No prosecution of any offense described in this section shall be undertaken by the United States except upon the certification in writing of the Attorney General or the Deputy Attorney General that in his judgment a prosecution by the United States is in the public interest and necessary to secure substantial justice, which function of certification may not be delegated.

(2) Nothing in this subsection shall be construed to limit the authority of Federal officers, or a Federal grand jury, to investigate possible violations of this section.

(b) Whoever, whether or not acting under color of law, by force or threat of force willfully injures, intimidates or interferes with, or attempts to injure, intimidate or interfere with—

    (1) any person because he is or has been, or in order to intimidate such person or any other person or any class of persons from—

        (A) voting or qualifying to vote, qualifying or campaigning as a candidate for elective office, or qualifying or acting as a poll watcher, or any legally authorized election official, in any primary, special, or general election;

        (B) participating in or enjoying any benefit, service, privilege, program, facility, or activity provided or administered by the United States;

        (C) applying for or enjoying employment, or any perquisite thereof, by any agency of the United States;

        (D) serving, or attending upon any court in connection with possible service, as a grand or petit juror in any court of the United States;

        (E) participating in or enjoying the benefits of any program or activity receiving Federal financial assistance; or

    (2) any person because of his race, color, religion or national origin and because he is or has been—

        (A) enrolling in or attending any public school or public college;

        (B) participating in or enjoying any benefit, service, privilege, program, facility or activity provided or administered by any State or subdivision thereof;

        (C) applying for or enjoying employment, or any perquisite thereof, by any private employer or any agency of any State or subdivision thereof, or joining or using the services or advantages of any labor organization, hiring hall, or employment agency;

        (D) serving, or attending upon any court of any State in connection with possible service, as a grand or petit juror,

        (E) traveling in or using any facility of interstate commerce, or using any vehicle, terminal, or facility of any common carrier by motor, rail, water, or air;

(F) enjoying the goods, services, facilities, privileges, advantages, or accommodations of any inn, hotel, motel, or other establishment which provides lodging to transient guests, or of any restaurant, cafeteria, lunchroom, lunch counter, soda fountain, or other facility which serves the public and which is principally engaged in selling food or beverages for consumption, on the premises, or of any gasoline station, or of any motion picture house, theater, concert hall, sports arena, stadium, or any other place of exhibition or entertainment which serves the public and (i) which is located within the premises of any of the aforesaid establishments or within the premises of which is physically located any of the aforesaid establishments, and (ii) which holds itself out as serving patrons of such establishments; or

(3) during or incident to a riot or civil disorder, any person engaged in a business in commerce or affecting commerce, including, but not limited to, any person engaged in a business which sells or offers for sale to interstate travelers a substantial portion of the articles, commodities, or services which it sells or where a substantial portion of the articles or commodities which it sells or offers for sale have moved in commerce; or

(4) any person because he is or has been, or in order to intimidate such person or any other person or any class of persons· from—

(A) participating, without discrimination on account of race, color, religion or national origin, in any of the benefits or activities described in subparagraphs (1) (A) through (1) (E) or subparagraphs (2) (A) through (2) (F); or

(B) affording another person or class of persons opportunity or protection to so participate; or

(5) any citizen because he is or has been, or in order to intimidate such citizen or any other citizen from lawfully aiding or encouraging other persons to participate, without discrimination on account of race, color, religion or national origin, in any of the benefits or activities described in subparagraphs (1) (A) through (1) (E) or subparagraphs (2) (A) through (2) (F), or participating lawfully in speech or peaceful assembly

opposing any denial of the opportunity to so participate— shall be fined not more than $1,000, or imprisoned not more than one year, or both; and if bodily injury results shall be fined not more than $10,000, or imprisoned not more than ten years, or both; and if death results shall be subject to imprisonment for any term of years or for life. As used in this section, the term "participating lawfully in speech or peaceful assembly" shall not mean the aiding, abetting, or inciting of other persons to riot or to commit any act of physical violence upon any individual or against any real or personal property in furtherance of a riot. Nothing in subparagraph (2) (F) or (4) (A) of this subsection shall apply to the proprietor of any establishment which provides lodging to transient guests, or to any employee acting on behalf of such proprietor, with respect to the enjoyment of the goods, services, facilities, privileges, advantages, or accommodations of such establishment if such establishment is located within a building which contains not more than five rooms for rent or hire and which is actually occupied by the proprietor as his residence.

(c) Nothing in this section shall be construed so as to deter any law enforcement officer from lawfully carrying out the duties of his office; and no law enforcement officer shall be considered to be in violation of this section for lawfully carrying out the duties of his office or lawfully enforcing ordinances and laws of the United States, the District of Columbia, any of the several States, or any political subdivision of a State. For purposes of the preceding sentence, the term "law enforcement officer" means any officer of the United States, the District of Columbia, a State, or political subdivision of a State, who is empowered by law to conduct investigations of, or make arrests because of, offenses against the United States, the District of Columbia, a State, or a political subdivision of a State.

Added Pub. L. 90–284, Title I; 101(a), April 11, 1968, 82 Stat. 73.

TITLE 18, CHAPTER 102—RIOTS

§ 2101—Riots

(a) (1) Whoever travels in interstate or foreign commerce or uses any facility of interstate or foreign commerce, including, but not limited to, the mail, telegraph, telephone, radio, or television, with intent—

(A) to incite a riot; or

(B) to organize, promote, encourage, participate in, or carry on a riot; or

(C) to commit any act of violence in furtherance of a riot; or

(D) to aid or abet any person in inciting or participating in or carrying on a riot or committing any act of violence in furtherance of a riot;

and who either during the course of any such travel or use or thereafter performs or attempts to perform any other overt act for any purpose specified in subparagraph (A), (B), (C), or (D) of this paragraph—

Shall be fined not more than $10,000, or imprisoned not more than five years, or both.

(b) In any prosecution under this section, proof that a defendant engaged or attempted to engage in one or more of the overt acts described in subparagraph (A), (B), (C), or (D) of paragraph (1) of subsection (a) and (1) has traveled in interstate or foreign commerce, or (2) has use of or used any facility of interstate or foreign commerce, including but not limited to, mail, telegraph, telephone, radio, or television, to communicate with or broadcast to any person or group of persons prior to such overt acts, such travel or use shall be admissible proof to establish that such defendant traveled in or used such facility of interstate or foreign commerce.

(c) A judgment of conviction or acquittal on the merits under the laws of any State shall be a bar to any prosecution hereunder for the same act or acts.

(d) Whenever, in the opinion of the Attorney General or of the appropriate officer of the Department of Justice charged by law or under the instructions of the Attorney General with authority to act, any person shall have violated this chapter, the Department shall proceed as speedily as possible with a prosecution of such person hereunder and with any appeal which may lie from any decision adverse to the Government resulting from such prosecution; or in the alternative shall report in writing, to the respective Houses of the Congress, the Department's reason for not so proceeding.

(e) Nothing contained in this section shall be construed to make it unlawful for any person to travel in, or use any facility of, interstate or foreign commerce for the purpose of pursuing the legitimate objectives of organized labor, through orderly and lawful means.

(f) Nothing in this section shall be construed as indicating an intent on the part of Congress to prevent any State, any possession or Commonwealth of the United States, or the district of Columbia from exercising jurisdiction over any offense over which it would have jurisdiction in the absence of this section; nor shall anything in this section be construed as depriving State and local law enforcement authorities of responsibility for prosecuting acts that may be violations of this section and that are violations of State and local law.

§ 2102—Definitions

(a) As used in this chapter, the term "riot" means a public disturbance involving (1) an act or acts of violence by one or more persons part of an assemblage of three or more persons, which act or acts shall constitute a clear and present danger of, or shall result in damage or injury to the property of any other person or to the person of any other individual or (2) a threat or threats of the commission of an act or acts of violence by one or more persons part of an assemblage of three or more persons having, individually or collectively, the ability of immediate execution of such threat or threats, where the performance of the threatened act or acts of violence would constitute a clear and present danger of, or would result in, damage or injury to the property of any other person or to the person of any other individual.

(b) As used in this chapter, the term "to incite a riot," or to organize, promote, encourage, participate in, or carry on a riot, includes, but is not limited to, urging or instigating other persons to riot, but shall not be deemed to mean the mere oral or written (1) advocacy of ideas or (2) expression of belief, not involving advocacy of any act or acts of violence or assertion of the rightness of, or the right to commit, any such act or acts.

Index

American Railway Union, 114
American Revolution, 4, 5, 37, 38
Americans for Democratic Action. *See* ADA
Andrews, George W., 196
Andry Revolt, 21–2
Anniston (Ala.), 188
Appalachiola Fort Affair, 41–2, 44, 50 n. 15, 16
Appalachiola River, 41, 42
Arbuthnot, Alexander, 43, 44, 59
Arkansas, 100
Armed Settler Bill, 60–1, 66 n. 12
Army. *See* U.S. Army
Arthur, Chester, 108–9
Articles of Confederation, 4, 7, 10, 38
Atlanta (Ga.), 129–31, 215
Atlanta race riot, 129–31
August, Ronald, 220
Aurand, Henry, 166, 167

Baird, Absalom, 96
Baker County (Ga.), 176
Baker, Frazier B., 116
Baker, Newton D., 146, 151, 153, 168
Baltimore (Md.), 221
Banks, Corinne, 161–2
Banks, Nathaniel, 82
Barbour, James, 26
Bard, David, 14
Barnett, Ross, 189, 190–1, 192, 193–4, 196
Barnwell (S.C.), 111–2
Barrancas (Fla.), 43
Barron v. Baltimore, 69
Battle of New Orleans, 41
Beattie, Taylor, 111
Beaumont (Tex.), 164
Bennett, Thomas, 25
Benton, Thomas Hart, 54, 55, 59, 60, 66 n. 12, 75
Biddle, Francis, 169–70
Bill of Attainder, 224
Bill of Rights, 69. See also *Constitution of the United States*

Birmingham (Ala.), 196–9, 218
Black Codes, 92. *See also* Reconstruction
Black, Hugo L., 176, 201
Black Legion, 165
Black liberation movement, 209–30, 236; nonviolent phase of, 209, 210–1, 212, 223; violent phase of, 222–3, 226, 227, 228–9. *See also* Black protest; Black radicalism; Civil rights movement
Black militancy, 222, 223, 226, 230
Black Muslims, 210, 211
Black nationalism, 209, 210
Black Panther Party, 222, 226, 227–8, 233 n. 28
Black power, 209, 214
Black protest, 111, 158; through bus boycott, 180; through civil rights organizations, 110, 118–9, 123, 140, 143, 145, 152–3, 159, 160–1, 162, 177, 178–9, 180, 185; through letters of, to government agencies, 116–7, 130, 143, 160, 161; and marches and mass meetings, 118, 163, 211; and migration, 107–8, 118; and petitioning, 110; through public statements of, 110, 131, 210, 211; and strikes, 111, 223. *See also* Black liberation movement; Civil rights movement, CORE; NAACP; SCLC; UNIA
Black radicalism, 151–2, 158–9
"Black Republicans," 77, 81, 106
Black Seaman's Act, 25
Black Seaman's Controversy, 28, 29
Blackburn, Thorton, 78 n. 6
Blaine, James, 106
Blair bill, 112
Blair, Henry, 112
Boggs, Hale, 219
Bolshevism, 144, 150, 152. *See also* Communism
Boston (Mass.), 72, 74–5
Bourbons, 105
Boutwell, Albert, 198

Bratton, U. S., 149
Brennan, William, 201–2
Brewer, David J., 127
Brewster, Benjamin, 108, 109
Brooke, George, 47
Brotherhood of Sleeping Car Porters and Maids, 161
Brown v. Board of Education, 180, 183, 187. *See also* Civil rights; Education
Brown, H. Rap, 223, 224, 226
Brown, John, 76, 77, 81
Brown, William, 148
Brownell, Herbert, 181, 182
Brownsville (Tex.), 128–9
Buchanan, James, 76
Bureau of Indian Affairs, 46
Burges, Tristam, 30–1
Burns, Anthony, 74
Bus boycott, 180
Butler, Benjamin, 64, 81–2
Butler, John M., 195–6
Byrd, Robert C., 212, 220
Byrd, William, 214

Calhoun, John C., 25, 29, 45, 75
Camp Chickamauga, 131
Camp Moultrie Treaty, 46, 47, 49
Camp Pike, 149
Camp Zachary Taylor, 152
Caraway, Thaddeus, 151
Carey, James, 178
Carmichael, Stokely, 223, 224, 226
Carolina (colony), 3
Cass, Lewis, 29
Cato, Willo, 125
Cavanaugh, Jerome, 215–6
Cease-and-desist proclamation, 193
Celler, Emanuel, 179
Chaney, James, 200, 201–2, 203, 218, 225
Charleston Employees' Strike, 223
Charleston (S.C.), 24–5, 110–1, 144
Cherokee Indians, 48, 51 n. 30, 57, 58. *See also* Indians; Seminole War

Chicago Commission on Race Relations, 147
Chicago Defender, 144
Chicago (Ill.), 115, 116, 118, 146–7, 221, 228
Chiles, Nick, 143
Choctaw Indians, 64. *See also* Indians; Seminole War
Christiana (Pa.), 73–4
Christopher, Warren, 216
Church of Jesus Christ of Latter-Day Saints (Mormons), 235
Cincinnati (Ohio), 70, 215
CIO, 178
Civil liberties, 71–2; freedom of assembly, 95–7, 118; freedom of the press; 22, 70, 71; freedom of speech, 69–70. *See also* Abolition movement; Civil rights
Civil rights, 90–1, 103, 183, 224; decisions of the Supreme Court, 126–9, 150, 161, 162–3, 183, 201–2, 203, 204, 217–8; right of equal accommodations, 107, 109–10, 177, 179, 188–9, 224, 226; right of equal employment, 165; franchise, 100, 103, 180; legislation, 161, 214, 224–5; right of petition, 75, 110, 203; violations, 160–1, 176. *See also* Black Codes; Black protest; Civil Rights Acts; *Civil Rights* cases; Civil rights movement; Commission on Civil Rights; Desegregation; Education; Integration; Interstate Commerce; Justice, U.S. Department of; National Guard; Racial murders; Riots, civil rights; Segregation; Supreme Court
Civil Rights Act, of 1866, 89–90, 92, 93, 95, 127, 128, 140, 202, 224; of 1875, 109; of 1957, 180, 195; of 1964, 199, 204 n. 1, 211; of 1965, 204; of 1966, 214
Civil Rights cases, 127, 136 n. 10
Civil Rights Commission, 180
Civil Rights Congress, 110

Civil rights movement, 187–90, 196–9, 200–2; fair employment campaign of, 196–7; freedom ride of, 188–90; Freedom Summer of, 200, 202–4; and marches, 196–9, 203; and sit-ins, 187, 188–9, 211. *See also* Black protest; Black liberation movement; Education; NAACP; CORE; Riots, civil rights; SCLC; SDS; SNCC

Civil War, 79–87, 92, 236, 239

Clark, Elmore, 162

Clark, Joseph S., 203

Clark, Mark, 228

Clark, Ramsey, 216, 218, 221, 232 n. 17, 233 n. 25

Clark, Tom C., 177, 178, 179, 201

Clay, Henry, 54

Clayton Antitrust Act, 139

Cleveland, Grover, 110, 114, 134

Clifford, Nathan, 63

Colmer, William, 203

Colonial period, 1–4

Colonization, 112

Columbia (Tenn.), 177

Commerce Clause. See *Constitution of the United States*

Commission on Civil Rights, 177

Communism, 212, 226, 227, 229. *See also* Bolshevism

Communist Party, 180

Compromise of 1850, 76

Compromise of 1877, 101, 103, 124, 223

Confederacy, 80, 84–7. *See also* Civil War

Confederate Congress, 85, 86

Confederation Congress, 16 n. 7

Confiscation Act of July 1862, 82–3, 84

Congress of Industrial Organizations (CIO), 178

Congress of Racial Equality (CORE), 188, 211

Congress of the United States; debates of, 11, 38, 54, 57, 73, 106, 112, 210; First, 10, 11; Fourth, 12; Gag Resolutions in, 54, 75–6; legislation of, 41, 80, 82–3, 89, 90, 91, 92, 97–8, 99–100, 114, 142, 192; powers of, 8, 10, 12, 44, 69, 82–3, 119, 176; Second, 10. *See also* Act of Congress of 30 June 1834; Act of Congress of 31 May 1870; *Congressional Record;* House of Representatives; U.S. Senate

Congressional Record, 184, 194, 195, 202, 219, 220, 224

Connor, Eugene Bull, 196, 198

Conrad, Charles M., 72

Constitution of the United States, 9, 23, 126, 196, 236, 237, 238, 239; apportionment of representation in, 8, 9; Bill of Rights, 6, 9; Article I of, 224; Article II of, 192; Article IV of, 64, 80, 98, 105, 217–8; Article VI of, 182; Commerce Clause of, 225, 228; Domestic Violence Clause of, 84, 101; enforcement of, 9; 15th Amendment of, 90, 123, 124, 129, 204; 5th Amendment of, 108; 1st Amendment of, 198, 224; 14th Amendment of, 90, 92, 98, 99–100, 101, 126, 136 n. 10, 153, 162, 180, 182, 188, 201, 225; Fugitive Slave Clause of, 9, 39, 74, 83; proslavery compromises in, 8, 9, 11, 13, 28, 31, 39, 45, 55–6, 64, 80, 81, 83, 84, 90; provisions for military aid requests in, 25, 28, 31, 105, 153, 184, 217–9, 221; Military Clauses of, 8, 9, 10, 39, 153; ratification of, 9–10, 39; 10th Amendment of, 14, 26; 13th Amendment of, 84, 89, 95, 101, 126, 127, 128; relegation of war-making power in, 44. *See also* Constitutional Convention; *United States Code*

Constitutional Convention, 7–9

Eisenhower, Dwight D., 175, 180, 181, 182, 183, 189, 190, 195, 219
Elaine (Ark.), 149–51
Election riots. *See* Riots, election
Elkison v. Deliesilline, 25–6
Ellender, Allen J., 195
Elliott, J. D., 28
Ellis, W. H., 134
Emancipation Proclamation, 83, 84, 86, 236–7
Emergency Plan White, 151, 166, 167, 168
Eppes, Richard, 27
Erie v. Tompkins, 194
Ervin, Sam, Jr., 180, 195, 225
Estill Springs (Tex.), 143
Everglades (Fla.), 58
Evers, Medgar, 199
Ex Parte Milligan, 92, 95
Export tax, 8

Fair Employment Practices Commission (FEPC), 177
Fair Housing Act, 224, 226
Farmer, James, 188, 189, 211
Faubus, Orval, 181, 182
FBI, 178, 184–5, 189, 200, 202, 211, 229
Federal Councils of Churches of Christ, 179
Federal intervention. See *Constitution of the United States*, provisions for federal aid requests; Justice, U.S. Department of; Marshals, U.S.; U.S. Army; U.S. Navy
Federal Party. *See* Whigs
Federalism, 1, 2, 10, 170
Federalists, 9
15th Amendment. See *Constitution of the United States*
5th Amendment. See *Constitution of the United States*
Fillmore, Millard, 72
1st Amendment. See *Constitution of the United States*

First Battalion of the District of Columbia, 145
Fisk University, 198
Fitts, William, 142, 143
503rd Military Police Battalion, 193
Florida, 35–67 *passim. See also* Adams-Onis Treaty; Armed Settler Bill
Foraker, Joseph, 129
Force Act of 31 May 1870, 105–6
Force Bill, 30
Ford, Gerald, 219
Forrester, Elijah, 183
Fortas, Abe, 201
Fortress Monroe, Va., 27, 28, 76, 81, 82, 93
Foster, William Z., 144
14th Amendment. See *Constitution of the United States*
Fowlton (Fla.), 42, 44
Franchise, 90, 100, 103, 114, 123, 124, 180, 203, 224–5; black attempts to exercise, 103; and black illiteracy, 92, 204; intimidation of blacks in exercise of, 100, 107, 124, 129–30, 153, 160. See also *Constitution of the United States*, 15th Amendment of; Freedom Summer; Force Act of 31 May 1870; Justice, U.S. Department of, and franchise; Lodge Bill; Riots, election; Republican Party; *United States Code*, Section 245; Voting Rights Acts of 1957, 1960, and 1965
Frankfurter, Felix, 176
Franklin (Tenn.), 98
Freedom ride, 188–90
Freedom Summer, 200, 202–4
Frelinghuysen, Theodore, 30
Fremont, John C., 83
French and Indian War. *See* Seven Years War
Fries Rebellion, 15, 17 n. 15, 28
Fugitive Slave Act, of 1793, 12, 35, 44–5, 46, 47, 64, 72, 78 n. 6; of

Meredith, James, 190–3, 194, 195, 196
Meridian (Miss.), 200
Mexican-Americans, 164, 235
Mexican War, 76
Mexico, 63
Miami (Fla.), 179
Migration of blacks. *See* Black protest
Militarism, 222
Military Police, 141–2, 193
Military Reconstruction Act, 97, 98
Militia, division of authority over, 10; establishment of, 2; in Fries Rebellion, 15; local responsibility for, 2, 19; Negro organization of, 21; and patrol, 19–20, 21, 85–6; in racial disturbances, 70–1, 73, 74, 104, 109, 110, 112, 118, 125, 130, 131, 133, 162; during Reconstruction, 91, 99, 100; during Seminole War, 56, 61, 62–3; and slave control, 2, 4, 22, 24, 26; state control of, 9; strengthening of, 3, 21; in strikebreaking, 105, 111; weaknesses of, 7, 20, 26; in Whiskey Rebellion, 15. *See also* Militia Acts of 1792 and 1795; Slavery
Militia Act of 1792, 10–1, 19, 20; of 1795, 11
Milwaukee (Wis.), 75
Mississippi, 80, 84, 85–6, 189
Mississippi River, 47, 57, 107
Missouri, 22–3
Missouri Compromise, 24, 64
Mitchell, William, 161
Mobile (Ala.), 98
Mohammed, Elijah, 210
Mondale, Walter F., 203, 212
Mondou v. New York, New Haven, and Hartford R. R. Co., 161
Monroe (Ga.), 178
Monroe, James, 20, 21, 26, 41, 43, 46
Monroe, John T., 95–6, 97, 98
Montgomery (Ala.), 180, 189
Moody, William H., 125–6

Moore v. Dempsey, 150
Moore, Harry T., 179
Morgan State College, 150
Mormons, 235
Morris, Gouverneur, 8–9
Morse, Wayne, 195, 196, 198
Moss, Theodore, 113, 114
Motley, Constance Baker, 192
Murder. *See* Police murders; Racial murders
Murphy, Frank, 163, 165, 168, 176
Murphy, Patrick V., 221

NAACP, 123, 132, 140, 143, 145, 146, 150, 151, 152–4, 158, 159, 160–1, 162, 164–5, 167, 171 n. 3, 11, 176, 177, 178, 179, 180, 185, 190, 192, 195, 199, 209, 210, 233
Nashville (Tenn.), 198
Natchez, 27
National Association for the Advancement of Colored People. *See* NAACP
National Association of Colored Women (NACW), 178
National Bar Association, 170
National Convention of Colored Men (NCCM), 110
National Guard, of Alabama, 189, 203; role of in enforcing civil rights, 163, 189, 197, 202, 203; role of in enforcing integration, 181–3, 193, 199; establishment of, 140; federalization of, 153; of Illinois, 141, 142; of Michigan, 166; and militarism, 222; of Mississippi, 193, 202; Negro units of, 145; role of in riot control, 128, 141, 142, 145, 147–8, 162, 166, 177, 212, 215–9, 220; riot training of, 221; of Texas, 128, 142–3
Navigation Acts, 2
Navy. *See* U.S. Navy
Nazis, 170
Neal, Claude, 163

DATE DUE

6 11 '81	
8 22 '81	
JUN 19 '__	